CHURCHILL

AND THE

SOVIET UNION

MANCHESTER
UNIVERSITY PRESS

TO TERESA

BY THE SAME AUTHOR

*MacDonald versus Henderson:
The Foreign Policy of the
Second Labour Government*

Anthony Eden: A Biography

Britain and the Suez Crisis

CHURCHILL

AND THE

SOVIET UNION

David Carlton

MANCHESTER
UNIVERSITY PRESS
Manchester and New York

distributed exclusively in the USA by St. Martin's Press

Published by Manchester University Press
Oxford Road, Manchester M13 9NR, UK
and Room 400, 175 Fifth Avenue, New York, NY 10010, USA
http://www.man.ac.uk/mup

Distributed exclusively in the USA by
St. Martin's Press, Inc., 175 Fifth Avenue, New York, NY 10010, USA

Distributed exclusively in Canada by
UBC Press, University of British Columbia, 6344 Memorial Road,
Vancouver, BC, Canada V6T 1Z2

British Library Cataloguing-in-Publication Data
A catalogue record for this book is available from the British Library

Library of Congress Cataloging-in-Publication Data
Carlton, David, 1938–
    Churchill and the Soviet Union / David Carlton
        p.   cm.
    Includes bibliographical references and index.
    ISBN 0–7190–4106–6 (hardcover). — ISBN 0–7190–4107–4 (pbk.)
    1. Great Britain—Foreign relations—Soviet Union. 2. Soviet
Union—Foreign relations—Great Britain. 3. Churchill, Winston,
Sir, 1874–1965—Views on Soviet Union. 4. Great Britain—Foreign
relations—20th century. I. Title.
DA47.65.C37   1999
327.41047'09'041—dc21   99–42908

ISBN 0 7190 4106 6 *hardback*
    0 7190 4107 4 *paperback*

First published 2000

07 06 05 04 03 02 01 00   10 9 8 7 6 5 4 3 2 1

Typeset in Aldus
by Koinonia, Manchester
Printed in Great Britain
by Bell & Bain Ltd, Glasgow

Contents

Acknowledgements

The research for this volume was mainly conducted in the Public Record Office (PRO), Kew; at Churchill College, Cambridge; and at the University of Warwick Library. In each case I owe a debt of gratitude to the staff for the assistance they gave me.

I am grateful for encouragement and helpful comments from two of my colleagues at the University of Warwick: Professor Wyn Grant and Professor Lord Skidelsky. But I hasten to add that neither should be assumed to be responsible for or be necessarily in agreement with the interpretations I offer here.

The editorial staff of Manchester University Press have been unfailingly patient and helpful. And I should also like to thank Dr John Stevenson of Worcester College, Oxford, who was responsible for introducing me to MUP.

Crown copyright material in the PRO appears here by permission of the Controller of Her Majesty's Stationery Office. Parliamentary copyright material from *Hansard* is reproduced with the permission of the Controller of Her Majesty's Stationery Office on behalf of Parliament. Extracts from the works of Sir Winston S. Churchill reproduced with permission of Curtis Brown Ltd, London on behalf of Winston S. Churchill Copyright © The Estate of Sir Winston S. Churchill. Every effort has been made to trace copyright holders but if any have been inadvertently overlooked the publishers will be pleased to make the necessary arrangements at the first opportunity.

David Carlton
University of Warwick, 1999

Introduction

'It is a riddle wrapped in a mystery inside an enigma.'[1] This was Winston Churchill's verdict on the Soviet Union on 1 October 1939. But the leaders of the Soviet Union must at times have felt like using the same words about Churchill. For in the course of the first four decades after the Bolshevik Revolution he oscillated in a seemingly bewildering fashion between extreme enmity and apparent friendship *vis-à-vis* the Soviets. Initially he achieved an astonishingly high public profile as a tireless advocate of Allied Intervention in Russia to eliminate the Bolshevik regime; by the late 1930s he was urging with almost as much publicity the forging with the Soviets of a Grand Alliance against Nazi Germany; during the winter of 1939–1940 he was apparently willing to see Great Britain come to the assistance of Finland in its war with the Soviet Union; in June 1941 he eagerly embraced the Soviet Union as a worthy ally against Nazi Germany; after the latter's defeat he rapidly moved to proposing a common Anglo-American front against the Soviet Union and global Communism in his famous Fulton speech, and soon afterwards he even called for an atomic 'showdown' with the Soviets; and finally, during the 1950s, he was to be an unexpected and lonely advocate of the early convening of a Western Summit with the regime in Moscow.

The purpose of the present volume is therefore to analyse this Churchillian enigma. For in the already vast literature on Churchill no single work has focused on this vital and even central aspect of his career. Of course the outline of the story can be teased out of Sir Martin Gilbert's admirable multi-volume authorised biography.[2] But Gilbert's approach is understandably and unapologetically not that of an analyst. Rather, his is a chronicle which allows the facts relating to Churchill's life, chronologically presented, largely to speak for themselves. There are also various specialised studies that throw much light on limited aspects of the theme of the present work. For example, at the time of writing, Michael Kettle is engaged on a multi-volume study of the role of the British in the Allied Intervention in Russia which will have much to say about Churchill. He has already published

Churchill and the Archangel Fiasco.[3] And John Young has recently produced an excellent scholarly account of Churchill's attempt during the 1950s to secure a *détente* with the Soviets.[4] Nevertheless there still seems to be a clear need for an analytical overview of the entire story of Churchill's dealings with the Soviets over four decades.

Precisely because such an overview is being attempted, research in archives has inevitably been less thorough than would have been appropriate if a shorter period of Churchill's life had been involved. Nevertheless, use has been made of material in the Public Record Office (PRO) at Kew, and of Churchill's Papers housed at Churchill College, Cambridge. Future researchers on Churchill may care to note, incidentally, that much of the material housed at Cambridge has been reproduced in Gilbert's multi-volume biography and in the numerous Companion Volumes of documentation; much of this is also duplicated at the PRO. Material in the PRO is of course normally Crown Copyright and hence it is not necessary to seek permission from literary executors to reproduce such material. The present writer has, therefore, when presented with a choice, normally given a PRO reference. *Hansard* and files of *The Times* have also been extensively scrutinised.

The main part of the book has the Bolshevik Revolution of 1917 as its starting point. Accordingly no attempt is made to present Churchill's background or his earlier political career in detail. Some critics will possibly deplore this. For they may believe that his views on the Soviet Union can only be understood in such a wider context. David Lloyd George was an early exponent of this approach: in his memoirs he saw Churchill's extreme support for intervention against the Bolsheviks as due to the fact that 'his ducal blood revolted against the wholesale elimination of Grand Dukes in Russia'.[5] Yet Churchill, elected to the House of Commons in 1900 as a Conservative, had crossed the floor in 1904 to join the Liberal Party – a rare example of a move from Right to Left in British politics (in which of course the reverse is much more common). He subsequently served as a Cabinet Minister under H. H. Asquith and strongly endorsed Lloyd George's 'People's Budget', a confrontation with the House of Lords and an attempt to bring in Home Rule for Ireland. How many grandsons of dukes behave in this way? At all events, his early career certainly does not suggest that Churchill was a die-hard or reactionary figure predisposed to oppose Bolshevism merely on traditionalist grounds – though his change of party may indicate a flexibility of mind that might be held partly to explain the subsequent apparent somersaults in his approach to the Soviet Union. All in all, however, dwelling extensively on Churchill's life before 1917 is as likely to mislead as it is to illuminate.

NOTES

1 *The Times*, 2 October 1939.
2 Martin Gilbert, *World in Torment: Winston S. Churchill, 1917–1922*, London, 1975 (Vol. IV); *Prophet of Truth: Winston S. Churchill, 1922–1939*, London, 1976 (Vol. V); *Finest Hour: Winston S. Churchill, 1939–1941*, London, 1983 (Vol. VI); *Road to Victory: Winston S. Churchill, 1941–1945*, London, 1986 (Vol. VII); and *'Never Despair': Winston S. Churchill, 1945–1965*, London, 1988 (Vol. VIII). There are also numerous Companion Volumes of documentation already in print and more are due to be published in future years. Details of such Companion Volumes utilised in the present work will be given in the various chapter notes.
3 Michael Kettle, *Churchill and the Archangel Fiasco, November 1918–July 1919*, London, 1992.
4 John W. Young, *Winston Churchill's Last Campaign: Britain and the Cold War, 1951–5*, Oxford, 1996.
5 David Lloyd George, *The Truth about the Peace Treaties*, London, 1938, p. 325.

1

CRUSADING FOR INTERVENTION

1917–1920

CHURCHILL'S reputation as the foremost Western enemy of the Bolsheviks during their struggle to consolidate their authority in Russia is undoubtedly deserved. But he was not alone in seeking the overthrow of Vladimir Lenin and his followers. And he only achieved a high public profile in this connection during 1919 – many months after the Bolsheviks had seized power in Petrograd on 7 November 1917. Indeed, even in private he seems to have been almost complacent during the whole of the Bolsheviks' first year. Why was this? First, he was fully occupied as Minister of Munitions, a post which did not give him regular access to the War Cabinet and which required him to concentrate primarily on military and technological developments relating to the Western Front. Second, he apparently did not take seriously the possibility that the Bolshevik regime would be able to survive for long in recognisable form in the face of the united resolve of Great Britain, France and the United States to intervene in the continuing civil war on the side of the so-called Whites (the groups opposed to Bolshevism). This resolve sprang of course from a belief that Russia, taken out of the War against the Central Powers by the Bolsheviks at the beginning of 1918, had a duty to its allies to recreate an Eastern Front. It is true that Churchill had briefly wondered, in a draft memorandum dated 7 April 1918, whether the Bolshevik leaders might resume hostilities against Germany in return for a compromise power-sharing deal with the Western Allies. But once this unrealistic hope was dashed Churchill became committed exclusively to the cause of the Whites, whom he thought could be relied upon to recreate a Second Front once they were restored to power in Petrograd – which he believed certain to come about, given vigorous Western help. As Churchill himself explained in 1929: 'Had the Great War been prolonged into 1919, intervention, which was gathering momentum every week, must have been militarily successful.'[1] Against all his expectations, however, the Great War ended prematurely with the Armistice of 11 November 1918.

The Armistice thus destroyed at a stroke the principal motivation of the Western Governments – and their peoples – for intervening in the Russian Civil War in any really determined fashion. Thereafter the priority of most Western statesmen was safely to remove their own forces from Russia and, as far as possible, not to let down too precipitately the Whites alongside whom they had been fighting during 1918. Churchill was unusual in that his priority quickly became that of urging the intensification of the Western intervention against Bolshevism. For he believed that otherwise it would soon constitute a severe threat to non-Communist governments throughout the Eurasian landmass and to Germany in particular.

Churchill first gave his colleagues in the British Government a foretaste of this somewhat distinctive line of thinking at the British War Cabinet on 10 November 1918, the very eve of the Armistice with Germany. He offered the opinion that 'we might have to build up the German Army, as it was important to get Germany on its legs again for fear of the spread of Bolshevism'.[2] This certainly did not meet with the approval of Prime Minister Lloyd George, who was about to enter a general election campaign at the head of a Coalition Government that was in effect to promise to squeeze Germany until the pips squeaked and to hang the Kaiser. Churchill did not in these circumstances immediately press his case with any vigour. Indeed, at a public meeting in Dundee, on 26 November, he proclaimed that 'practically the whole German nation was guilty of the crime of aggressive war conducted by brutal and bestial means' and added that 'they were all in it, and they must all suffer for it'.[3] But this may only show that even Churchill had to concede that politics can at least occasionally be local politics. For he might otherwise have failed to secure re-election as one of Dundee's Members of Parliament. At all events, he was soon to revert to the line concerning Germany that he had taken on 10 November. Many years later, for example, Lady Violet Bonham Carter recalled his telling her around this time that his policy was 'Kill the

Bolshie, Kiss the Hun'.[4] And in the same spirit, on 24 March 1920, he informed Lloyd George with some exaggeration: 'Since the Armistice my policy would have been "Peace with the German people, war on the Bolshevik tyranny." Willingly or unavoidably, you have followed something very near the reverse.'[5]

A profound divergence between Churchill and Lloyd George concerning Bolshevism did undoubtedly develop over time. But its importance evidently did not loom large in the Prime Minister's thinking until some way into 1919. Indeed, Lloyd George clearly still saw Churchill as a friend and ally until at least the end of 1918. For in the Conservative-dominated Coalition he was the most senior colleague of the Prime Minister to share his nominally Liberal affiliation. No doubt this goes far to explaining why the Prime Minister, having secured a new mandate from the electorate at the end of December 1918, decided to promote Churchill to full War Cabinet membership and to give him major responsibility as Secretary of State for War and Air. But if Lloyd George saw Churchill as a friend worth promoting, it is not so certain that his goodwill was fully reciprocated. For by 1919 the 45-year-old Churchill may secretly have been increasingly jealous of Lloyd George's spectacular rise to the Premiership and his role as an architect of victory in the First World War. And if he was looking for scapegoats to blame for the fact that his own climb up the 'greasy pole' had been less spectacular than he would have wished and expected, Lloyd George may have been among the leading candidates.

Churchill had originally entered the House of Commons in 1900 as a Conservative. However in May 1904, as a strong supporter of free trade, he had chosen literally to cross the floor and sit next to Lloyd George – thereby signalling a desire to associate himself with the Opposition Liberal Party's most notable radical and reformer. Soon the two had struck up a close friendship and at first it had been unusually free from any competitive spirit. For Churchill, as a newcomer, needed to work his passage with the Liberals and in any case, at the time he crossed the floor, he was still under 30, whereas Lloyd George was already entering his forties and almost at the peak of his powers. Thus, during the pre-war Liberal Administrations from 1905 to 1914 Lloyd George was a Cabinet Minister, and Chancellor of the Exchequer after 1908, whereas Churchill had to work his way up from a junior ministerial appointment to a series of Cabinet appointments (President of the Board of Trade, Home Secretary and First Lord of the Admiralty). Clearly, then, Lloyd George was seen as the more senior figure before the outbreak of the First World War and Churchill had no reason to resent this. Indeed, the two worked closely together during the critical years between 1908 and 1911 when the early welfare state was being created and the challenge of the House of Lords was being met. But as Churchill matured he was increasingly seen, and presumably saw himself, as at least a potential long-term rival to his friend for the Liberal Party Leadership. As Norman Rose has written about this phase:

> Lloyd George had visited Germany in August 1908 and had come away 'tremendously impressed' at what he had seen of the German social insurance system. He immediately passed on these impressions to Churchill. For the next few years Lloyd George and Churchill were to work in close tandem. It was the period of their most intimate collaboration. They were nicknamed 'the two Romeos' or 'the Heavenly Twins'. It was only natural that Lloyd George should take the lead. As Chancellor of the Exchequer he outranked Churchill, his radical credentials were more impeccable, and his was the authentic voice of the common man. Nor had he blotted his copybook by betraying one party to seek preference with another. They were a formidable combination; dynamic, restless, visibly anmbitious, blessed with brilliant powers of persuasion. Togther they succeeded in pulling an often hesitant and suspicious Cabinet towards their goal of extensive social reform. But their fruitful partnership masked a rivalry no less acute because of their collaboration. Both considered themselves as potential leaders of the Liberal Party; Lloyd George with more cause, but with Churchill's confidence growing as he clambered up the political ladder. Apprehensive lest one snatch the glory from the other, they viewed each other with misgivings.
>
> Two such ebullient personalities, egocentric, enamoured of their own abilities, could not fail, on occasion, to irritate each other. For all that, they appreciated each other's talents. In time, through force of circumstance, Churchill accustomed himself to Lloyd George's pre-eminent position. He thought him 'the greatest political genius of the day', with more 'political insight than any other statesman', and admitted later that he had acted as Lloyd George's 'chief lieutenant'.[6]

The First World War, however, brought acute strains into their relationship. Early in 1915 Churchill lost credibility with his Cabinet colleagues, Lloyd George included, through his involvement in initiating the ill-fated Dardenelles/Gallipoli campaign. Then in May 1915 Asquith decided that the intensifying war required the creation of a Coalition administration in partnership with the Conservatives. This meant there were fewer posts for Liberals and this in turn led to a vulnerable Churchill being dropped as First Lord of the Admiralty. He became Chancellor of the Duchy of Lancaster and in that capacity had so few serious duties that by November 1915 he felt he had no alternative other than to resign from the Government. These developments left him literally inconsolable. And among those he blamed for his downfall was Lloyd George whom he rebuked for not attempting to save him.[7] Nor did their relations improve in December 1916 when Lloyd George became Prime Minister but felt constrained to allow the Conservatives to veto any post being offered to Churchill. By July 1917, however, Lloyd George had succeeded in overcoming Conservative opposition and Churchill was restored to office – though only in the relatively junior role of Minister of Munitions outside the War Cabinet. Churchill was certainly grateful to Lloyd George and was even more so when he was offered the War and Air portfolios with a seat in the War Cabinet at the end of 1918. But there must nevertheless be a doubt whether the former ever really fully forgave the latter for his earlier alleged disloyalty. And certainly this possibility should be borne in mind as we seek to understand how the differences between them developed between 1919 and 1922.

However that may be, Churchill, assuming his new post on 14 January 1919, had thus suddenly become the minister with principal responsibility for handling the delicate task of extricating British armed forces from Russia while organising the provision of such various supplies to the Whites as were from time to time thought to be appropriate to enable them to continue to fight their civil war within Russia. In giving him this responsibiliity Lloyd George surely believed that Churchill would fall in with the thinking of the majority of his colleagues on these matters – which Churchill initially seemed prepared to do. On 23 December 1918, for example, he had argued at the Imperial War Cabinet that the choice was to 'leave the Bolsheviks to "stew in their own juice"' and to allow the Russians to freely murder each other or 'in the name of order, to interfere and do it thoroughly' with large forces 'abundantly supplied'. The second policy meant, he acknowledged, that the country must be 'stirred up' and a large voluntary army collected. But while it was obvious that he personally favoured this policy his main argument appeared to be that in one way or another indecision must end.[8]

Churchill's line seemed to be similarly accommodating when the War Cabinet gave extremely detailed attention to the Russian issue on 12 February 1919. As he succinctly put it: 'The Great Powers were still delaying the decision on this matter. If we were going to withdraw our troops, it should be done at once. If we were going to intervene, we should send larger forces there. He believed that we ought to intervene.' But then he was challenged by Lloyd George, who stated that he 'understood the military view to be that, if we were going to do any good, we should need a million men at least, and these should be despatched in the spring'. Churchill evidently realised at once that such a proposal would be unacceptable to his colleagues. For the Chancellor of the Exchequer, Austen Chamberlain, was desperately seeking to cut back public spending. And in any case, the War Secretary himself only weeks earlier had had to order a rapid speeding up of the demobilisation of conscripts following mutinous demonstrations against the delays that had followed the Armistice. Hence he readily appreciated that only volunteers could possibly be sent to Russia. And Churchill appeared further to yield to Lloyd George by expressly acknowledging that in these circumstances 'intervention on a large scale was not possible'. The meeting concluded by asking Field-Marshal Sir Henry Wilson, the Chief of the Imperial General Staff, to prepare a statement showing the military effect which would ensue from the adoption of each of the following policies with regard to Russia:

(i) Intervention
(ii) Evacuation
(iii) A middle policy of giving all possible help by way of arms and money to the anti-Bolshevik Governments of Russia
(iv) The defence of all those States which depended upon the Great Powers for their protection.[9]

When, on the following day, 13 February, a further meeting of the War Cabinet took place, Wilson, according to his own account, in effect refused to oblige, saying that 'there are too many unknown quantities for me to offer an opinion'.[10] But Churchill for his part drew a conclusion that seemed to be acceptable to his colleagues:

there was no doubt that the only chance of making headway against the Bolsheviks was by the use of Russian armies. If Russian armies were not available, there was no remedy. Large British and French armies were not to be thought of …
… If we were unable to support the Russians effectively, it would be far better to take a decision now to quit and face the consequences, and tell these people to make the best terms they could with the Bolsheviks, than to leave our troops there and continue without a policy.

Churchill and Lloyd George went on to agree that the Allies should be consulted about how to proceed. In particular, it was deemed essential that US President Woodrow Wilson, who was then attending the Peace Conference in Paris but who was on the point of returning home, 'ought to share the decision and face the responsibility'. But Lloyd George himself felt unable immediately to visit Paris because of a worsening domestic crisis involving the possibility of something approaching a general strike. The Prime Minister accordingly asked Churchill to meet the President on his behalf – an indication that the Prime Minister had at this stage no lack of confidence in his colleague's essential reasonableness on the Russian issue. Indeed, in a private conversation involving the two men and Henry Wilson on the evening immediately following this War Cabinet, Churchill modestly stated that at Paris he would put some 'direct questions' rather than make proposals. For 'there must be some intelligible policy which could be explained and defended in the House of Commons'.[11]

On the following day, 14 February, the War Secretary duly arrived in Paris and at once found himself in the presence of world leaders at a session of the so-called Supreme War Council. Among those present were Georges Clemenceau and Ferdinand Foch of France, Italian Foreign Minister Baron Sidney Sonnino, British Foreign Secretary Arthur Balfour, and Wilson himself. Churchill was in no way over-awed and virtually compelled a reluctant Wilson to respond to questions about Russia. He did not at this stage, however, depart far if at all from the spirit of the previous day's War Cabinet discussion. For he conceded that 'none of the Allies could send conscript troops to Russia' and he accepted that total withdrawal would be 'a logical and clear policy'. At the same time, he ventured to wonder whether 'volunteers, technical experts, arms, munitions, tanks, aeroplanes etc' should be despatched in order to prevent the collapse of the Whites which would leave only 'an interminable vista of violence and misery' for the whole of Russia. But Wilson was discouraging. He thought that 'conscripts could not be sent and volunteers could probably not be obtained'. He stated that 'his conclusion ... was that the Allied and Associated Powers ought to withdraw from all parts of Russian terrritory'. But he was then further pressed by Churchill about the possibility 'of arming the anti-Bolshevik forces in Russia'. Anxious not to miss his train, the President merely replied that he 'hesitated to express any definite opinion'. He rather weakly added that whatever the Supreme War Council decided, 'he would cast in his lot with the rest'.[12] He then left for home and the meeting adjourned until the following day.

Churchill seems to have decided at this point to attempt, in the absence of Wilson, to secure the support of France, Italy and Japan for a vigorous policy of granting as much assistance as possible to the Whites, once forlorn efforts to promote a peace settlement among the various Russian factions at a conference intended to be held on the Turkish island of Prinkipo could be deemed to have failed. And he was evidently no longer minded to operate on the British War Cabinet assumption that any British assistance would necessarily be extremely modest in scale. This led Philip Kerr, a close associate of Lloyd George, after dining with Churchill and other British delegates on the evening of Wilson's departure, to send a message to his chief that concluded:

> in my opinion Mr Churchill is bent on forcing a campaign against Bolshevik Russia by using Allied volunteers, Polish and Finnish and any other conscripts that he can get hold of, financed and equipped by the Allies. He is perfectly logical in his policy, because he declares that the Bolsheviks are the enemies of the human race and must be put down at any cost ... I think you ought to watch the situation very carefully, if you do not want to be rushed into a policy of a volunteer war against the Bolsheviks in the near future.[13]

Churchill's more robust approach did indeed become apparent even to other delegations on the following day, 15 February, when the Supreme War Council reconvened. In his own words, he 'proposed the setting up of an Allied Council for Russian affairs with political, economic and military sections'. The military section would be asked to draw up 'a complete military plan and an expression of opinion from the highest military authorities as to whether within the limit of our available resources there is a reasonable prospect of success'. At this point the Supreme War Council, that is the Allies acting collectively, 'would then be in a position to make a definite decision whether to clear out altogether, or to adopt the plan'.[14] Churchill appears to have favourably impressed the Supreme War Council and especially the French members of it. But the US Secretary of State, Robert Lansing, wanted time for consultation. Hence it was decided to adjourn for two days before taking a final decision.

The delay proved fatal to Churchill's hopes and maybe also to those of the Whites. For, having been alerted by Kerr to the way in which an attempt was being made to 'bounce' him, on 16 February Lloyd George intervened to decisive effect. He simply sent critical messages to Churchill via Kerr and gave the latter an instruction to show them to Balfour, then the nominal acting head of the British delegation who had hitherto allowed Churchill on the two previous days to speak on behalf of the British War Cabinet; and, more drastically, to show them also to Colonel E. M. House of the US delegation. Among Lloyd George's blunt words were the following:

> Am very alarmed at ... planning war against the Bolsheviks. The Cabinet have never authorized such a proposal ... An expensive war of aggression against Russia is a way to strengthen Bolshevism in Russia and create it at home. We cannot afford the burden. Chamberlain says we can hardly make both ends meet on a peace basis, even at the present crushing rate of taxation; and if we are committed to a war against a continent like Russia, it is the road to bankruptcy and Bolshevism in these islands.
>
> The French are not safe guides in this matter. Their opinion is largely biased by the enormous number of small investors who put their money into Russian loans and who now see no prospect of ever recovering it. I urge you therefore not to pay too much heed to their incitements ...
>
> I also want you to bear in mind the very grave labour position in this country. Were it known that you had gone over to Paris to prepare a plan of war against the Bolsheviks it would do more to incense organised labour than anything I can think of; and what is still worse, it would throw into the ranks of the extremists a very large number of thinking people who now abhor their methods.[15]

On the following day, 17 February, the Prime Minister sent a further message: 'Have consulted my colleagues. They approve of my telegram.'[16]

Churchill was understandably angered. Above all, he was shaken by the news that the Americans had been informed about the rebuke he had received. As Henry Wilson put it in his diary: 'This was a low down trick.'[17] The upshot was that when the Supreme War Council reassembled, on the afternoon of 17 February, Churchill faced open opposition not only from the Americans but also from his own colleague Balfour, who now for the first time began to assert his authority. Nevertheless Churchill persisted with his plea for the establishment of a joint military commission to report on the options open to the Supreme War Council. But, despite having the support of Clemenceau, he was compelled to accept defeat after much acrimonious discussion. As Henry Wilson recorded in his diary: 'in the end it was agreed that each country should ask its Military Adviser who should report separately, no Joint Note being allowed.'[18] This effectively destroyed the prospects for any early collective action against the Russian Bolsheviks by the Allies. And there turned out to be no possibility of reopening the issue when President Wilson let his delegation know on 19 February that he was 'greatly surprised by Churchill's Russian suggestion'. He added: 'It would be fatal to be led further into the Russian chaos.' The US delegation reassured him on 23 February that 'Churchill's project is dead and there is little danger that it will be revived again by the Conference'.[19]

On his return to London Churchill found himself therefore in an unenviable situation: for all his colleagues knew that he had been defeated by the Prime Minister. Yet his political base was so weak that resignation would probably have been suicidal. Hence he decided to serve on – no doubt clinging to the hope that he would be able to take full advantage in a fluid situation of opportunities to assist the Whites at least to a marginal degree. He could draw some comfort, for example, from the knowledge that many Conservative backbenchers were more eager than their leaders to get into a crusade against Bolshevism. And there was also the fact that British troops were still in various parts of Russia in considerable numbers. True, Churchill was now supposed to be working for their early withdrawal. But as Henry Wilson, himself a fanatical anti-Bolshevik, hopefully put it: 'Once a military force is involved in operations on land it is almost impossible to limit the magnitude of its commitments.'[20]

The ensuing months of 1919 saw Churchill manoeuvring constantly to prolong British involvement in Russia. In this he was able to count on the influential support of *The Times*. And on occasion he had some limited encouragement from the War Cabinet. For the majority did not actually share Lloyd George's private preference for the Bolsheviks as against the reactionary Whites. Hence whenever the Whites began to prosper, Churchill's arguments for giving them relatively inexpensive additional assistance tended to win support. But conversely, when the Whites lost ground then Lloyd George's case for the British to cut their losses usually prevailed. But matters were never straightforward. For various independent states had emerged in the territory of former Imperial Russia, notably in the Caucasus and the Baltic areas. Then there was a scattered array of White forces in Russia itself, led by such as Admiral A. V. Kolchak (in the east), General Anton Denikin (in the south) and General Nikolai Yudenich (in the north), whose fortunes did not tend to ebb and flow in a synchronised fashion. And in any case no British withdrawal from any

Russian theatre could be affected instantaneously or without risk to the forces concerned. All this naturally gave Churchill as War Secretary scope for opportunistic activity. As the historian D. G. Boadle has written:

> The War Office and its political head thus had wide latitude and discretion, for it was their prerogative to decide on the necessity for offensive operations as preliminaries to ensure the safety of withdrawal. And how difficult it was for outsiders to differentiate between an offensive as the prelude to a renewed attempt at a deeper and more far-reaching involvement, and a covering offensive to permit a breathing-space for safer withdrawal. So while his colleagues continued to believe that he was preparing for a safe winding up of Britain's commitment, Churchill was, in reality, utilizing the opportunity to dispatch fresh contingents, thereby greatly increasing the extent and magnitude of British intervention. All that was needed to ensure his colleagues' tacit approval was definite proof of absolute military necessity, and this the General Staff was only too ready to provide.[21]

On 4 March, for example, the War Cabinet had to face the seeming fact that the British forces in Northern Russia, that is those based at Archangel and Murmansk, would be in acute danger once the region's ice melted. They accordingly decided that all such forces must be withdrawn by June. For Churchill, however, this was only seen as grounds for sending more troops in the meantime in order to help 'to extricate' safely the ones already there.[22]

Similarly Churchill was able to exploit a War Cabinet decision on 6 March to withdraw British forces from the Caucasus. For it prompted the question whether White Russian forces under Denikin could be induced not to try to eliminate the newly-independent states which had emerged there – enabling Churchill, with Lloyd George absent, to persuade his colleagues 'to compensate General Denikin ... with material and munitions of war, and with a military mission' provided he agreed not to 'interefere with the Georgians and other independent States in the Caucasus'. Fearing that the Prime Minister would try to evade carrying out this decision Churchill had a personal meeting with his chief two days later. The historian Michael Kettle has recorded the sequel:

> Immediately on return to the War Office he [Churchill] wrote a very careful letter to Lloyd George confirming that 'it is your decision and the decision of the War Cabinet' that British troops and those Russians who wished to leave were to be evacuated from Murmansk

and Archangel 'as soon as the ice melts in the White Sea', and that more British troops could be sent to cover this operation. It was 'also decided by you and the War Cabinet' that Britain should withdraw from the Caucasus as soon as possible, and compensate Denikin by the despatch of arms and munitions and a British Military Mission of 2,000 special volunteers, in return for an undertaking from him not to attack the Caucasus states south of a line 'which the Foreign Office are tracing'. Lloyd George had 'also decided' that the two British Regiments at Omsk should be replaced by another British Mission.

'On these lines and within these limits', wrote Churchill carefully, 'I should be prepared to be responsible for carrying out the policy on which you and the War Cabinet have decided.' He presumed that either Lloyd George or Balfour would inform the Allies of this decision. 'If, however, I have wrongly interpreted your decisions in any respect, I hope you will let me know what you really wish', he concluded pointedly, 'in order that I may see whether it can be done.'

Churchill probably knew that he would not receive an answer to his letter ... But he gave the Prime Minister every chance to reply. Finally, on March 21, Churchill simply informed the General Staff that his letter, nevertheless, was to be taken as their Russian policy.[23]

British withdrawals were thus confusingly accompanied by new commitments. And if Churchill had had his way Germany would have also been drawn actively into the struggle for the future of Russia. For in a speech at the Aldwych Club on 11 April, he reminded the new German authorities that the Kaiser's Government had triggered the Bolshevik revolution by sending Lenin back to Russia in a sealed train and suggested that a way of atonement now lay open to the successor regime in Berlin. 'By combating Bolshevism, by being the bulwark against it,' he proclaimed, 'Germany may take the first step towards ultimate reunion with the civilised world.' And to give further encouragement to the Germans Churchill added: 'Of all the tyrannies in history, the Bolshevist tyranny is the worst, the most destructive, and the most degrading. It is sheer humbug to pretend that it is not far worse than German militarism.'[24] He accordingly wanted the War Cabinet to make appropriate bilateral overtures to the German Government even though at this time the Armistice had not yet been superseded by a formal peace treaty. But knowing that France in particular would greatly resent anything of this kind, Churchill's colleagues rejected the idea on 29 April.[25]

The onus was thus now clearly on both the Whites and the newly-independent states to work out their own salvation. For despite all

Churchill's indefatigable endeavours, it had become obvious that assistance from London (and from the West in general) was destined to be of no more than marginal importance. At first Kolchak's forces, based in Omsk, Siberia, showed the greatest promise by advancing rapidly in a westward direction at the end of March 1919. They eventually reached almost halfway between the Ural Mountains and Moscow. Churchill's response was to spend April and May consistently and obsessionally urging on his colleagues that the Kolchak regime be accorded formal diplomatic recognition; and that the British forces based in Archangel and Murmansk should not now be withdrawn as previously agreed but should instead be sent in a southeasterly direction to the town of Kotlas with a view to achieving a junction with Kolchak's forces. In the first aim he was to be effectively frustrated. But by 11 June he finally secured War Cabinet agreement to the Kotlas plan. By this stage, however, the Bolsheviks had begun a successful counterattack against Kolchak's forces, from which the latter were never to recover. The upshot was that Churchill had to postpone the implementation of the Kotlas plan. And on 9 July the War Cabinet, with his concurrence, accepted that it must be finally abandoned.[26]

Now Lloyd George was able to go on the offensive against Churchill. At a War Cabinet meeting on 29 July the Prime Minister pointed out that definite pledges had been given to the British troops in Northern Russia that 'our policy was to clear out'. He went on to ask whether 'after our pledges had been broken', any troops kept there for a further winter 'could possibly be relied upon'. He therefore favoured withdrawal from Archangel and Murmansk. Churchill for his part said that 'he was very sorry to be associated with such an operation'. 'It would,' he stated, 'be repugnant to everyone to feel that we were leaving a small Government to fall to pieces.' But Lloyd George said that 'it was a mistake to treat the present operations as though they were a campaign against Bolshevism' and held that the War Cabinet had accepted the view that 'it was not our business to interfere in the internal affairs of Russia'. And he even singled out Churchill for criticism in front of his colleagues, saying:

> If the Allies had decided to defeat Bolshevism, great armies would have been required. The small British force in Russia had not been sent there for this purpose. It was true that one member of the Cabinet had always urged this policy, but he himself [Lloyd George] had always protested against it.[27]

Churchill was thus again isolated and humiliated. The result was that all British forces were withdrawn from Archangel by 27 September and from Murmansk by 12 October.

Churchill was to prove astonishingly resilient, however, in the aftermath of his historic defeat at the War Cabinet of 29 July 1919. For he was soon able to draw comfort from a timely rally on the part of Denikin's forces in the South during August, September and October. Odessa, Kiev and Voronezh all fell to them – leaving them less than 250 miles from Moscow. Soon Churchill was brimming with optimism and began again to bombard both the War Cabinet and Lloyd George personally with demands that increased assistance be given to Denikin (and also to Yudenich who by September was threatening to overrun Petrograd). Now it was Lloyd George's turn to retreat. At a War Cabinet meeting on 12 August he stated that 'he felt himself that there was hardly an even chance of Denikin's reaching Moscow' and he lamented that Great Britain was 'spending £100 million a year on operations in Russia'. Nevertheless, he evidently sensed that many of his colleagues were now increasingly sympathetic to Churchill's pleas. The Prime Minister accordingly summed up as follows: 'He himself would give Denikin one last "packet", so to speak, and he suggested that the Secretary of State for War should state what the contents of the "packet" should be, and estimate its cost. We should say to Denikin: "You must make the most of it ... we cannot give you gratis any more supplies."'[28]

Lloyd George's irritation with his War Secretary was, however, growing. In particular, he believed that Churchill had become so obsessed with Russia that he was neglecting his other duties. Above all, insufficient attention was being given to tackling the bloated War Office budget as a whole. The Prime Minister sent Churchill a relatively friendly warning about his concerns on 30 August.[29] But the latter continued as before to concentrate on Russia. He urged without success, for example, that Yudenich be supported in what turned out to be a vain attempt to capture Petrograd; that recognition be given to the breakaway Baltic states; and that still more aid be sent to Denikin. At the same time, the popular press had recognised that Churchill was increasingly pursuing a personal policy over Russia and that he was making little effort in his public statements to conceal the fact. This led editors to charge Lloyd George with being unable to keep his subordinate under control. The Prime Minister's patience was thus brought to exhaustion point. He accordingly sent Churchill an almost insulting letter of reprimand on 22 September. It contained the following:

> I wonder whether it is any use my making one last effort to induce you to throw off this obsession, which if you will forgive me for saying so, is upsetting your balance. I again ask you to let Russia be, at any rate for a few days, and to concentrate your mind on the quite unjustifiable expenditure in France, at home and in the East, incurred by the War Office and the Air Department. Some of the items could not possibly have been tolerated by you if you had given one-fifth of the thought to these matters which you devoted to Russia ...
>
> The reconquest of Russia would cost hundreds of millions. It would cost hundreds of millions more to maintain the new Government until it had established itself.
>
> You are prepared to spend all that money, and I know perfectly well that it is what you really desire. But as you know that you won't find another responsible person in the whole land who will take your view, why waste your energy and your usefulness on this vain fretting which completely paralyses you for other work?[30]

Then, on 7 October, Lloyd George raised with Churchill his concern about the 'treatment of the Jews by your friends'.[31] This was a reference to the anti-Semitic behaviour of the Whites under the leadership of Denikin and his associates in the South, where, according to Churchill's authorised biographer, 'during 1919, more than 100,000 Jews were murdered'.[32] In his reply Churchill did not flinch from acknowledging that anti-Semitism was widespread among the enemies of Russian Bolshevism:

> 1. There is a very bitter feeling throughout Russia against the Jews, who are regarded as being the main instigators of the ruin of the Empire, and who certainly have played a leading part in the Bolshevik atrocities ...
> 2. This feeling is shared by the Volunteer Army and the army of the Don under General Denikin ...

But his conclusion was of course that the anti-Bolsheviks must nevertheless be supported.[33] Does this mean that Churchill himself was anti-Semitic? Surely not – at least not as the term would normally have been used in the pre-Holocaust era. For in his earlier career, when he was involved in politics in the Greater Manchester conurbation, no hint of hostility to local Jews is to be found. And, as is well-known, he was to be a consistent friend of Zionism over many years both before and after the creation of Israel. It seems certain, therefore, that in 1919 Churchill genuinely regretted the anti-Semitism of 'his friends'. But he nevertheless saw them, for all their faults, as infinitely preferable to the Bolsheviks. Moreover, he was hopeful that their excesses might be curbed. In this spirit, on 9 October, he wrote to Denikin, whom he considered to be an opponent of extremism, as follows: 'I know the efforts you have already made and the difficulty of restraining Anti-Semitic feeling. But I beg you, as a sincere well-wisher, to redouble these efforts and place me in a strong position to vindicate the honour of the Volunteer Army.'[34] At the same time he warned Lloyd George that 'by cutting ourselves adrift from National Russia on the eve of its restoration, we should lose all power to influence events either in the direction of mercy or democracy, and the very weakness which would be caused to the Russian National leaders by our defection would render them powerless to stand against the tide of popular vengeance'.[35] This kind of reasoning no doubt made equal sense during the late 1930s to some of the 'appeasers' of European Fascism. But by then, as will be seen, Churchill himself seemed no longer sure that the Bolsheviks were the foremost enemies of the human race or at least of Great Britain.

Lloyd George had yet another cause for rebuking Churchill in the autumn of 1919. It was that he was failing to observe collective Cabinet responsibility. On 5 October Churchill had sent a message to the now beleagured Kolchak indicating that he had 'personally hoped' that recognition of his regime would have been accorded in the previous June. Seizing on this, Lloyd George sent Churchill five days later a minute stating that 'it is very undesirable and quite contrary to the accepted traditions of Cabinet responsibility for a Minister to suggest that he holds a different view from that which has finally been adopted by the Cabinet of which he is a member and which he has himself accepted'.[36] But Churchill still did not offer to resign and Lloyd George evidently did not feel politically strong enough to dismiss him.

Churchill's position was to be greatly undermined, however, during the course of the following month. For Denikin's 'National Russia' turned out after all not to be 'on the eve of its restoration'. Instead, a series of decisive defeats ensued – with the result that by the beginning of 1920 an outright Bolshevik victory in the South seemed increasingly likely. Simultaneously, Kolchak's efforts in Siberia collapsed: he himself was captured, interrogated and, finally, on 7 February 1920, executed by the Bolsheviks.

Now Lloyd George felt able to humiliate Churchill in public. On 8

November 1919 he accordingly made a dramatic statement at a banquet at the Guildhall to the effect that the British intervention, including all financial assistance, was at an end. Churchill, sitting in the audience and having apparently had no prior warning, heard the Prime Minister proclaim:

> We have sent a hundred millions' worth of material, and support in every form, and not a penny of it do I regret in spite of the heavy burdens which are cast upon us ... We cannot, of course, continue so costly an intervention in an interminable civil war. Our troops are all out of Russia – frankly, I am glad.[37]

Churchill for his part was not glad. And throughout 1920, as previously, he did not fail to make this clear both in private and in a variety of public statements. Above all, he took full advantage of a Cabinet policy, reaffirmed as late as 18 November 1920, that permitted members to denounce Bolshevism.[38] One historian, Clive Ponting, has even gone to the trouble to collect together some of his wilder utterances over a period of years:

> He told the House of Commons ...: 'Bolshevism is not a policy; it is a disease. It is not a creed; it is a pestilence.' This image of Bolshevism as a disease was one of Churchill's favourites. In the *Evening News* in July 1920 he wrote of 'a poisoned Russia, an infected Russia, a plague bearing Russia'. Nine years later in *The Aftermath* he described the Bolsheviks as 'swarms of typhus-bearing vermin'.
>
> The Bolsheviks were also a 'league of the failures, the criminals, the morbid, the deranged and the distraught'. In a speech in the Connaught Rooms in April 1919 they were a 'foul combination of criminality and animalism'. Animals were another favourite source of imagery. In a speech in Dundee in November 1918 Bolshevism was described as 'an animal form of Barbarism' and its adherents were 'troops of ferocious baboons amid the ruins of cities and the corpses of their victims' although the 'bloody and wholesale butcheries and murders [were] carried out to a large extent by Chinese executioners and armoured cars'. Again in a speech at the Mansion House in February 1919 he spoke of the 'foul baboonery' of Bolshevism ... although a month later the Bolsheviks were portayed as vampires.[39]

The same historian has also usefully drawn attention to Churchill's various outbursts relating to the linkage between Russian Bolshevism and Jewry:

> In private to [Lord] Curzon the Foreign Secretary [from 1919 to 1922] he described the Soviet Government as a 'tyrannic government of these Jew commissars' and even in public he called it 'a world wide

communistic state under Jewish domination'. In a public speech in Sunderland in 1920 he spoke of 'the international Soviet of the Russian and Polish Jew'. In April 1922 he drafted a letter ... in which he described the Bolsheviks as 'these semitic conspirators'. On another occasion they were 'these cold Semitic internationalists' and he usually referred to [Leon] Trotsky as Bronstein.[40]

Another historian, Norman Rose of the Hebrew University, Jerusalem, has also noted that Churchill 'made the unfortunate but common error of equating Jews and Bolsheviks'. He commented:

> Jews certainly played a leading part in the Bolshevik revolution, well out of proportion to their numbers among the Russian population. Four out of seven members of the first Politburo ... were Jews. But this was a far cry from Churchill's intemperate conjectures. Apart from this outburst, Churchill was remarkably free from anti-semitic prejudice.[41]

To Lloyd George, Churchill's various outbursts continued to be an irritation during 1920. But for much of the time the War Secretary seemed to have been reduced to mere impotent ranting. On 16 January 1920, for example, the Prime Minister told Henry Wilson in an almost patronising fashion: 'Winston has gone mad.'[42] And on the following day Frances Stevenson, Lloyd George's secretary and mistress, recorded in her diary: 'He [Churchill] has arrived [in Paris] simply *raving* because of the decision of the Peace Conference with regard to trading with Russia, which absolutely and finally ruins his hopes of a possible war in the East. At times he became almost like a madman.'[43]

The possibility of Great Britain, in common with its Allies, commencing trading with the Soviets naturally became the next issue on which Churchill became obsessive. But by May 1920 Lloyd George had decided that negotiations should definitely begin with Soviet representatives. On 31 May Leonid Krassin duly arrived at Number Ten to meet the Prime Minister and various colleagues. Churchill, who was not present, was filled with scorn. In his view, those concerned had grasped the 'hairy paw of the baboon'.[44]

Meanwhile Churchill had become increasingly alarmed at the linkages that were developing between the British Labour Movement and the Russian Bolsheviks. He saw this as a two-way process. British trade union leaders, to an extent impressed and emboldened by the Russian Bolshevik example, were frequently tempted to challenge the rule of law and were willing to threaten to call strikes in sympathy with one another's demands concerning hours and pay. In particular, a so-called Triple Alliance of miners, railwaymen and transport workers periodically caused panic throughout the Lloyd George Administration. But the Russian Bolsheviks were also increasingly beneficiaries of the new mood of industrial militancy in Great Britain that they had helped to create. For no effective military moves against them were likely to be possible if the British trade union leaders could be persuaded to organise resistance to any anti-Bolshevik decisions made by the British Government.

An example of the former tendency could be seen, according to Churchill and his followers, during the early months of 1920. Then an attempt was made by the miners to persuade the Trades Union Congress (TUC) to call a general strike to force the Government to nationalise the coal mines. This attempt failed – but not before many in Whitehall had become greatly alarmed. For example, Henry Wilson, still at Churchill's side in the War Office, wrote in his diary on 15 January :

> Transport Sub Committee of the Cabinet ... One after another got up and said there was nothing to be done, that the police were powerless, that the Citizen Guard had been forbidden by the Unions and that now the Unions would not allow Special Constables to be sworn and treated them like blacklegs ...
>
> It is a truly terrifying state of affairs and not one of them except Walter [Long, the First Lord of the Admiralty] and Winston seem prepared to put up a fight. [45]

An example of the tendency in the other direction, that is for the British trade unions to assist the Russian Bolsheviks, came in May 1920. At this time the armies of the latter were apparently losing ground in the Ukraine to the forces of newly-independent Poland, which had placed an order for munitions in Great Britain. The London dockers, with the support of the wider Labour Movement, accordingly decided to prevent the order being sent to Poland by refusing to load the munitions on the commissioned vessel – named *The Jolly George*. To Churchill's annoyance it was eventually forced to sail without its controversial cargo; industrial muscle had thus successfully shaped an aspect of Great Britain's international policy.

The two tendencies to some degree came together, however, in August 1920. On the home front the Triple Alliance appeared to be on the verge of calling a collective strike – on this occasion in support of a miners' wage claim. But meanwhile the Poles had begun to lose in their struggle with the Russian Bolsheviks to such an extent that even Warsaw itself was thought to be vulnerable. Lord Riddell recorded in his diary on 23 July how Churchill saw matters:

> He said, 'What I forsaw has come to pass. Now they are invading Poland, which they mean to make a jumping-off ground for propaganda in the rest of Europe. They will make peace with the Poles and endeavour to form a Soviet Government in Poland. The Bolsheviks are fanatics. Nothing will turn a fanatic from his purpose ... Their view is that their system has not been successful because it has not been tried on a large enough scale, and that in order to secure success they must make it world-wide'.[46]

Fearful that a complete Polish collapse would bring Bolshevism to the borders of an unstable Germany and that a German-Soviet 'conjuncture' against the Western powers would then occur, Churchill was naturally anxious that Great Britain should not adopt a passive stance. He was an eager advocate of Anglo-French military action to try to save Poland; and if that did not prove possible or adequate he hoped at least to prevent the 'Poison Peril from the East' spreading into Germany. He recognised that this might mean co-operating actively with the new moderate German Government. As he put it to Lord Riddell on 22 July: 'It may well be that Great Britain and France will have to call upon the Germans for their assistance [against Bolshevik Russia].'[47] And in these circumstances even Lloyd George seemed resigned to contemplating at least some show of force in support of Poland. Hence he threatened to send the fleet to the Baltic. But now the British Labour Movement decided to intervene. On 9 August at a meeting of representatives of the Trades Union Congress, the Labour Party's Executive and the Parliamentary Labour Party a resolution was passed stating that a war over Poland would be 'a crime against humanity' and warning that 'the whole industrial power of the organised workers' would be used to prevent it.[48] A Council of Action was then established. And on the following day the Prime Minister agreed to meet Ernest Bevin and other Labour leaders at Number Ten. A. J. P. Taylor related the sequel: 'On 10 August Bevin presented Labour's ultimatum. Lloyd George was delighted to turn the storm against his unruly colleagues. Labour, he said, was knocking at an open door so far as he was concerned; he even urged Bevin to act as negotiator between Russia and the British government.'[49] On the same day Lloyd George made it clear in the House of Commons that British armed intervention to save Poland had been ruled out.[50]

Nevertheless local Councils of Action sprang up all over the country in case he again changed his mind. And even Labour Party moderates echoed J. H. Thomas of the railwaymen when he spoke of challenging 'the whole Constitution of the Country'.[51]

Churchill and Henry Wilson in particular were dismayed at Lloyd George's capitulation to Bevin. And they further feared that he would yield to the unions again on domestic matters. At the same time, they became aware, through intercepts obtained by the intelligence services, that the Councils of Action that had emerged during the Polish crisis had been actively inspired by the Russian Bolshevik representatives supposedly present in London only to discuss opening trade with Great Britain. Naturally Churchill and Wilson demanded that Lloyd George immediately expel the Russians but they found that he was not apparently minded to do so. The Chief of the Imperial General Staff drew from this the astonishing conclusion, and not for the first time, that the Prime Minister might be a traitor working for the Bolsheviks. On 18 August, according to an entry in his diary, Wilson raised his suspicion with Churchill. He recorded the latter's reaction: 'Winston was much excited. He said it was quite true that LG was dragging the Cabinet step by step towards Bolshevism.' Wilson, according to his own account, even told Churchill that the attitude of Lloyd George and the Cabinet towards the intercepts 'put a severe strain on our (soldier) loyalty to the Cabinet as though we wished to be loyal to the Government we had a still higher loyalty to our King and to England'.[52]

By 24 August Wilson had persuaded Churchill that both men should send notes to the Cabinet demanding that the Soviet representatives be expelled. He added in his diary:

> I told Winston it was the chance of his life to come out as an Englishman and that in one bound he would recover his lost position and be hailed as saviour by all that is best in England. I think I have got him pretty well fixed. I warned him that we soldiers might have to take action if he did not and in that case his position would be impossible. He agreed. He said he was 'much worried' about LG's attitude and so am I, and it will take some explaining to ease my mind of the suspicion that LG is a traitor.
>
> [Air-Marshal Sir Hugh] Trenchard [the Chief of the Air Staff] with whom I discussed this matter later ... thinks, like [Sir] Basil Thomson [the Director of Intelligence based at the Home Office], that LG is a traitor. I *hate* to think it but cannot help getting very suspicious.[53]

Churchill duly sent, on 25 August, an alarmist note to Lloyd George and a few other other ministers. It included the following:

> I feel bound to bring to the notice of my colleagues the peturbation which is caused to the British officers who are concerned with this intelligence work when they see what they cannot but regard as a deliberate and dangerous conspiracy aimed at the main security of the State unfolding before their eyes and before the eyes of the executive Government without any steps being taken to interfere with it. In these circumstances the Government might at any time find itself confronted with disclosures and resignations which would be deeply injurious.
>
> I therefore ask specifically, What is the service which [L. B.] Kameneff and Krassin are expected to render this country which justifies us in delaying their expulsion? Their presence here is a source of continued and increasing danger. It is an encouragement to every revolutionary enterprise. The miners' strike, with all its indefinite possibilities, is drawing steadily nearer. Are we really going to sit still until we see the combination of the money from Moscow, the Kameneff-Krassin propaganda, the Council of Action, and something very like a general strike, all acting and reacting on one another, while at the same time our military forces are at their very weakest?[54]

With the Cabinet on protracted leave Lloyd George decided to ignore this plea. But now even Churchill and Wilson rather unexpectedly calmed down and no resignations were tendered. Probably this was mainly due to the fact that the threat to Warsaw had receded. The so-called 'Miracle of the Vistula' had occurred and the Bolsheviks had begun to be driven back into the Ukraine. And by 12 October the two sides duly agreed on a compromise peace that left anti-Communist Poland with borders far to the East but that denied any independent existence to the Ukraine which fell under Russian Bolshevik control. But if Warsaw had actually fallen in August 1920 who can say what would have happened next in British politics? Perhaps Wilson and others would have attempted a military coup against the 'traitor' Lloyd George. And possibly Churchill himself might have been headstrong enough to have become involved. But fortunately for all concerned the immediate crisis had passed.

Churchill now decided that after all the excitement a holiday in France would be appropriate and he duly left London on 2 September. In his absence Lloyd George convened a Conference of Ministers on 10 September which decided not to expel the entire Soviet trade delegation but simply to ask Kameneff alone to leave and merely to warn Krassin 'that his conduct had given rise to suspicion'.[55] And in the following month revolutionary (and counter-revolutionary) possiblities were further defused when Lloyd George managed to buy off the miners with a temporary pay rise and to secure a postponement of a looming rail strike. The threat posed by the Triple Alliance thus disappeared – at least for the remainder of 1920.

Churchill's anguish was not, however, at an end. For the negotiations with Krassin now began in earnest. And by 18 November 1920 Lloyd George was ready to ask the Cabinet to accept in principle that trading with Bolshevik Russia should begin. Only three colleagues joined Churchill in opposing the proposal.[56] Humiliated once more, he was only with difficulty dissuaded from resigning by Lord Birkenhead, a long-standing personal friend. But he consoled himself on the same evening by addressing the Oxford Union in terms that surely went beyond the freedom that Cabinet Ministers still had to denounce Bolshevism, in that it seemed to demand active intervention to eliminate it:

> all the harm and misery in Russia has arisen out of the wickedness and folly of the Bolsheviks, and ... there will be no recovery of any kind in Russia or in eastern Europe while these wicked men, this vile group of cosmopolitan fanatics, hold the Russian nation by the hair of its head and tyrannizes over its great population. The policy I will always advocate is the overthrow and destruction of that criminal regime.[57]

Lloyd George still evidently did not feel strong enough to dismiss Churchill. But he now determined that his War Secretary must at least be moved to another post much less involved with matters relating to Russia.

NOTES

1 Martin Gilbert, 'Churchill and the European Idea', in R. A. C. Parker (ed.), *Winston Churchill: Studies in Statesmanship*, London, 1995, p. 203; Martin Gilbert, 'From Yalta to Bermuda and Beyond: In Search of Peace with the Soviet Union', in James W. Muller (ed.), *Churchill as Peacemaker*, Cambridge, 1997, p. 304; and Winston S. Churchill, *The Aftermath*, London, 1929, p. 273.

2 War Cabinet Minutes, 10 November 1918, CAB 23/14, Public Record Office, London (hereafter PRO).

3 *The Times*, 27 November 1918. See also Churchill, *The Aftermath*, p. 47. Here he admitted: 'I cannot pretend not to have been influenced by electoral currents so far as verbiage was concerned.'

4 Quoted in Gilbert, *World in Torment*, p. 278.

5   Churchill to Lloyd George, 24 March 1920, Churchill Papers, in Martin Gilbert, *Winston S. Churchill: Vol. IV, Companion*, London, 1977, p. 1053.
6   Norman Rose, *Churchill: An Unruly Life*, London, 1994, pp. 70–1.
7   John Grigg, 'Churchill and Lloyd George', in Robert Blake and Wm. Roger Louis (eds), *Churchill*, Oxford, 1993, p. 104.
8   Imperial War Cabinet Minutes, 23 December 1918, CAB 23/42, PRO. See also Kettle, *Churchill and the Archangel Fiasco*, p. 60.
9   War Cabinet Minutes, 12 February 1919, CAB 23/9, PRO.
10   Diary of Henry Wilson, 13 February 1919, in Gilbert, *Churchill: IV, Companion*, p. 525.
11   War Cabinet Minutes, 13 February 1919, CAB 23/15, PRO; Lloyd George Papers, F 202/1/1, quoted in Kettle, *Churchill and the Archangel Fiasco*, p. 122.
12   Council of Ten Minutes, 14 February 1919, in Gilbert, *World in Torment*, pp. 244–5.
13   Kerr to Lloyd George, 15 February 1919, Lloyd George Papers, in *ibid.*, pp. 531–2.
14   Churchill to Lloyd George, 16 February 1919, Lloyd George Papers, in *ibid.*, p. 535.
15   Lloyd George to Churchill, Churchill Papers, in *ibid.*, pp. 538–9.
16   Lloyd George to Churchill, 17 February 1919, in *ibid.*, p. 540.
17   Diary of Henry Wilson, 17 February 1919, in *ibid.*, p. 541.
18   *Ibid.* See also John M. Thompson, *Russia, Bolshevism and the Versailles Peace*, Princeton, New Jersey, 1966.
19   Seth P. Tillman, *Anglo-American Relations at the Paris Peace Conference of 1919*, Princeton, New Jersey, 1961, p. 141.
20   Quoted in D. G. Boadle, *Winston Churchill and the German Question in British Foreign Policy, 1918–1922*, The Hague, 1973, p. 77.
21   *Ibid.*, p. 86.
22   War Cabinet Minutes, 4 March 1919, CAB 23/15, PRO; War Office Papers, 32/5682, PRO, in Gilbert, *Churchill: IV, Companion*, p. 571; and *Hansard*, vol. 114, cols 483–7, 26 March 1919.
23   War Cabinet Minutes, 6 March 1919, CAB 23/9, PRO; and Churchill to Lloyd George, 8 March 1919, WO 0149/6699, PRO, as quoted and summarised in Kettle, *Churchill and the Archangel Fiasco*, pp. 190–1.
24   *The Times*, 12 April 1919.
25   War Cabinet Minutes, 29 April 1919, CAB 23/10, PRO.
26   *Ibid.*, 11 June and 9 July 1919, CAB 23/15, PRO.
27   *Ibid.*, 29 July 1919, CAB 23/11, PRO.
28   *Ibid.*, 12 August 1919.
29   Lloyd George to Churchill, 30 August 1919, Churchill Papers, in Gilbert, *Churchill: IV, Companion*, pp. 826–7.
30   Lloyd George to Churchill, 22 September 1919, Churchill Papers, in *ibid.*, p. 869.
31   Lloyd George to Churchill, 7 October 1919, Churchill Papers, in *ibid.*, p. 899.
32   Gilbert, *World in Torment*, p. 342 n.
33   Churchill to Lloyd George, 10 October 1919, Churchill Papers, in Gilbert, *Churchill: IV, Companion*, p. 912.
34   Churchill to Denikin, 9 October 1919, Churchill Papers, in *ibid.*, p. 907.
35   Churchill to Lloyd George, 10 October 1919, Churchill Papers, in *ibid.*, pp. 912–13.
36   Churchill to Kolchak, 5 October 1919; and Lloyd George to Churchill, 10

October 1919, Churchill Papers, in *ibid.*, pp. 896, 910.

37 *The Times,* 10 November 1919.

38 Cabinet Minutes, 18 November 1920, CAB 23/23, PRO.

39 Clive Ponting, *Churchill,* London, 1994, pp. 229–30.

40 *Ibid.,* p. 230.

41 Rose, *Churchill,* p. 147. See also Norman Rose, 'Churchill and Zionism', in Robert Blake and Wm. Roger Louis (eds), *Churchill,* Oxford, 1993.

42 Diary of Henry Wilson, 16 January 1920, in Gilbert, *Churchill: IV, Companion,* p. 1004.

43 A. J. P. Taylor (ed.), *Lloyd George: A Diary by Frances Stevenson,* London, 1971, p. 197.

44 Stephen Roskill, *Hankey: Man of Secrets: Vol. II, 1919–1931,* London, 1972, p. 170.

45 Diary of Henry Wilson, 15 January 1920, in Gilbert, *Churchill: IV, Companion,* p. 1002.

46 Lord Riddell, *Lord Riddell's Intimate Diary of the Peace Conference and After,* New York, 1934, p. 224.

47 Gilbert, *World in Torment,* ch. 24; and Riddell, *Intimate Diary,* p. 222. For Churchill's fears concerning a possible German–Soviet 'conjuncture' see Boadle, *Winston Churchill and the German Question,* ch. 2. See also Draft Cabinet Memorandum (unsent), 29 August 1920, in Gilbert, *Churchill: IV, Companion,* pp. 1190–4.

48 Charles Loch Mowat, *Britain between the Wars, 1918–1940,* London, 1955, p. 41.

49 A. J. P. Taylor, *English History, 1914–1945,* Oxford, 1965, p. 144.

50 *Hansard,* 10 August 1920, vol. 133, cols 253–72.

51 Ralph Miliband, *Parliamentary Socialism: A Study in the Politics of Labour,* London, 1961, p. 80. See also L. J. Macfarlane, 'Hands Off Russia: The British Labour Movement and the Russo-Polish War, 1920', *Past and Present,* no. 38, December 1967, pp. 126–57.

52 Diary of Henry Wilson, 18 August 1920, in Gilbert, *Churchill: IV, Companion,* p. 1172.

53 Diary of Henry Wilson, 24 August 1920, in *ibid.,* p. 1178.

54 Churchill to Lloyd George, 25 August 1920, Lloyd George Papers, in *ibid.,* p. 1183.

55 Conference of Ministers Minutes, 10 September 1920, CAB 23/22, PRO. For more detail on the events of August and September 1920 see David Stafford, *Churchill and the Secret Service,* London, 1997, pp. 94–103.

56 War Cabinet Minutes, 18 November 1920, CAB 23/23, PRO. See also M. V. Glenny, 'The Anglo-Soviet Trade Agreement, March 1921', *Journal of Contemporary History,* V , 1970.

57 *The Times,* 19 November 1920.

2

IRRECONCILABLE ADVERSARY

1921–1933

IN FEBRUARY 1921 Churchill was moved from the War Office to the Colonial Office. This meant that he no longer had any direct responsibility for dealing with the Soviet Union. Indeed, not until he became First Lord of the Admiralty in Septemeber 1939 was he again to be in that position. But however limited his real influence on policy-making in this area, he clearly remained fascinated by everything connected with Bolshevism. And, being Churchill, he did not hesitate to offer his views both in private and in public – sometimes at considerable apparent risk to his chances of political advancement.

During 1921 he was perhaps too immersed in handling the pressing problems of the Middle East and Ireland to trouble his colleagues unduly over the relatively stable situation that had by now emerged in Soviet Russia. And in December of that year he was even briefly persuaded by the *émigré* Boris Savinkov that the Western Powers should offer help with economic reconstruction to the Bolsheviks provided they would, at a time when their so-called New Economic Policy was being implemented, agree also to 'mollify the tyranny' – which Churchill, in a moment of gullibility, thought they might be willing to do. He even speculated that the 'tyrannic Government of these Jew Commisars' might be so desperate for foreign aid that they might broaden the basis of their government in order to secure it. But Foreign Secretary Curzon, for once even more uncompromising than Churchill, rejected the idea out of hand.[1]

During 1922, however, Churchill swung back to unambiguous

hostility. What provoked him was Lloyd George's decision in March to move decisively towards arranging terms for general European *de jure* recognition of the Soviets. The idea was to invite them to send representatives for informal discussions at the forthcoming international conference in Genoa at which a number of outstanding issues relating to European pacification were to be considered. According to Lloyd George's initial plan, the Soviets were in effect to be offered full recognition provided they agreed that they would not make Bolshevik propaganda in countries with which they had diplomatic relations. The Prime Minister thought that he had already arranged French support for his position. But as he wrote to Frances Stevenson:

> The fat is well in the fire again. Austen [Chamberlain] writes to say that Winston says he will resign if I am to recognise the Bolsheviks at Genoa, and that he (Austen) cannot face the Tories on a resignation over that issue. If that is the case then I go, and I go on an issue that suits me. It puts Labour right on my side. I have written to Austen to say that I am not going to Genoa unless I am free to recognise the Bolsheviks if they accept the conditions and that the Cabinet must decide between Winston and me ... If the Unionists take Winston's view I go without any hesitation.[2]

The upshot was that the Cabinet held on 28 March reached a compromise: Lloyd George would go to Genoa and discuss recognition but of a kind that would originally fall short of full diplomatic recognition; and he would have to communicate with the Cabinet in London. In effect Churchill left his resignation on the table pending developments at the conference – though he had proclaimed to his colleagues on the previous day his opposition to a move which he thought was 'taking sides against Russia as a whole in favour of a band of dastardly criminals'.[3] In the event, however, the long-awaited showdown between Churchill and Lloyd George was averted because the French revealed themselves to be unexpectedly uncooperative at Genoa on many issues, including that of Soviet recognition, with the result that the conference broke down in failure. In the aftermath, in July 1922, Churchill felt strong enough to renew his resignation threat when Lloyd George seemed poised to try to reopen the issue of Soviet recognition and again it was the latter who backed down.

These developments cannot be understood, however, other than in their domestic political context. For in 1922 Lloyd George's Coalition Administration was widely seen to be approaching collapse. And Churchill, as the most prominent of Lloyd George's Liberal followers, cannot have been unaware that the most likely outcome would be a general election that would produce a new House of Commons polarised between Conservative and Labour – with Liberals like himself badly squeezed. It is possible therefore that his anti-Soviet line in 1922 was partly intended to strengthen his appeal to Conservatives in case he should wish to abandon Liberalism. But there were also risks involved in being an anti-Soviet extremist. For he must have known that he was annoying several prominent Conservatives who wished to maintain the Coalition and did not relish the prospect of being outflanked on this issue by a so-called Liberal. For example, Austen Chamberlain had written to Lloyd George on 23 March: 'he [Churchill] is, as I have said, your follower, and therefore doubly dangerous to me and my colleagues if he parts from us on a question where he would have the sympathy of a large section of Unionist opinion.'[4]

In the event the Coalition was terminated by the Conservatives in October 1922 – with the Soviet issue being of little importance in their decision. Nor was Churchill, temporarily hospitalised with an appendicitus, active in precipitating the final collapse. So he was left with no alternative other than to try to retain his seat at Dundee with the Liberal Party label – though with no Conservative candidate opposing him. But in this he was unsuccessful. In what was a two-member constituency he came fourth, his personal vote having fallen by 5,000 since 1918. Socialists took the two winning places. This election campaign was notable not only for Churchill's failure but also for his increasingly obvious alienation from Liberal mainstream attitudes. For apart from having a unique anti-Soviet reputation, he now began to describe the Labour Party and the trade unions in venomous language that even most Conservatives would have repudiated. He had come to believe, as has been seen, that Labour's attitudes had been fatally affected by events in Russia and that respect for British constitutional proceedures had been undermined. For example, he linked E. D. Morel, his Labour opponent, with Communism in this crude fashion: 'Mr [William] Gallagher [the Communist candidate] is only Mr Morel with the courage of his convictions, and Trotsky is only Mr Gallagher with the power to murder those whom he cannot convince.'[5]

Once out of Parliament Churchill sought to move as rapidly as he could back into the Conservative Party. For the latter now dominated the political scene – with the Liberals of various types all being evidently in terminal decline. But his transition was delayed by the decision of Prime Minister Stanley Baldwin to adopt full-blooded protectionism and seek a new electoral mandate for this policy in December 1923. As a long-standing opponent of this approach – he had deserted the Conservatives for the Liberals on the same issue in 1904 – Churchill was stymied. He accordingly fought West Leicester as a Liberal candidate. He was defeated by Labour.

The outcome of the 1923 General Election was a setback for the Conservatives. For, though remaining the largest single party, they lost their overall majority in the Commons. This led to the formation of the First Labour Government headed by Ramsay MacDonald. It was supported by the Liberal Party which shared its outlook on free trade. Churchill saw this as a decisive moment. He announced his bitter hostility to the Liberal move, declaring that 'the enthronement of a Socialist Government will be a serious national misfortune such as has usually befallen great states only on the morrow of defeat in war'.[6] This meant that he could now plausibly head towards the Conservative Party, which moreover seemed likely to abandon extreme protectionism in the light of the electorate's negative verdict.

By March 1924 Churchill was back on the hustings in a by-election in the Westminster Abbey division. He called himself an Independent Anti-Socialist. He sought and received much support from leading Conservatives notwithstanding the candidature of an official Conservative. He criticised Bolshevism in severe terms and warned, as he had done at Dundee, about the 'Socialist Peril' at home. He was defeated by the official Conservative by the narrow margin of 43 votes. Impressed rather than enraged, the Conservative leadership decided to find him a safe seat for the next General Election which ensued in October 1924 following the collapse of the minority Labour Government. He was presented with Epping and even allowed to call himself a Constitutionalist rather than a Conservative.

This friendly gesture did not lead Churchill to behave with greater prudence. On the contrary, while a prospective candidate he simply became wilder than ever in his denunciations of the Labour Party. What he now objected to was the formal diplomatic recognition MacDonald had accorded to the Soviets and the subsequent decision to present a treaty to Parliament which, if it had not been defeated, would have allowed them a trade-promoting loan in return for a debt settlement. In a speech at Edinburgh on 25 September he said that he objected 'to subsidising tyranny'. He considered it 'an outrage on the British name' that loans should be given to the Soviets 'to pay for the ammunition to murder the Georgians, to enable the Soviet sect to keep its stranglehold on the dumb Russian nation, and to poison the world, and as far as they can the British Empire, with their filthy propaganda'.[7] Churchill also objected in the most extreme fashion to the Labour Government's decision to abandon the prosecution of the editor of the Communist *Weekly Worker*, J. R. Campbell, who had allegedly urged sedition on the armed forces. He correctly anticipated that it would lead to the Government being defeated in a vote of confidence in the House of Commons and that a general election would ensue. A public statement given to the Press Association by Churchill on 7 October included the following:

> An appeal to the country on the grave issues of this dropped Prosecution would in my judgment be very serious for Ministers … The prominence of such a question would in no way diminish the importance of the Russian Treaty. On the contrary there is in my opinion a very close connection between the conduct of the Government in stopping the prosecution of a Communist Editor, and their surrender against their better judgment to the extremists of their Party and to the dictation of Moscow in the matter of the guaranteed loan to the Russian Bolsheviks. In both cases you see His Majesty's Socialist Ministers forced to go back upon their better judgment in consequence of subterranean, and possibly external pressure. In both cases they knew what was the right course to take. The Prime Minister refused to give a guaranteed loan to Russia. The Attorney-General set out to do his duty in prosecuting the Communist Editor for sedition. In both cases they recoiled from the clear, plain path of duty; and in both cases their recoil is acclaimed in Moscow as a result of the influence exerted upon a British Cabinet and British Ministers by a foreign organisation and by the friends of that foreign organisation in London. There are in the ranks of the Socialist Government many men of high reputation, men who stood by their country in the war, men who have lived their lives in the public eye and in the House of Commons for a whole generation. The position of these men is pathetic. They have been unable to keep their feet upon the slippery slopes on which they tried to stand. Well was it said of the French Revolutionary: 'No one knows how far he will go when he tries to work with men who are ready to go to all lengths.'[8]

During the course of the 1924 election campaign the Labour Party's chances were further damaged by the Zinoviev Affair. A letter, apparently signed by G. Y. Zinoviev of the Communist International based in Moscow and urging British Communists to engage in subversive acts, was intercepted and leaked to the *Daily Mail*. It is now widely thought among historians to have been a forgery – though it was in no way out of character with Zinoviev's public line. But it was rather unscrupulously used by opponents as a means of implying that the Labour Party was somehow linked to Moscow's plans. None was more extreme than Churchill who, in a speech in his new constituency, denounced MacDonald for demonstrating 'a sense of comradeship with these foul, filthy butchers of Moscow'. He continued:

> They write from their Praesidium, or centre of control, in order that germ cells shall be established in our regiments and on our ships, that propaganda shall be developed in our streets and villages. They write to order that preparations shall be made for bloody revolt to be started and for civil war, flames and carnage to disturb and defile our streets. They write to order these things in this country at the very moment when they are here discussing with the British Government a treaty for a loan, asking for more of our money. I say such a situation has never occurred in the history of this country.[9]

Safely elected at Epping, Churchill seemed destined to become a maverick figure in the new House of Commons. But Baldwin, returned to Number 10 with an overall majority, was clearly worried about the prospect and agreed with Austen Chamberlain who told him: 'If you leave him [Churchill] out, he will be leading a Tory rump in six months' time.'[10] So Baldwin decided to make Churchill the extraordinarily generous offer of the Chancellorship of the Exchequer – gambling correctly that as long as he held such a senior post he would be reasonably contented and broadly loyal. A grateful and astonished Churchill naturally seized his 'glittering prize'.

During his stint as Chancellor, which lasted for more than four years, Churchill did not, however, abandon his obsession concerning the Soviet Union. But his ability to influence developments was, if anything, rather less than it had been during his time in Lloyd George's Cabinet. For though he now held a much more senior post, he was no longer serving in a vulnerable coalition but in a one-party administration with a secure majority. Baldwin, in short, was in a much stronger position than Lloyd George to face Churchill down if he threatened resignation. In fact, three trials of strength over the Soviet Union took place during the first year of the new administation – with Churchill defeated on all occasions. Shortly after entering office, on 14 November, the Chancellor urged the incoming Foreign Secretary, Austen Chamberlain, to cancel the formal recognition which the Labour Government had accorded to Moscow. But the Foreign Secretary temporised before announcing in the Commons that relations would continue with a Soviet chargé staying in London. And he also turned down Churchill's demand to be allowed to see intelligence cables – a decision , on Churchill's appeal, upheld by the Prime Minister. Then in July 1925 Chamberlain was faced with evidence from intelligence sources of hostile activities by London-based Soviets 'such as I suppose we have never tolerated from any government'.[11] He accordingly suggested the establishment of a five-man Cabinet Committee to review the situation. But Churchill was pointedly excluded from it and he cannot have been pleased with its conclusion that, in effect, nothing should be done by way of publishing evidence or breaking off relations.[12]

Churchill did not, however, have to wait long for an opportunity to undermine Chamberlain on the Soviet issue. For in the second half of 1925 and in the early months of 1926 the prospect of industrial strife at home greatly increased, and with it fears in Conservative circles of Soviet encouragement for trade union extremism. True, on 30 July 1925 Churchill surprisingly agreed with Baldwin that the Government should provide a nine-month subsidy to preserve exist-ing wages and hours in the troubled coal industry. Meanwhile a Royal Commission headed by Herbert Samuel was to investigate the crisis in the pits. But the suspicion must be that Churchill, at least, was only engaged in a tactical manoeuvre in order that adequate preparations could be made for a later showdown with the entire domestic Labour Movement which, despite the timidity on most matters that had been revealed by the Labour Government, he continued to believe had been dangerously infected with the Bolshevik virus. He had never doubted that some Labour leaders wished to be moderate but he thought they were frequently manipulated by wilder followers.[13] Now with Labour again in opposition in Parliament, Churchill thought the extremists would seek to advance on the industrial front.

In this mood he risked making a speech on 11 December 1925 at Battersea which was something of a challenge to his colleagues:

> Behind Socialism stands Communism; behind Communism stands Moscow, that dark, sinister, evil power which has made its appear-ance in the world. This band of Cosmopolitan conspirators are aiming constantly to overthrow all civilised countries and reduce every nation to the level of misery in which they have plunged the great people of Russia. They strike everywhere, by every method, through every channel which is open to them. But there is no country at which they strike so much as at this island of ours.[14]

As a result Baldwin was faced with a difficult Parliamentary Question and he accordingly asked Churchill to prepare a draft reply. This led the Chancellor, now somewhat in retreat, to pen words that for the first time conceded the case for continued relations with the Soviet Union despite its faults: 'in an endeavour to foster trade between Great Britain and Russia and as a *modus vivendi*, we have resumed and are maintaining diplomatic relations with the Soviet Government.'[15]

Churchill's hand was to be strengthened, however, when the threatened General Strike materialised in May 1926. He saw it as a dramatic and conscious challenge to the Constitution and, according to Neville Chamberlain (then Minister of Health), in the days before its commencement was 'getting frantic with excitement and eagerness to begin the battle'.[16] Baldwin put him in charge of the *British Gazette*, remarking privately that 'it will keep him busy, stop him doing worse things' and adding 'I'm terrified of what Winston is going to be like'.[17] In the event the moderate anti-Bolshevik leaders of the TUC rapidly called off the General Strike once they had grasped the constitutional implications. The miners were simply left to face eventual defeat. But Churchill continued to believe that sinister pro-Soviet forces had been seriously involved. It is true of course that the Soviets welcomed the British General Strike and even contributed some funds to assist strikers and their families. But it seems unlikely that their role in any phase of British interwar industrial relations, perhaps in some contrast say to the period 1972–1985, was of any great importance. After all, industrial relations had also been extremely strained in the years before 1914 when no Soviet regime existed. And, above all, few if any of the TUC General Council members during the interwar years were Leninists or even Marxists. Churchill, however, saw matters in a different light. For on 19 June 1926, knowing that he had the support of a group in the Cabinet led by Home Secretary William Joynson-Hicks, he spoke as follows about the Soviets:

> If the Russian Bolsheviks could only pull down Britain, ruin its prosperity, plunge it into anarchy, obliterate the British Empire as a force in the world, the road would be clear for a general butchery, followed by a universal tyranny of which they would be the heads and out of which they would get the profits. They would not succeed in their aim. They did not understand at all the resources of tempered strength on which this nation rested. They thought of it as if it were a part of their own ignorant slave state.
>
> They thought the same kind of stuff with which they bamboozled their own moujiks would suit Britain. They are always expecting to

wake up and find that we are cutting each other's throats for their benefit. They had their dupes, they had their feather-headed hirelings and allies in this country, but they will be disappointed ... His Majesty's Government understand exactly their aims and their methods. The Socialist Party in the House of Commons was now labouring to prove that the Russian Government had nothing to do with the sending of money to foment the general strike. But what were the facts? The Russian Government, the Third International, and the Russian trade unions are all of them only off-shoots of the Russian Communist Party. The inner committee of the Communist Party was the sole central governing, controlling body in Russia. It is the real Cabinet of Russia. They work all the marionettes. They animate and direct every part of the diabolical machinery which is in action all over the world. When they knew the hand that fires the pistol, what does it matter which finger pulls the trigger?

The Government were under no illusions. He had heard the question asked several times, and it was a perfectly fair question: Why do you let them stay here? Why do you not throw them out?

I am sure it would give me a great deal of satisfaction if they were thrown out. Personally, I hope I shall live to see the day when either there will be a civilised Government in Russia or that we shall have ended the present pretence of friendly relations with men who are seeking our overthrow.[18]

In the year following the collapse of the General Strike Churchill gradually gained support for his outlook and he decided to try to internationalise his anti-Bolshevik appeal by heaping extraordinary praise on Benito Mussolini and his Fascist Government in Italy. According to *The Times*, at a press conference in Rome on 20 January 1927 he said:

it is quite absurd to suggest that the Italian Government does not rest upon popular bases or that it is not upheld by the active and practical assent of the great masses.

If I had been an Italian I am sure that I should have been wholeheartedly with you from start to finish in your triumphant struggle against the bestial appetites and passions of Leninism. But in England we have not had to fight this danger in the same deadly form. We have our own way of doing things. But that we shall succeed in grappling with Communism and choking the life out of it – of that I am absolutely sure.

I will, however, say a word on an international aspect of Fascismo. Externally, your movement has rendered a service to the whole world. The great fear which has always beset every democratic leader or working-class leader has been that of being undermined or overbid by someone more extreme than he. It seems that continued progression to the Left, a sort of inevitable landslide into the abyss, was characteristic of all revolutions. Italy has shown that there is a way of fighting the subversive forces which can rally the mass of the people, properly led, to value and wish to defend the honour and stability of civilised society. She provided the necessary antidote to the Russian poison. Hereafter, no great nation will be unprovided with an ultimate means of protection against cancerous growths, and every responsible labour leader in every country ought to feel his feet more firmly planted in resisting levelling and reckless doctrines. The great mass of the people love their country and are proud of its flag and history. They do not regard these as incompatible with a progressive advance towards social justice and economic betterment.[19]

The last paragraph was not reproduced either in Gilbert's authorised biography nor in the companion volume of documents but was summarised in a sentence.[20] Yet it is perhaps the most extreme endorsement of right-wing dictatorship that he was ever to utter. Indeed, it could be said to amount to nothing less than an invitation or even an incitement to those who were serious about seeking 'the necessary antidote' to a likely takeover by Red revolution to follow in the ultimate the example of the Italians. When some in Germany, East-Central Europe and Spain did just that in the 1930s, they may therefore have wondered why Churchill withheld his wholehearted public endorsement.

Meanwhile in May 1927 Churchill had the satisfation of seeing Austen Chamberlain forced at last to acquiesce in decisive action being taken against the Soviet community in London. Warned by intelligence sources that the All Russian Co-operative Society (ARCOS), a vehicle for Anglo-Soviet trade, was being used as a base for subversion, the Prime Minister reluctantly consented to a police raid. This produced sufficient evidence, in the Government's opinion, to justify the suspension of relations with Moscow and the expulsion of the Soviet chargé. The impression thus created was that Churchill had triumphed over his more pragmatic colleagues. He did not hesitate to capitalise on this. For on 27 May, the day the Soviet mission was informed of the breach, Churchill sent a public letter to a Conservative by-election candidate. It included these words:

> The fact that we are falling behind other countries in recovering from the war is due more than anything else to the misuse of the great Trade Union Movement by the Socialists. Unless they are checked, they will ruin the country. In fact some of them want to ruin the country, because they hope to clamber on top of the wreckage ...
>
> Just as the Trade Unionists have let themselves be led by the nose by the Socialist extremists, so the Socialist extremists have fallen

increasingly under the influence of Moscow. Many of them are fascinated by the spectacle of a gang of conspirators having succeeded in toppling over the Russian Empire and now ruling it with a rod of iron. They think they might with a little luck do the same sort of thing here and get the country into their grip by violence, and hold it down afterwards by terror. The Russian Bolsheviks are always urging them to try. They send them money, they help them to organise, they teach them how to poison people's minds, and how to spread the propaganda of Revolution ...

We have shown the patience of Job. Perhaps contempt has led us to show more patience than was wise. But at last, after every warning had been disregarded and their bad faith was shown to be bottomless, the House of Commons by an overwhelming majority has resolved to utter the short, simple but useful word – 'Go!'.[21]

The Soviets were not gone for long. For after the General Election of 1929 the Labour Party returned to office (again dependent on Liberal support) and quickly restored relations with Moscow despite Conservative objections. And now for the first time a Soviet Ambassador, Gregory Sokolnikov, came to London and actually had to be invited to shake hands with a horrified King George V. Who could then have foreseen that relations would never again be broken off, and that Sokolnikov's immediate successor, Ivan Maisky, who served from 1932 until 1943, would become a close associate of Churchill?

Meanwhile the fall of the Conservative Government was followed by a period of extreme personal and political turbulence in Churchill's life. On the face of it he left office in May 1929 with every reason to travel hopefully. For at 54 he was significantly younger than his outgoing principal Conservative colleagues, namely Baldwin, Austen Chamberlain and Joynson-Hicks, all of whom were over 60. But within three years he had become a largely discredited backbencher without a serious following. A mixture of conviction, poor judgment and sheer bad luck brought this about. He seems first to have been genuinely dismayed at the decision of Baldwin and his frontbench colleagues to give broad approval to the Labour Government's summoning of a Round Table Conference to discuss the future of India. Probably his anti-Sovietism helped to push him in this direction. For as early as 2 January 1920 he had made a close connection between Bolshevism and the Indian clamour for self-rule:

We may abandon – the Allies may abandon – Russia. But Russia will not abandon them. The ghost of the Russian bear comes padding across the immense field of snow. Now it stops outside the Peace

Conference in Paris, in silent reproach at their uncompleted task. Now it ranges widely over the enormous countries which lead us to the frontiers of India, disturbing Afghanistan, distracting Persia, and creating far to the southward great agitation and unrest among the hundreds of millions of our Indian population, who have hitherto lived in peace and tranquility under British rule.[22]

But Churchill was mistaken in supposing that most Conservatives would share his die-hard opposition to the granting of any degree of self-government to India. Hence, when he somewhat capriciously quit the 'Shadow Cabinet' on the issue in January 1930 he found himself more completely in the wilderness than he expected. He continued, however, to stress his concerns about India and, in particular, the Soviet propaganda aimed at destabilising it. For example, on 18 May 1931 he spoke as follows in the House of Commons:

> Let me read to the Prime Minister [MacDonald] what is published in the official Press of Russia about India ... This is what is said by the International Press Correspondence, the organ of the Communist International, and it is dated 26th February 1931. 'We need in India to build class proletarian trade unions at a feverish pace, instantly, every day and under all circumstances [...] The preparations for a general political strike must be brought to the front [...] We must rouse the masses [...] We must inspire them with the spirit of war to the bitter end, and the spirit of struggle for India in which there will be no place for British Imperialism.' These things are published under the full authority of the Government of the day in a country where ... no newspaper opinion is allowed which is not in accord with the opinions of the Government of the day.[23]

This linking of his twin obsessions concerning the Soviet Union and India may not have increased Churchill's popularity with the Conservative Front Bench. But he may well have expected that there would in due course be moves to reconcile divergent forces within the Conservative Party and that he would thus be able to return to the Front Bench before the end of a Parliament that appeared likely to run for near to a full term. Hopes for anything of this kind were to be fatally undermined, however, when in August 1931, during a severe international financial crisis, a so-called National Government was formed under MacDonald's leadership and with Baldwin and the Conservative Front Bench in full support. For the sudden emergence of another coalition meant that the Conservatives could not, on returning to office, have the usual number of Cabinet posts and hence no reconciling gesture to Churchill could be made. Meanwhile his personal finances had been undermined by loss of office and by the Wall Street Crash; and he had been seriously injured in a motor accident in New York. The upshot was that he was forced to try to rebuild his political career in unenviable circumstances. Some inconsistency and opportunism based on desperation was therefore only to be expected. What was to be surprising, however, was the bewildering extent of his moves back and forth across the political spectrum during the next decade, although he contrived to remain nominally a Conservative Member of Parliament throughout.

At first Churchill's approach was to make himself the principal right-wing extremist on the issue of India – an obsesssion that was to occupy most of his attention until July 1934, when the House of Commons as a whole decisively came down against his attempt to use the Committee of Privileges to discredit Sir Samuel Hoare, the Secretary of State for India. But if India was for several years Churchill's main concern, he played up to the same die-hard constituency in other respects too. For example, he was to be unfashionably severe, both in public and in private, about all attempts to achieve disarmament and arms control by international agreement. And he continued, as before, to condemn the Soviet Union and Communism. On 13 May 1932, for example, he warned of the 'threat to peace' from Moscow:

> We must also remember that the great mass of Russia, with its enormous armies and with its schools of ardent students of chemical warfare, poison gas, its tanks and all its appliances, looms up all along the frontier of Europe and that the small States, Finland, Estonia, Latvia, Lithuania, Poland – not a small State, but for this purpose in the line – and Romania, are under the continued preoccupation of this enormous and to them in many ways unfriendly Russian power.[24]

Then, when the Japanese, having invaded Chinese-owned Manchuria, threatened to move into China proper, he attempted to excuse their conduct in view of the threat from Communism. On 17 February 1933 he addressed the Anti-Socialist and Anti-Communist Union in these terms:

> I hope we shall try in England to understand a little the position of Japan, an ancient state with the highest state sense of national honour and patriotism and with a teeming population and a remarkable energy. On the one side they see the dark menace of Soviet Russia. On the other the chaos of China, four or five provinces of which are actually now being tortured, under Communist rule.[25]

Clearly, then, he was no enthusiast for the League of Nations but on the contrary saw fit to give aid and comfort to its foremost enemy at this time. Indeed, the Japanese aggression in 1932–1933 was widely seen as the League's first major test – which it unambiguously failed. Churchill's conscience was apparently untroubled – though he was later to posture as a League supporter.

As for European developments, Churchill offered a relatively muted reaction to the rise of the Nazis and Adolf Hitler, who became Chancellor of Germany in January 1933. Given the blimpish constituency Churchill was then courting, this is perhaps unsurprising. For though Hitler was clearly a potential bulwark against Bolshevism he could hardly be praised in quite the same fulsome way as Mussolini – given that Germany, in contrast to Italy, had so recently been at war with Great Britain. Churchill was similarly prudent with respect to the implications for British relations with France. For example, less than a month after Hitler's victory Churchill told his constituents that 'there was no likelihood of a war in which Great Britain would be involved'. 'The Government,' he added, 'had very rightly refused to extend our obligation in Europe or elsewhere.'[26] And on 14 March he stated: 'I hope and trust that the French will look after their own safety, and that we shall be permitted to live our life in our island ... without again being drawn into the perils of the Continent of Europe. But if we wish to detach ourselves, if we wish to lead a life of independence from European entanglements, we have to be strong enough to defend our neutrality.'[27] But by 13 April 1933 he had moved sufficiently to feel able in a speech in the Commons to criticise the 'grim dictatorship in Germany'. And he opined that 'as surely as Germany acquires full military equality with her neighbours while her own grievances are unredressed and while she is in the temper which we unhappily see, so surely would we see ourselves within a measurable distance of general European war'. On the other hand, he still gave no signs of wanting to ally with France: 'We should be very careful not to mix ourselves up too deeply in this European scene.'[28] True, by 7 November 1933 Churchill was paying lip-service to the League of Nations. But what apparently he had in mind at this time was to use the League not as a means of confronting the Germans but rather of appeasing them:

> Whatever way we turn there is risk. But I believe that the least risk and the greatest help will be found in re-creating the Concert of Europe through the League of Nations, not for the purpose of fiercely quarrelling and haggling about the details of disarmament but in an

attempt to address Germany collectively, so that there may be some redress of the grievances of the German nation and that that may be effected before this peril of rearmament reaches a point which may endanger the peace of the world.[29]

As 1934 dawned, then, Churchill was still seen as a 'die-hard' Tory. And there was so far no indication that he had any intention of softening his hostility to the Soviets, let alone of favouring alliance with them against Germany.

NOTES

1 Churchill to Curzon, 24 December 1921, Curzon Papers, in Gilbert, *Churchill: IV, Companion*, pp. 1699–1701; and Curzon to Churchill, 30 December 1921, in Stephen White, *The Origins of Detente: The Genoa Conference and Soviet–Westen Relations, 1921–1922*, Cambridge, 1985, p. 44. Churchill had previously flirted with the idea, in April 1918 and again in the spring of 1920, that the Bolshevik leaders, potentially 'with ropes around their necks', might be interested in some form of compromise settlement with their enemies. See Martin Gilbert, *Churchill's Political Philosophy*, London, 1981, pp. 78–81.

2 Lord Beaverbrook, *The Decline and Fall of Lloyd George*, London, 1963, p. 138. For further details see also White, *Origins*, pp. 83–94.

3 Stephen White, *Britain and the Bolshevik Revolution: A Study in the Politics of Diplomacy, 1920–1924*, London, 1979, pp. 64–5.

4 Chamberlain to Lloyd George, 23 March 1922, Lloyd George Papers, quoted in Gilbert, *World in Torment*, p. 777.

5 Robert Rhodes James, *Churchill: A Study in Failure, 1900–1939*, London, 1970, p. 148.

6 *The Times*, 18 January 1924.

7 *Ibid.*, 26 September 1924.

8 Martin Gilbert, *Winston S. Churchill: Vol. V, Companion, The Exchequer Years*, London, 1979, pp. 213–6.

9 *The Times*, 27 October 1924.

10 David Dilks, *Neville Chamberlain: Vol. I, Pioneering and Reform, 1869–1929*, Cambridge, 1984, p. 398.

11 Chamberlain to Baldwin, 24 July 1925, Austen Chamberlain Papers, quoted in David Dutton, *Austen Chamberlain: Gentleman in Politics*, Bolton, 1985, p. 275.

12 Christopher Andrew, 'British Intelligence and the Break with Russia in 1927', *The Historical Journal*, XXV, 1982, p. 958.

13 See above, p. 33.

14 Gilbert, *Churchill: V, Companion, The Exchequer Years*, p. 621n.

15 *Ibid.*, p. 621.

16 Neville Chamberlain to his wife, 21 May 1926, Neville Chamberlain Papers, quoted in Ponting, *Churchill*, p. 308.

17 Robert Rhodes James, *Memoirs of a Conservative: J. C. C. Davidson's Memoirs and Papers, 1910–37*, London, 1969, p. 238.

18 *The Times*, 21 June 1926. For the views of Joynson-Hicks at this period see Gabriel Gorodetsky, *The Perilous Truce: Anglo-Soviet Relations, 1924–27*, Cambridge, 1977, pp. 175–7.

19 *The Times*, 21 January 1927. For a slightly different version see Churchill's Chartwell Papers, 9/82, Churchill College, Cambridge.

20 Gilbert, *Prophet of Truth*, p. 226. Parts of the paragraph in question appear in Paolo Pombeni, 'Churchill and Italy, 1922–40', in Parker (ed.), *Winston Churchill*, p. 73.

21 Gilbert, *Churchill: V, Companion, The Exchequer Years*, pp. 1001–2.

22 *The Times*, 5 January 1920.

23 *Hansard*, 18 May 1931, vol. 252, col. 1663.

24 *Ibid.*, 13 May 1932, vol. 265, col. 2352.

25 *The Times*, 18 February 1933.

26 *Ibid.*, 25 February 1933.

27 *Hansard*, 14 March 1933, vol. 275, col. 1820.

28 *Ibid.*, 13 April 1933, vol. 276, cols 2791–3. The version of this Commons speech in Gilbert, *Prophet of Truth*, pp. 462–3, does not correspond to that in *Hansard*.

29 *Hansard*, 7 November 1933, vol. 281, col. 142.

3

GUARDED
RAPPROCHEMENT

1934–1939

ONCE INDIA ceased, in the summer of 1934, to be Churchill's main concern, some shift in his other attitudes soon emerged but no great consistency was apparent. Perhaps the reality was that, for several years, he was at a loss to know how to rebuild his career. He had clearly lost faith in an approach that appealed only to Conservative die-hards but, for whatever reason, he could not bring himself loyally to back MacDonald and Baldwin, who dominated the middle ground of British politics until May 1937. And so he continued to be a critic of the National Government. This did not prevent him, however, from feeling acute disappointment at not receiving an offer to return to the Cabinet when, in March 1936, a new post for Defence Co-ordination was created. Thereafter personal animosity towards Baldwin may have become an increasingly important element in shaping his outlook. For example, Henry ('Chips') Channon, a Conservative MP, wrote of Churchill in his diary on 15 May 1936: 'He is consumed with contempt, jealousy, indeed hatred, for Baldwin, whom he always denigrates.'[1] At all events, he became increasingly unpredictable. And on most issues he seemed, as Labour's Arthur Greenwood claimed as early as October 1935, to be 'boxing the compass'[2] and to be desperately seeking friends in the most unlikely quarters.

Two of his 'issues', the need for British rearmament and his support in the Abdication Crisis of 1936 for King Edward VIII, who was incidentally well-known in elite circles for his sympathy for Nazi Germany, may have gained him additional approval, so far as it went, from parts of the Right. But a tendency from time to time to berate Germany, and a belated decision, after rather than before the Italian conquest of Abyssinia, to ally with Viscount Cecil of Chelwood in defence of the League Covenant, won him some rather guarded plaudits from the Left and also from Jews across the political spectrum. But there were two other matters on which he was to face considerable difficulty in deciding whether, and to what extent, he was with the Right or the Left. One centred on the Soviet Union: should he soften his hostility towards it in view of the possible threat from Germany? The other not unrelated matter was his need to decide how to react to the Spanish Civil War, which broke out in July 1936.

So far as the Soviet Union was concerned, his first serious move in its direction came in 1934. Ambassador Maisky wrote in 1966: 'In the middle of 1934 Churchill on his own initiative made my acquaintance and thereafter made every effort to develop our relations.'[3] This claim is not endorsed by Churchill's authorised biographer, who appears to place their first meeting in 1936.[4] But in any case such a meeting, if it actually occurred in 1934, would undoubtedly have been a private affair and hence may not have signified much. What is beyond question, however, is the date of Churchill's first public gesture indicating a new approach towards Moscow. This was 13 July 1934, when he told the House of Commons: 'I believe that the statement which the Right Honourable Gentleman [Sir John Simon, then Foreign Secretary] has made as to the welcome which would be extended to Soviet Russia in the League of Nations is one about which there will be no dispute in this country, even among those who have the greatest prejudices against the political and social philosophy and system of government which the Russian people have, I will not say chosen for themselves but have found it necessary to adopt.'[5] This was an astonishing intervention on two counts. First, it clearly signalled an end to his long crusade against all forms of diplomatic recognition of the Soviet Union. Second, he blatantly passed up the opportunity to point out that the Soviet Union's traditional doctrines relating to international affairs were absolutely incompatible with the aims of the League of Nations, which placed almost exclusive emphasis in its Covenant on the sanctity of national frontiers, and which gave absolutely no recognition to 'class' as a basis for justifying the use of armed force. (Lenin had initially seen Geneva as the seat of what he called a 'League of Burglars'.) But Churchill did not just address the issue of Soviet membership of the League. He went on to suggest that the Soviets might now be genuinely interested in promoting world peace:

> I notice that for some time the speeches of Mr. [Maxim] Litvinoff [then Soviet Foreign Minister] had seemed to give the impression, which I believe is a true one, that Russia is most deeply desirous of maintaining peace at the present time. Certainly, she has a great interest in maintaining peace. It is not enough to talk about her as 'peace-loving' because every Power is peace-loving always. One wants to see what is the interest of a particular Power and it is certainly the interest of Russia, even on grounds concerning her own internal arrangements to preserve peace.[6]

But however startling this volte-face seemed at the time, Churchill was still very far from advocating any direct or indirect British alliance with the Soviets. Gradually, however, he was forced during the next several years to contemplate this possibility. For he became persuaded, at least intermittently, of the desirability of backing France against Germany, despite knowledge that in May 1935 the former had signed an alliance with the Soviet Union and had proceeded to ratify it in March 1936. And the case for giving British support to France was greatly strengthened in Churchill's eyes by Germany's decision in the same month, ostensibly as a retaliation for this ratification, to remilitarise the Rhineland in defiance of the Versailles and Locarno Treaties. Although he did not call for war on this issue, he clearly did think that the Anglo-French response was too feeble and that steps must be taken to deter further aggressive acts on Germany's part. But the French link to Moscow undoubtedly put off many British Conservatives who otherwise might have agreed with Churchill. And his embarrassment was made worse by the outcome of the French General Election of April 1936, which resulted in the creation of a Popular Front Government, headed by Socialist Léon Blum, and supported by Communists. For example, Lord Londonderry, a friend and relative, wrote to Churchill on 4 May 1936:

> When I saw Hitler in the course of a two hours' interview he spoke chiefly of the Communistic menace and I found myself in agreement with a great deal of what he said. His prophesies of the French Election have been absolutely fulfilled, and I view with grave apprehension the Communistic influences, which have assumed such a large proportion in France. We in this country, owing to the fact that Communism is non-existent, take the view that Germany is exaggerating the Communistic danger, but I am quite sure that they

are doing nothing of the kind and I deeply regret first of all, the Alliance which the French were forced to make with Russia.[7]

Churchill, in his reply on 6 May, was evasive on the Communist/ Soviet aspects but did state that the only chance of avoiding a European war would be 'to have a union of nations, all well-armed and bound to defend each other, and thus confront the Nazi aggression with over-whelming force'.[8] That he wanted the Soviet Union to be one of these nations was implied, though not clearly stated, in a letter published in The Times on 13 May.[9]

The fact was, however, that Churchill at this point was not wholly consistent in his approach. On 19 April he had told Maurice Hankey, the Cabinet Secretary, that he favoured what amounted to encirclement of Germany by Great Britain in alliance, under League auspices, with 'the various countries of the Baltic, Holland, Belgium, France, Italy, Switzerland, Austria, the Balkan States, Russia and Poland'.[10] But by 25 May he was able to write to Lady Violet Bonham Carter, a prominent Liberal, announcing that his anti-German encirclement scheme involving the Soviet Union was wholly dependent on Italian collaboration. For if Mussolini 'refused to work with us and leaves the League of Nations, then I would say sorrowfully and openly that nothing remains for us but to provide for our own interests and security'. 'This,' he added, 'would be done by a strictly limited regional pact among the Western States.' His latest vision continued: 'In this second case we should have to expect that the Germans would soon begin a war of conquest east and south and that at the same time Japan would attack Russia in the Far East. But Britain and France would maintain a heavily-armed neutrality in the north and the Mediterranean powers would hold Mussolini completely gripped on all sides so that he would have to be neutral too.'[11] In the event Italy did indeed leave the League of Nations and gradually aligned itself with Germany. But by then Churchill had again changed his line; he was in the last resort to favour any kind of 'Grand Alliance' against the Axis Powers rather than the Anglo-French heavily-armed neutrality he had suggested to Lady Violet. It was left to Neville Chamberlain and other appeasers when Czechoslovakia came under pressure to try faithfully to implement Churchill's vision of 25 May 1936.

Meanwhile, back in 1936 many Conservatives were showing their concern at the possibility of British involvement with the Soviets. As early as 4 April Thomas Jones of the Cabinet Office recorded: 'In two party meetings of back-benchers last week, the first, addressed by Austen [Chamberlain] and Winston, was on the whole pro-French; but two or three days later opinion had swung round to a majority of perhaps 5 to 4 for Germany. Part of the opposition to France is influenced by fear of our being drawn in on the side of Russia.'[12] Then, at the end of June, 48 backbench Conservatives signed a Commons motion in these terms: 'That this House looks confidently to His Majesty's Government to eschew any military or other commitments which have the appearance of an alliance between Great Britain and France and the Soviet Union and adheres firmly to the desire for close relations between Great Britain, Germany, and France, which was stressed by the Prime Minister in this House on 23 June.'[13] Churchill was certainly to some degree responsive to these feelings. For example Leopold Amery, a former Conservative Cabinet Minister, recorded in his diary on 16 July:

> Foreign Affairs Committee. I was interested to find that I had them practically solid with me not only on the impossibility of a League based on coercion but also on keeping out of any continental arrangements that committed us to Russia ... Even Winston, who afterwards argued against declaring that we washed our hands of Russia and Eastern Europe, qualified that by saying that we should not commit ourselves to military intervention on her behalf.[14]

The intensifying anti-Soviet mood and Churchill's reluctance to challenge it was, however, most strikingly revealed on 29 July when, in the course of a private meeting with a deputation of senior Conservatives, including Austen Chamberlain and Churchill, to discuss the pace of British rearmament, Baldwin himself offered a few candid reflections on the wider context:

> We all know the German desire ... to move East, and if he [Hitler] should move East I should not break my heart ... There is one danger, of course, which has probably been in all your minds – supposing the Russians and the Germans got fighting and the French went in as allies of Russia owing to that appalling pact they made, you would not feel you were obliged to to go and help France, would you? If there is any fighting in Europe to be done, I should like to to see the Bolshies and the Nazis doing it.[15]

Churchill was allowed to make the final contribution to the discussion. But the minutes reveal that he ducked Baldwin's remarkably penetrating question about France and merely stuck to details relating to British rearmament.[16] Had he taken up the challenge he would almost certainly have been able to count on strong support from Austen Chamberlain.[17] But Churchill, for whatever reason, did not see fit to contradict Baldwin.

This apparently uncharacteristic circumspection on Churchill's part was probably connected with the fact that a Popular Front Government had been elected in Spain earlier in 1936 and the disorders this produced had culminated in the outbreak of a full-scale Left–Right civil war on 17 July. As the historian Maurice Cowling has written, 'most Conservative MPs sympathised with [General Francisco] Franco from the start'.[18] And Churchill was undoubtedly one of them. But it is less clear how most Conservative MPs felt about the implications of the Spanish Civil War for British relations with Germany. As another historian, Richard Griffiths, has written:

> On the Right, the Spanish Civil War impinged on Anglo-German affairs to the extent that the question of intervention became one more item on the international agenda and the Bolshevik threat appeared, to some, to need Germany as its champion. Not everyone on the Right, however, saw the connexion.[19]

Churchill personally had clearly never been an enthusiast for appointing Nazi Germany as a champion of anti-Bolshevism or anything else. But he was probably not unaffected during the second half of 1936, and also during 1937, by the fact that many of his fellow sympathisers with Franco saw matters differently. As he put it to Foreign Secretary Anthony Eden on 7 August: 'This Spanish business cuts across my thoughts.'[20] In short, unambiguous ideological polarisation in Spain may have driven him for a time much nearer to his appeasement-minded colleagues than most of his admirers would today wish to recognise. For example, William Manchester has claimed without adequate evidence that Churchill saw Baldwin's line at the private meeting held on 29 July as 'begging the question'. Manchester continued: 'Germany, not Russia, threatened the peace. His [Churchill's] fear was that the Tory rank and file, championing Franco's style of Red-baiting, would join Hitler's camp followers.'[21] And Churchill's authorised biographer has written:

> Churchill did not share Baldwin's view that if there were to be fighting in Europe it would be good 'to see the Bolshies and the Nazis doing it'. Indeed, with the outbreak of the Spanish Civil War, he was afraid that Conservative sympathies, veering as they did to Franco and anti-Commmunism, would go too far, and move closer to Germany. 'I do not like to hear people talking of England, Germany

and Italy forming up against European Communism,' Churchill
wrote to the French Ambassador.

In whatever way the Spanish Civil War ended, Churchill wrote
in an article in the *Evening Standard,* the violence, the cruelties and
the drawing in of outside forces, could only help the ever-increasing
Nazi power.[22]

These interpretations are, however, open to challenge. Above all,
Churchill's purpose in writing to the French Ambassador in London,
Charles Corbin, has to be seen in the context of France having a
Popular Front Government. Churchill's principal fear at this stage
may not, then, have related solely to Germany, as Manchester and
Gilbert appear to suppose, but may have been that Paris would give
active support to the left-wing Government in Spain and thereby help
bring about an ultimate victory there for Communism. It is of course
clear that he hoped, as did the British Government, that France, like
Great Britain, would remain neutral in the Civil War. But it has also to
be borne in mind that it was politically impossible and unthinkable for
Blum's Government actively to assist Franco as Germany and Italy
were able to do. Thus Churchill may have initially urged French
neutrality because the only realistic alternative would have been
active support for the Republican Government in Madrid. For it is
certain that he himself was not really neutral in outlook but sympathised with the anti-Communist side in Spain. He refused, for
example, to shake hands with the Spanish Ambassador. And he wrote
in the *Evening Standard* on 10 August 1936: 'A revivified Fascist
Spain in closest sympathy with Italy and Germany is one kind of
disaster. A Communist Spain spreading its snaky tentacles through
Portugal and France is another, and many will think the worse.'[23] So
when he wrote to the French Ambassador that he did not like to hear
people talking of England, Germany and Italy forming up against
European Communism, what he probably meant to convey to Paris
was that France was in danger of being written off as an ally or even
seen as drifting into a Communist grouping. In short, Churchill was
perhaps not primarily and certainly not solely afraid that British
Conservative 'sympathies would go too far, and move closer to
Germany' (in Gilbert's words) but was, above all, apprehensive lest
French sympathies go too far in a Communist direction.

The plausibility of this interpretation of Churchill's line is
bolstered if one considers his response to a letter sent to him by
General Sir Hugh Tudor, a long-standing personal friend who was

occasionally a guest at his Chartwell retreat. Tudor wrote on 4 August 1936:

> The situation in Europe certainly seems to be getting worse. Spain is a new complication. If the rebels win the Fascist group will be strengthened in Europe, and Spain may line up with Italy and Germany.
>
> If the red Government wins Bolshevism will come very near us. With Spain Bolshie, France half Bolshie, and Russia subsidising our communists are we going to line up with them and Russia?
>
> I know how important even vital our friendship with France is, but I feel many in England would rather make a strong western pact with Germany and France and let Germany settle Russia and Bolshevism in her own way. No doubt Germany would *eventually* be stronger after defeating Russia but in the meantime we and France would have time to get our defences right; and it would take years before Germany would be in a position to make war again, nor do I suppose she would want to having got a satisfactory expansion. Even Germany cannot like war.
>
> Russia deserves what is coming to her, as she will never stop undermining capitalistic governments in every way she can. If she is left alone, in 10 years or so she will be the strongest power on earth and *she* may want to take in India and may be a more dangerous enemy than Germany.[24]

This was an unusually lucid exposition of the case for the appeasers. And it surely had the great merit so far as Churchill was concerned that it envisaged France being part of the anti-Red grouping. But is it possible that Churchill was also seriously attracted even to the German aspect of Tudor's case as the Communist menace to the western end of Europe seemed to be fully revealing itself? The answer in the present writer's opinion is in the affirmative. For his reply to Tudor on 16 August leaned towards the appeasers' side of the argument. Instead of offering any kind of rebuke, he merely wrote:

> I have, as you divine, been much perturbed in my thoughts by the Spanish explosion. I feel acutely the weight of what you say ... I am sure it represents the strong and growing section of Conservative opinion, and events seem to be driving *us* in that direction.[25] [Italics added.]

Actually, this highly significant hint as to Churchill's private views would not be at all astonishing to us today if we had not been misled by his own memoirs (in which, for example, he claimed to be neutral in the Spanish Civil War),[26] and by the writings of some of his admirers into thinking that he had become a single-minded anti-Nazi by the late 1930s. For would it otherwise have seemed plausible to us that his earlier anti-Communist principles, not to say emotions, would have so completely left him?

What perhaps requires further explanation is why Churchill in his return to anti-Communist attitudes showed at least some restraint and why, in particular, he appeared at times to have an ambiguous line concerning the Soviet Union itself. Why, for example, did he not break off all contact with Maisky? The answer probably lies in his growing obsession with Great Britain's need to accelerate its rate of rearmament. To maximise his influence in this direction he had to take account of the views of potential sympathisers on both the Right and the Left of British politics. So far as the Left was concerned, he could not ignore the fact that most of those willing to support him on rearmament were almost exclusively motivated by hatred of Nazi Germany and Fascist Italy and by belief in 'collective security' under League of Nations auspices; and he must have been conscious that his own standing as a self-proclaimed League supporter had scarcely been enhanced by his recent equivocal attitude concerning the sanctions applied against the Italians in the wake of their attack on Abyssinia. Indeed, on 9 April 1936 Churchill had written frankly about the tactical importance of the League as a potential umbrella to further his aims in a private letter to A. R. Wise, a Conservative backbencher:

> if we can bring all the others [states in the East including the Soviet Union] in against German aggression before the end of the year, the forces with which we ourselves are associated would be overwhelming, and we might be able to come to terms with the Germans without a war. At the same time it would be folly to go in for such a policy unless we are prepared to face a war. The League of Nations is the only means by which all these overwhelming forces can be assembled. It is also the means by which the greatest unity can be obtained in this country.[27]

At the same time, Churchill was aware that the most influential Conservative backbench advocate of rearmament was not in fact himself but Austen Chamberlain, the former Party Leader and elder statesman. Despite their earlier lack of closeness of outlook, particularly on matters relating to the Soviet Union in 1919 and during the 1920s, the two men were indeed co-operating closely in 1936 on the rearmament issue and, as we have seen, were the leading figures in a deputation received by Baldwin. Churchill may therefore have hesitated to adopt too strident an anti-Soviet tone during the second half of 1936 if this was likely to alienate Chamberlain. The two men were in communication on the Soviet issue at the beginning of July 1936, when Churchill lent his colleague a letter he had received from an anti-Soviet backbench Conservative MP, Reginald Purbrick. The latter was primarily concerned about the possibility that the British Government might decide to agree to Turkey's desire to see the ending of the Demilitarised Zone of the Dardanelles and hoped that Churchill and Chamberlain would take a stand against it. But he also warned against any British alliance with the Soviet Union, France and Turkey against Germany. Churchill sent it to Chamberlain without any comment of his own but with a request for the latter's reaction. Chamberlain rather testy reply to Churchill, dated 4 July, read:

> I am afraid I differ from him [Purbrick] *in toto*.
>
> I regard it as impossible to maintain the Demililtarized zone in the Straits since we have allowed Germany to fortify the demilitarized zone on the Western frontier ...
>
> Secondly, I do not regard Russia as a military menace to us or to Europe. Nor do I regard Germany as a defence of Europe against Communism. That is part of Hitler's propaganda, but if my safety depended upon him, I should think myself very insecure. Communism is an internal menace in many countries and no doubt wherever it appears to have a chance to flourish, it is encouraged and aided by the Third International which is indistinguishable from the Soviet Government, but against this kind of attack Germany can offer no guarantee to other countries, and I think the German menace to our own safety so real and so imminent that it would be folly to dissipate our strength and energies over a number of minor perils when we need to concentrate them all to save us from the greater peril.
>
> I dictate in haste and therefore, I fear, rather dogmatically, but 'them's my sentiments' shortly put.[28]

It is at least suggestive that Chamberlain wrote in this vein to Churchill and not the other way round.

Possibly, then, Churchill was influenced somewhat by the need to avoid alienating unduly either the British non-Communist Left or Austen Chamberlain by engaging in strident anti-Communist and still less anti-Soviet rhetoric during the early months of the Spanish Civil War. All the same, during the remainder of Baldwin's Premiership, which ended in May 1937, Churchill was to continue to lean towards Franco's side – even though he accepted the British Government's decision to favour and to try to promote non-intervention by all foreign powers. On 10 August 1936, for example, he wrote in the

Evening Standard that the Republic was 'sliding steadily toward the Left ... falling into the grip of dark, violent forces coming ever more plainly into the open, and operating by murder, pillage and industrial disturbance'.[29] And on 2 October he wrote for the same newspaper: 'No one can now pretend that the issue bears the slightest resemblance to a struggle between a constitutional Parliamentary Government and a militarist-Fascist revolt. What a lesson these events should be to advanced Radical or moderate Socialists who in alliance with extreme forces form constitutional governments!'[30] This indicates that Churchill accepted Franco's line (which is by no means one that many historians, rightly or wrongly, would unreservedly endorse today) that the Government in Madrid really was heading for Communism in 1936. At first he was reluctant, however, to believe that the Soviet Union itself would any longer want actively to promote Communism throughout Western Europe. For example, on 10 August he wrote in the *Evening Standard* in terms that hinted at a willingness on his part to see Stalin as a 'revisionist' interested only in 'Socialism in One Country': 'Two antagonistic modern systems are in mortal grapple [in Spain]. Fascism confronts Communism. The spirit and prowess of Mussolini and of Hitler strive with those of Trotsky and Bela Kun [who had briefly been the leader of an unsuccessful and extreme Bolshevik experiment in Hungary in 1919].'[31] And on 4 September he wrote in the same newspaper about the meaning, as he then saw it, of the Moscow Purges which had seen the execution of such members of the Bolshevist Old Guard as Kameneff, Zinoviev and Mikhail Tomsky. Churchill commented that 'certainly, if ever human tears were rightly lacking on such occasions' it would be in this case. For, as well as recalling that these were 'men whose names and crimes are by-words throughout the world', he saw the executions as a welcome 'lurch to the Right' in the Soviet Union. The fact that 'these victims were nearly all Jews' clearly troubled him: 'Evidently the Nationalist elements represented by [Josef] Stalin and the Soviet armies are developing the same prejudices against the Chosen People as are so painfully evident in Germany. Here again extremes meet, and meet on a common platform of hate and cruelty.' But the main point was that, as the Soviet Union became more like Nazi Germany, it was potentially more valuable as a factor in the European power balance:

> Russian nationalism and discrowned Imperialism present themselves more crudely but also more solidly. It may well be that Russia in her old guise of a personal despotism may have more points of contact

with the West than the evangelists of the Third International. At any rate it will be less hard to understand. This [the staging of show trials] is in fact less a manifestation of world propaganda than an act of self-preservation by a community which fears, and has reason to fear, the sharp German sword.[32]

Then, he wrote to his wife from Paris on 13 September as follows:

Everything gets worse, except the Nationalists (as they insist on being called) are winning [in Spain]. *Secret.* F. [Pierre-Etienne Flandin, the former French Foreign Minister] thinks that the French Communists were paid at the election, not by Russia but by *Germany* – in order to weaken France. Pretty cynical if true. This would explain why Stalin executed the Bolshevik old guard: i.e. in order to break the orthodox Communists who were disobeying his orders about not disturbing France. On this showing it looks as if the Russians are trying to move to the right – and with sincerity. Of course this is only surmise.[33]

The evidence about Soviet international conduct, especially in Spain and France, reaching Churchill in the ensuing weeks served, however, to a considerable extent to undermine this hope. By 16 October he had accordingly arrived at this rather nuanced conclusion as presented to the readers of the *Evening Standard*:

It would be premature and far too sweeping to say that Russia is a military dictatorship rather than a Communistic State. In fact Russia enjoys the blessings of both dispensations at the present time; but there is no doubt which is on the wane …

The external action of Moscow proceeds along two contradictory paths: the first tries to bring about the world revolution. It has played its part in giving birth to the Spanish Horror. The second seeks to become a serviceable factor in European relationships, and is, whatever we may feel about it, an essential element in the balance of power.[34]

Next, on 30 October, he wrote in the same newspaper that 'Soviet Russia has taken not a few steps likely to render difficult, if not impossible, her association with the western democracies, and with the League of Nations'.[35] Then, on 5 November, addressing the House of Commons, he vigorously condemned Soviet 'intrigues' in Spain as 'insensate folly'. He elaborated:

so far as I have been able to ascertain, there is practically no doubt that an enormous influence in creating revolutionary conditions in Spain was the most imprudent and improvident action of Soviet Russia. I say that it would be quite impossible for the free nations of the western world to interest themselves in the fate of Russia, let alone make incursions on her behalf, if she continues to present herself in this guise. It would be a crime to call upon French or British soldiers, or upon the good peoples of these two countries, to go to the aid of such a Russia. Why it would be worse than a crime; it would be an act of supreme futility. But there is another Russia, which seems to be growing stronger as the years pass, which only wishes to be left alone in peace … Such a Russia has its rights in the comity of the nations, if, by foolish conduct, these rights are not destroyed and … such a Russia would be an indispensible element in the equipoise of peace both in the West and in the East. But we have not such a Russia at the present moment.[36]

Gradually, then, Churchill in some respects distanced himself during the winter months of 1936–1937 from many of his prospective allies on the British Left. On 15 December, for example, he made it clear to the left-leaning Duchess of Atholl, who was still nevertheless at this stage nominally a Conservative MP, that he would not accept an invitation to speak with her at the Annual Congress of Peace and Friendship with the USSR.[37] And this may not have been entirely due to his changing evaluation of Soviet conduct. For he must have been aware that Baldwin was approaching a decision to retire. His successor was widely expected to be Chancellor of the Exchequer Neville Chamberlain, who might conceivably have been willing to bring Churchill into his Cabinet provided that he did not give the appearance of having entirely lost touch with those in the Conservative Party who shared his own outlook, which involved feeling near-contempt for most representatives of the British Left of that period and visceral hatred, above all, for the Soviet Union and Communism. And any worries Churchill may have had about thereby falling out of step with his new Conservative partner Austen Chamberlain, whose views on foreign policy had come to differ greatly from those of his half-brother, ended on 16 March 1937 with his sudden death. Speaking in the Commons on 14 April, Churchill thus found the courage to say: 'I will not pretend that, if I had to choose between Communism and Naziism, I would choose Communism.'[38] It was seemingly the first time he had ever said this in so many words in public. As for Spain, he reaffirmed to the Commons in the same speech his support for the official British Government line backing non-intervention. But his private view remained what it had been from the outset: as he had written to his wife on 5 September 1936, it would be 'better for the safety of all if the Communists are crushed'.[39] And his journalistic references to the

Spanish struggle during the winter of 1936–1937 were undoubtedly broadly in line with the outlook of the Conservative Right. On this alleged 'bias' the historian Robert Rhodes James has written:

> Although he expressed repugnance at the atrocities committed by both sides, it was unfortunate that Churchill always managed to differentiate between them. Thus, the Communists indulged in 'butcheries' while Franco was only guilty of a grievous error of military judgement by not offering fair terms of surrender to beaten foes, for 'such a course would markedly help the winning side'. But the Madrid Government, he declared (2 October 1936), had committed the 'hideous series of nightly butcheries which have robbed [it] of the lineaments of a civilised power', and Largo Cabellero was referred to as the 'Lenin of Spain'. It would appear, from Churchill's version of events, that the Government forces dragged 'helpless and defenceless political opponents' whose only crime was that 'they belong to the classes opposed to Communism' to slaughter whereas the Franco-ist forces never decended to this 'lowest pit of human degradation'. He averred that:
>
> > Although it seems to be the practice of the Nationalist forces to shoot a proportion of their prisoners taken in arms, they cannot be accused of having fallen to the level of committing the atrocities which are the daily handiwork of the Communists, Anarchists, and the POUM (...) It would be a mistake alike in truth and wisdom for British public opinion to rate both sides at the same level. (9 October 1936.)[40]

By May 1937, therefore, Churchill appears to have been ready to work closely with the new Prime Minister, Neville Chamberlain, if only the latter had offered him a Cabinet post. As it was, even though disappointed in this respect, he felt able as the senior Privy Councillor on the Conservative benches to second the nomination of Chamberlain as Party Leader and to make a friendly speech about him. In fact the two men remained on reasonably cordial personal terms until Chamberlain's death in 1940. For Churchill respected Chamberlain as he had never been able to respect MacDonald and Baldwin in the years after 1931. All the same, Churchill and Chamberlain gradually drew apart and, as is well known, by September 1938 they stood for completely divergent approaches to the question of whether or not to go to war with Germany. Nominally, the narrow issue addressed at this time turned on whether Czechoslovakia should be required to surrender the German-speaking Sudetenland to Germany. But the reality was that in 1938 Chamberlain still favoured giving Germany a free hand to overrun Eastern Europe and ultimately the Soviet Union exactly as Baldwin (and Tudor) had envisaged in the summer of 1936. On the earlier occasion there had been, as has been seen, no consistently clear objections from Churchill. But now, in 1938, he decisively came out on the other side of the argument: he favoured war rather than see Czechoslovakia humiliated; he appeared to assume that Great Britain, if it stood firm, would have the support not only of France but also of the Soviet Union (whose public backing he urged Chamberlain to seek); and he was confident that Hitler would either be deterred, overthrown or defeated in war. We must now ask why Churchill had moved so far in so short a time.

The most lurid possible explanation would centre on the fact that Churchill faced financial ruin in March 1938, following stock market losses and the termination of his journalistic contract with Lord Beaverbrook. Having placed Chartwell, his country home, on the market, he was suddenly saved when an anti-Nazi acquaintance volunteered to carry a then vast debt of more than £18,000 for three years. The rescuer was Sir Henry Strakosh who happened to be a Jew born in Moravia, Czechoslovakia. The historian John Charmley has accordingly asked: 'So was Churchill a "hired help" [the words of David Irving] for a Jewish lobby, which, regarding Jewish interests as superior to those of the British Empire, was determined to embroil that Empire in a war on their behalf?' But his sensible conclusion is that 'no one would argue that Churchill only opposed Hitler because he was receiving cash for it'.[41] And there is, moreover, absolutely no evidence known to this writer that afterwards Strakosh ever regarded Churchill as an 'agent of influence' or behaved with the slightest impropriety towards him.

Another unfriendly explanation for Churchill's strong divergence from Chamberlain in 1938, however, is a good deal more plausible. It is simply that he had lost hope of being asked to serve under Chamberlain and accordingly decided to gamble all at the age of 63 on being catapulted into power on a wave of anti-German emotion. In such circumstances Churchill would have had to be ready to work with left-wing forces and to move back towards favouring British align-ment with the Soviet Union. For this cynical gamble, if such it was, to succeed Chamberlain's 'appeasement' policy had of course to be seen to fail. And indeed by 26 September 1938 Churchill's career-driven hopes, on this interpretation, stood high. For the Cabinet had just rejected Chamberlain's wish to accept Hitler's latest terms concerning the Sudetenland. And Foreign Secretary Lord Halifax, without Chamberlain's knowledge, had issued a statement that read: 'If, in spite of the efforts made by the British Prime Minister, a German attack is made upon Czechoslovakia, the immediate result must be that France will be bound to come to her assistance, and Great Britain and Russia will certainly stand by France.'[42] Two days later a buoyant Churchill thus sat behind Chamberlain as he began to address the House of Commons in terms that suggested war must be imminent. But suddenly the Prime Minister was handed a note which allowed him to announce in theatrical fashion that Hitler had agreed to a four-power meeting in Munich: a compromise outcome was now being signalled. Most MPs expressed their joy and Churchill himself felt obliged to shake the Prime Minister's hand. According to his author-ised biographer, Churchill then wished Chamberlain 'God speed'.[43] But other accounts have him saying sourly, 'By God, you were lucky!'[44] This latter remark would of course fit in well with the interpretation that Churchill, in a certain sense, was at this hour more an ambitious politician than a high-minded statesman.

Less discreditable explanations for Churchill's divergence from Chamberlain cannot, however, be discounted. First, it may well be that, like a great number of his compatriots, he had come to believe that Hitler was simply not 'appeaseable' to any degree and that British interests now required that a stand be taken, even in the East, at the earliest possible opportunity. But Churchill had seemingly been here before. For, as has been seen, he had talked robustly to Hankey in April 1936 about encircling Germany with Russian support – only to draw back within a few months. The timing of this retreat may, however, give us the ultimate clue enabling us to explain his course: the extent of the menace represented by the Soviet Union and Communism. Quite simply, in the summer of 1936 he feared a Red victory in Spain with potential implications elsewhere in Western Europe and especially in France (where the early outbreak of another civil war was not to be ruled out) and in Portugal. Hence, as we have seen, he became highly critical of the Soviets – for example, in his Commons speech of 5 November 1936 – while still keeping open lines of communication to the non-Communist British Left. But by 1938 it was clear that Franco was approaching victory and that the pro-Communist tide in France, marked in 1936 by widespread sit-ins in factories, had receded. So now Churchill could return with relative safety to an unambiguous anti-German line and even contemplate a

British alliance with the Soviets given that their influence was once again largely confined to the East. But if this interpretation is persuasive we have to ask a searching question: what if, in 1938, it had been the Reds who had been on the brink of triumph in Spain with all the Europe-wide ramifications that could have been involved? Is it not plausible that in such circumstances Churchill ('I will not pretend that if I had to choose between Communism and Naziism, I would choose Communism') might have supported Munich and might even have saluted Hitler as a bulwark against Bolshevism?

Churchill's contacts with Maisky also provide some guidance to his thinking. In April 1936 Hankey wrote that he was 'apparently a bosom friend of M. Maisky'.[45] And it is known that Churchill had two meetings in May 1936 with the Soviet Ambassador, 'on whom he urged the need for Russian support of the League of Nations Covenant'.[46] But after the outbreak of the Spanish Civil War relations cooled. For example, on 10 November 1936 Maisky took Churchill to task for allegedly claiming that Moscow was responsible for its outbreak.[47] And it was indeed not until the onset of the Czechoslovak Crisis early in 1938 that they began a serious collaboration. Even then Churchill was at first cautious. For in March, when the Soviets proposed a four-power meeting among themselves, the French, the British and the Americans he declined to endorse the idea – which was also decisively rejected by Chamberlain, who told his sister that he believed that the Soviets were 'steadily and cunningly pulling all the strings behind the scenes to get us involved with Germany'.[48] Instead, Churchill, in his speeches and articles at this time, stuck to relatively vague demands for preparations for collective action under the auspices of the League – with only France openly envisaged as a leading potential partner for Great Britain. On 9 May 1938, for example, in a speech at the Free Trade Hall in Manchester he clearly chose his words with particular care when referring to Moscow: 'To the east of Europe lies the enormous power of Russia, a country whose form of government I detest, but which at any rate seeks no military aggression upon its neighbours, a country whose interests are peace, a country profoundly menaced by Nazi hostility, a country which lies as a great background and counterpoise at this moment to all those states of Middle Europe I have mentioned.' He went on to urge the British Government not to go 'cap in hand to Russia, or count in any definite manner upon Russian action'. He concluded: 'But how improvidently foolish we should be when dangers are so great, to put needless barriers in the way of the general association of the great Russian mass with resistance to an act of Nazi aggression.'[49] And even when the Czechoslovak Crisis peaked in the autumn of 1938 he was careful about what he said in public about the Soviet Union. But behind the scenes at least, he now made repeatedly clear to both Chamberlain and Halifax that he believed the only hope of deterring Hitler from invading Czechoslovakia would be for Great Britain and France to join with the Soviets in proclaiming a joint intention to assist if it was attacked. On 3 September, for example, acting on information received from Maisky, he eagerly told Halifax that the Soviets would be interested in making such a declaration – an approach that the British Government at the time found unhelpful. After all, if Maisky had a message for Halifax why did he not deliver it himself? Churchill seems, incidentally, to have been unwilling in this period to admit to having any doubts of the kind he had expressed in the Commons as recently as 5 November 1936 about Soviet good faith, whereas Chamberlain in particular supposed that the Soviet aim was merely to provoke a war among capitalist powers from which they would seek to benefit.

It is unsurprising, therefore, that Churchill came to be seen as something of a nuisance in Whitehall. For example Alexander Cadogan, the Permanent Under-Secretary at the Foreign Office, wrote in his diary on 1 October 1938: 'Winston, G. Lloyd [Lord Lloyd], and others are intriguing with [Jan] Masaryk [the Czechoslovak Ambassador] and Maisky.'[50] And even some of Chamberlain's Conservative critics, particularly Amery, were privately dismayed at Churchill's enthusiasm for trying, behind the scenes, to push the Government into public association with Moscow.

In the aftermath of the Munich Agreement Chamberlain's reputation naturally soared and Churchill's standing vis-à-vis the Conservative activists in his Epping constituency began to look precarious. Churchill accordingly once again distanced himself from Maisky for a time and avoided making demands for cooperation with the Soviet Union. The furthest he felt able to go in Moscow's direction was to hint, on 30 December 1938, at some apparent remorse for his earlier hostility towards the Left in the Spanish Civil War. For now, with the Republican cause obviously doomed, he claimed to have arrived at the view that 'it would seem that today the British Empire would run far less risk from the victory of the Spanish Government than from that of General Franco'.[51] But once Germany had occupied

Prague in March 1939 he was able gradually to reveal more of his thinking. His first opportunity came following the Cabinet's decision, made at Halifax's insistence against Chamberlain's better judgment, that Poland should be guaranteed against a German attack. A statement to this effect having been made by Chamberlain in the House of Commons on 3 April, Churchill, in welcoming the move, was enabled to speak of the Government 'having begun to create a Grand Alliance against aggression'. As for Moscow:

> Why should we expect Soviet Russia to be willing to work with us? Certainly we have no special claim upon her good will, nor she on ours. But Soviet Russia is profoundly affected by the German Nazi ambitions ... No one can say that there is not a solid identity of interest between the Western democracies and Soviet Russia, and we must do nothing to obstruct the natural play of that identity of interest.[52]

Afterwards he was observed by Channon, still an unreconstructed appeaser and anti-Soviet, who wrote in his diary in terms reminiscent of the Churchill of earlier days: 'after the debate, I saw him with Lloyd George, [Robert] Boothby and Randolph [Churchill], in a triumphant huddle surrounding Maisky. Maisky, the Ambassador of torture, murder and every crime in the calendar.'[53] And in the *Daily Telegraph* on 20 April Churchill deliberately cut any remaining links he had with the likes of Channon by writing of Franco's ultimate victory in Spain: 'The Conservative Right Wing, who have given him such passionate support, must now be prey to many misgivings.'[54]

During May Churchill increased the pressure for a direct British appeal for an alliance with the Soviets. On the 4th he published an article in the *Daily Telegraph* pointing out that the guarantee of Poland only made sense in military terms if supported by Moscow. But he also knew that the Poles feared the Soviet Union no less than Germany and that they had therefore, so far, shown no interest in seeking Moscow's 'assistance'. There was also the difficulty, as seen from Moscow, that Germany might see fit to attack the Soviets from its East Prussian territories not through Poland but through the Baltic States of Lithuania, Latvia and Estonia, none of which had been offered or had sought Anglo-French 'guarantees'. Nevertheless to the British and Polish Governments Churchill's advice was:

> These are days when acts of faith must be performed by Governments and peoples who are striving to resist the spread of Nazidom. The British Government, who have undertaken to go to war with Germany if Poland is the victim of aggression, have a right

to ask the Polish leaders to study the problem of a Russian alliance with a sincere desire to bring it into lively and forceful action.[55]

At first Chamberlain resisted Churchill's advice as he made clear on the following day in the Commons. Channon recorded gleefully: 'He was most scathing and clearly revealed both his dislike of the "Bollos" and of Russia.'[56] But on 19 May, also in the Commons, Churchill, having been briefed by Maisky, returned to the issue in the light of what had now become a public Soviet offer to create a triple alliance with Great Britain and France. 'What is wrong,' he asked, 'with this simple proposal?' He continued: 'It is said: "Can you trust the Russian Soviet Government?" I suppose in Moscow they say "Can we trust Chamberlain?" I hope that we may say that the answer to both questions is in the affirmative. I earnestly hope so.'[57] Lloyd George took the same line. Once again Chamberlain stood firm. But Channon was now unsure about what would happen next:

> He [Lloyd George] challenged us again and again on Russia, why didn't we come out into the open and embrace her? I looked up at Maisky, the smirking cat, who leant over the railing of the Ambassadorial gallery and sat so sinister and smug (are we to place our honour, our safety in those blood-stained hands?)[58]

On the following day Cadogan recorded Chamberlain as saying that he would 'resign rather than sign an alliance with Soviet'. But by the 24th Chamberlain was ready to give way. As Cadogan again wrote in his diary: 'PM apparently resigned to idea of Soviet alliance, but depressed.'[59] On that day the Cabinet in fact agreed formally to approach Moscow and Chamberlain had to be satisfied with a form of words that avoided the use of 'alliance' and stressed Article XVI of the League Covenant. The House of Commons were immediately informed.

Churchill had thus apparently won over the Government to that reversal of policy towards the Soviet Union for which he had been so ardently working. But the sequel was not to be that which he had seemingly anticipated. For the Soviets at first proved elusive and then, in late summer 1939, rejected the Anglo-French combination entirely. Instead, on 24 August Vyacheslav Molotov, now Soviet Foreign Minister, met in Moscow with his German counterpart, Joachim von Ribbentrop. They signed a non-aggression treaty and secretly agreed to partition much of Eastern Europe, including Poland, into spheres of influence. Then, on 3 September, Great Britain and France declared war

on Germany after its invasion of the western part of Poland allotted to
it under this agreement. On the same day Chamberlain invited
Churchill to join his War Cabinet as First Lord of the Admiralty.

The outbreak of war has usually been seen as a vindication of
Churchill's uniquely prescient warnings about the aggressive nature
of Nazi Germany – though it seems fair to add that it had, after all, not
attacked in the West but rather in the East as his critics, especially
Baldwin, had always foreseen that it would. And Churchill's demands
for rapid rearmament, inevitably given no detailed attention in the
present work, also count strongly in his favour when historians
examine his record. But there is a good deal less to be said for his
supposed farsightedness with respect to the Soviet Union. For in the
end he had seen his policy of seeking alliance with Moscow adopted
and it had ended in catastrophic failure. This was particularly tragic for
the Poles whom he had urged to join a 'Grand Alliance' and whom,
after they had done so, he had counselled to collaborate with the
Soviets. Now they were to be brutally partitioned between Hitler and
Stalin. Churchill's defenders would presumably say that the Soviets
were what he claimed – they had a 'loyal attitude to the cause of
peace'[60] as he had written on 24 March 1939 – but that the appeasers
had alienated them by their behaviour at the Munich Conference and
then by subsequently failing to approach them until May 1939.
Alternatively, they might wish to emphasise the lack of urgency shown
even after May – allegedly proved by the failure of the Chamberlain
Government to send a high-level personage such as Eden, the former
Foreign Secretary, or Churchill himself, to take the negotiations out of
the hands of the professional diplomats. Or they might see fit to argue
that the Soviets would have behaved differently if only the British and
the French had compelled Poland and Romania and even perhaps the
Baltic States to be more welcoming towards Soviet demands for access
to their territory – though quite how that could have been done is
something nobody has yet explained. Maybe the archives in Moscow
will one day decisively prove the correctness of one or other of these
contentions. But it seems more likely that the Soviets were never
genuinely tempted by what the British and the French had to offer
during the late 1930s – however enthusiastically propounded.[61] For
Great Britain had no land forces worth considering – conscription only
being introduced in April 1939. And France had a military strategy of
responding to war with Germany by digging in behind their elaborate
fortifications known as the Maginot Line. No wonder, therefore, that

Stalin declared in public on 10 March 1939 that he would never allow his country 'to be drawn into conflicts by warmongers who are accustomed to have others pull the chestnuts out of the fire for them'.[62]

Possibly the Soviets would have been more interested in serving in a 'Grand Alliance' in 1938, when Czechoslovakia was still in existence and apparently keener on working with the Soviets than Poland and Romania were to be a year later. But this must remain speculative. For Prague capitulated rather than fight – much to Churchill's regret. And supposing Czechoslovakia had stood firm in 1938, would Soviet help, if given, have proved effective? Churchill seemingly thought the answer was in the affirmative. But the Soviet forces were at the time rather distant from the Sudetenland. Maybe, then, there is unusual force in A. J. P. Taylor's question: 'In 1938 Czechoslovakia was betrayed. In 1939 Poland was saved. Less than one hundred thousand Czechs died during the war. Six and a half million Poles were killed. Which was better – to be a betrayed Czech or a saved Pole?'[63]

However this may be, it seems certain that few Conservative MPs in September 1939 would have thought that the new First Lord of the Admiralty, whatever his other merits, had been seriously vindicated with respect to the Soviets. But Churchill could console himself with the knowledge that his courting of Maisky and the Soviet Union had not been entirely a waste of effort. For it had helped to give him a hitherto unexpected respectability on the British Left which served to strengthen his chance of obtaining the Premiership when Chamberlain's narrowly-based administration had to be widened. Had he perhaps foreseen this all along?

NOTES

1 Robert Rhodes James (ed.), *Chips: The Diaries of Sir Henry Channon*, London, 1967, p. 60.
2 *Hansard*, 22 October 1935, vol. 305, col. 368.
3 Ivan Maisky, *Spanish Notebooks*, London, 1966, p. 72.
4 Gilbert, *Prophet of Truth*, p. 720.
5 *Hansard*, 13 July 1934, vol. 292, col. 732.
6 *Ibid.*
7 Londonderry to Churchill, 4 May 1936, Churchill Papers, in Martin Gilbert, *Winston S. Churchill: Vol. V, Companion, The Coming of War, 1936–1939*, London, 1982, p. 131.
8 Churchill to Londonderry, 6 May 1936, Churchill Papers, in *ibid.*, p. 142.
9 *The Times*, 13 May 1936.

10   Gilbert, *Churchill: V, Companion, The Coming of War*, p. 108. Later in 1936 Hankey was to write in a private memorandum: 'In the present state of Europe, with France and Spain menaced by Bolshevism, it is not inconceivable that before long it might pay us to throw our lot in with Germany and Italy.' (Quoted in Lawrence R. Pratt, *East of Malta, West of Suez: Britain's Mediterranean Crisis, 1936–1939*, Cambridge, 1975, p. 39.)

11   Churchill to Violet Bonham Carter, 25 May 1936, Churchill Papers, in Gilbert, *Churchill: V, Companion, The Coming of War*, p. 173.

12   Thomas Jones to a friend, 4 April 1936, Thomas Jones Papers, in *ibid.*, p. 90.

13   Neville Thompson, *The Anti-Appeasers: Conservative Opposition to Appeasement in the 1930s*, Oxford, 1971, p. 39.

14   John Barnes and David Nicholson (eds), *The Empire at Bay: The Leo Amery Diaries, 1929–1945*, London, 1988, pp. 424–5.

15   PREM 1/193, PRO.

16   *Ibid.*

17   On Austen Chamberlain's attitude, see below, pp. 53–4.

18   Maurice Cowling, *The Impact of Hitler: British Politics and British Policy, 1933–1940*, Cambridge, 1975, p. 266.

19   Richard Griffiths, *Fellow Travellers of the Right: British Enthusiasts for Nazi Germany, 1933–9*, London, 1980, p. 264.

20   Churchill to Eden, 7 August 1936, Churchill Papers, in Gilbert, *Churchill: V, Companion, The Coming of War*, p. 307.

21   William Manchester, *The Caged Lion: Winston Spencer Churchill, 1932–1940*, London, 1988, p. 207.

22   Martin Gilbert, *Winston Churchill: The Wilderness Years*, London, 1981, p. 161.

23   Winston S. Churchill, *Step by Step, 1936–1939*, London, 1939, p. 40.

24   Tudor to Churchill, 4 August 1936, Churchill Papers, in Gilbert, *Churchill: V, Companion, The Coming of War*, pp. 306–7.

25   Churchill to Tudor, 16 August 1936, Churchill Papers in *ibid.*, p. 313.

26   Winston S. Churchill, *The Second World War*, 6 vols, London, 1948–54, vol. I, p. 214.

27   Churchill to Wise, 9 April 1936, Churchill Papers, in Gilbert, *Churchill: V, Companion, The Coming of War*, pp. 94–5. See also Graham Somerville Stewart, 'Winston Churchill and the Conservative Party, 1929–1937', unpublished Ph.D. thesis, University of Cambridge, esp. p. 245.

28   Purbrick to Churchill, 29 June 1936, Churchill (Chartwell) Papers, 2/255, Churchill College, Cambridge; and Churchill to Austen Chamberlain, 2 July 1936, *ibid.*, 2/266; and Austen Chamberlain to Churchill, 4 July 1936, in Gilbert, *Churchill: V, Companion, The Coming of War*, p. 232.

29   Churchill, *Step by Step*, pp. 38–9.

30   Winston Churchill, 'An Object Lesson from Spain', article prepared for the *Evening Standard*, 2 October 1936, as preserved in Churchill (Chartwell) Papers, 8/543. Churchill College, Cambridge.

31   Churchill, *Step by Step*, pp. 39–40.

32   *Ibid.*, pp. 47–9.

33   Mary Soames (ed.), *Speaking for Themselves: The Personal Letters of Winston and Clementine Churchill*, London, 1998, p. 417. Incidentally, when Churchill wrote of his hope that the Soviets were moving to the 'Right' nobody in 1936 would have been in any doubt what he meant by that. Had he

been able to revisit us in the 1980s he would thus presumably have spoken of Gorbachev as also attempting to move to the 'Right' in his struggles with the unreconstructed supporters of the late Leonid Brezhnev. But, if so, he would no doubt have been corrected by many commentators, including some of those working for the BBC, who frequently described Gorbachev as a left-winger opposing the benighted forces of the Soviet 'Right'. In short, 'Right' is nowadays becoming a pejorative word with no particularly clear meaning. It was not always so.

34 Churchill, *Step by Step*, p. 59.

35 *Ibid.*, p. 63.

36 *Hansard*, 5 November 1936, vol. 317, col. 318.

37 Atholl to Churchill, 8 December 1936; and Churchill to Atholl, 15 December 1936, Churchill (Chartwell) Papers, 2/261, Churchill College, Cambridge. Atholl interestingly informed Churchill that she feared a Soviet–German rapprochement and that Alexander Kerensky, the exiled former Premier of the Menshevik-dominated Russian Provisional Government of 1917, had told her that a strong party in Moscow favoured that course.

38 *Hansard*, 14 April 1937, vol. 322, col. 1063.

39 Churchill to his wife, 5 September 1936, Spencer-Churchill Papers, in Gilbert, *Churchill: V, Companion, The Coming of War*, p. 338.

40 Rhodes James, *Churchill: A Study in Failure*, pp. 319–20. It is perhaps of interest that the author, writing in 1970, was 'politically correct' enough to have regarded it as 'unfortunate' that Churchill showed 'bias' towards the Nationalists in the Spanish Civil War. He later wrote an 'authorised' biography of Anthony Eden and served as a not notably 'dry' Conservative Member of Parliament in the era of Margaret Thatcher.

41 John Charmley, *Churchill: The End of Glory: A Political Biography*, London, 1993, pp. 336–7; and David Irving, *Churchill's War: Vol. I: the Struggle for Power*, Western Australia, 1987, ch. 6.

42 Gilbert, *Prophet of Truth*, p. 984.

43 *Ibid.*, p. 987.

44 N. A. Rose (ed.), *Baffy: The Diaries of Blanche Dugdale, 1936–1947*, London, 1973, p. 108. See also, Nigel Nicolson (ed.), *Harold Nicolson: Diaries and Letters, 1930–1939*, London, 1966, p. 371.

45 Gilbert, *Churchill: V, Companion, The Coming of War*, p. 108.

46 Gilbert, *Prophet of Truth*, p. 737.

47 Maisky to Churchill, 10 November 1936, Churchill Papers, in Gilbert, *Churchill: V, Companion, The Coming of War*, pp. 396–8.

48 Thompson, *The Anti-Appeasers*, p. 164. In private Churchill did, according to Soviet records, encourage Maisky on 23 March 1938 by saying that he hated Nazi Germany and was 'working unceasingly towards the creation of a "grand alliance" within the framework of the League of Nations to fight Germany and the aggressors in general', in which the main role 'must naturally be played by England, France and Russia'. He added: 'We desperately need a strong Russia; many tell me that as a result of recent events [the purges in the Red Army] Russia has ceased to be a serious factor in international politics.' He considered that it was vital 'that the USSR demonstrate, by some firm act or other before the whole world, that all the cock-and-bull stories about would-be weakness are entirely without foundation'. What he had in mind was, for example, 'a solemn and totally

firm statement' by the Soviet Union that it 'would render serious aid to Czechoslovakia in the event of aggression against it'. Maisky to Moscow, 23 March 1938, translated and quoted in Jonathan Haslam, *The Soviet Union and the Struggle for Collective Security in Europe, 1933–39*, London, 1984, p. 169. The Soviets ignored Churchill's suggestion.

49 Quoted in Thompson, *The Anti-Appeasers.*, p. 176.

50 David Dilks (ed.), *The Diaries of Sir Alexander Cadogan, 1938–1945*, London, 1971, p. 111.

51 Churchill, *Step by Step*, p. 299.

52 *Hansard*, 3 April 1939, vol. 345, cols 2501–2.

53 Rhodes James (ed.), *Chips*, p. 192.

54 *Daily Telegraph*, 20 April 1939, quoted in Manchester, *The Caged Lion*, p. 204.

55 *Daily Telegraph*, 4 May 1939, in Churchill, *Step by Step*, p. 344.

56 Rhodes James (ed.), *Chips*, p. 197.

57 *Hansard*, 19 May 1939, vol. 347, col. 1841.

58 Rhodes James (ed.), *Chips*, p. 199.

59 Dilks (ed.), *Cadogan*, pp. 182, 184.

60 Churchill, *Step by Step*, p. 330.

61 For a survey of some of the conjectures on differing sides of these debates see Andrew J. Crozier, *The Causes of the Second World War*, Oxford, 1997, pp. 250–2. He draws attention, in particular, to Jiri Hochman, *The Soviet Union and the Failure of Collective Security, 1934–1938*, Ithaca, New York, 1984, as a proponent of the view that Stalin never sincerely sought agreement with the Western Powers; and, as taking broadly the contrary view, to Haslam, *The Soviet Union and the Struggle for Collective Security*; and to Geoffrey Roberts, *The Soviet Union and the Origins of the Second World War: Russo-German Relations and the Road to War, 1933–1941*, Basingstoke, 1995.

62 Sidney Aster, *1939: The Making of the Second World War*, London, 1973, p. 156.

63 A. J. P. Taylor, *The Origins of the Second World War*, London, 2nd edn., 1963, p. 26.

4

KEEPING IN STEP
WITH PUBLIC OPINION?

1939–1941

B ACK IN OFFICE for the first time for more than a decade, Churchill
seemed determined to control such anti-Soviet emotions as the
Molotov–Ribbentrop Pact may have reawakened in him. When last a
Cabinet Minister he had campaigned ceaselessly to bring about a break
in diplomatic relations with Moscow on the flimsiest of pretexts. But
now he was to be the main exponent in the War Cabinet of the view
that Soviet misconduct should, as far as possible, be condoned. Hence,
a week after the Soviets invaded eastern Poland on 17 September
1939, the First Lord urged Chamberlain to see how promising a
development this might be from a British viewpoint. As Patrick
Cosgrave has written:

> Given the inevitable ultimate hostility of Germany and Russia, he
> pointed out 'an Eastern front is therefore potentially in existence' and
> then offered a hypothesis regarding the possible development of a
> war of strangulation and attrition in company with Russia. Germany,
> he saw, would have to break out of her present central European
> position:
>
>> The left paw of the Bear has already closed the pathway from
>> Poland to Roumania. Russian interest in the Slavonic people of
>> the Balkans is traditional. The arrival of the Germans on the
>> Black Sea would be a deadly threat to Russia and also to Turkey
>> (…) None of this conflicts with our main interest, which is to
>> arrest the German movement towards the East and South-East
>> of Europe.[1]

By 1 October Churchill even proved willing to make a public broadcast which virtually welcomed the Soviet act of aggression against Great Britain's hapless ally:

> Russia has pursued a policy of cold self-interest. We could have wished that the Russian armies should be standing on their present line as the friends and allies of Poland, instead of as invaders. But that the Russian armies should stand on this line was clearly necessary for the safety of Russia against the Nazi menace. At any rate the line is there, and an Eastern Front has been created which Nazi Germany does not dare assail.[2]

In taking this line, Churchill may have been genuinely convinced that Great Britain and the Soviet Union would soon be allies. But it is also possible that he was primarily motivated by a desire to keep in step with public opinion and to avoid alienating powerful potential allies on the British Left. Certainly Gallup polls from the period show, in P. M. H. Bell's words, 'no clear-cut hostile response to the Nazi–Soviet Pact'.[3]

After crushing Polish resistance the Soviets next turned their attention to Finland. They demanded the right to establish naval bases on Finnish territory. This met with Churchill's private approval. And on 16 November he told the War Cabinet:

> No doubt it appeared reasonable to the Soviet Union to take advantage of the present situation to regain some of the territory which Russia had lost as a result of the last war, at the beginning of which she had been the ally of France and Great Britain. This applied not only to the Baltic territories but also to Finland. It was to our interests that the U.S.S.R. should increase their strength in the Baltic, thereby limiting the risk of German domination in that area. For this reason it would be a mistake for us to stiffen the Finns against making concessions to the U.S.S.R.[4]

Given no clear guidance by the British, Finland refused to yield and was duly attacked by the Soviet Union on 30 November. The War Cabinet, meeting the same day, decided merely to express their 'strong sense of disapproval'. Churchill concurred in a rather flippant fashion, stating that he 'thought we ought not to be deterred from expressing disapproval by consideration of the possible effects on the Russians, who were impervious to words'.[5]

Despite the attack on Finland, then, Churchill was seemingly content to remain one of London's most influential appeasers of the Soviet Union. And when his friend Admiral the Earl of Cork and Orrery, Director of Plans at the Admiralty, wrote to him on 5 December arguing that the attack on Finland 'affords us a wonderful chance – and perhaps the last – of mobilising the anti-Bolshevik forces of the world on our side', the First Lord coldly replied: 'I still hope war with Russia may be avoided and it is my policy to try to avoid it.'[6] But within days Churchill had performed a bewildering volte-face. He now wanted to see Great Britain and France intervene in Scandinavia in a very dramatic fashion, violating if necessary the sovereignty of neutral Norway and Sweden. The aim apparently was to deny Germany access one way or another to the Swedish iron-ore deposits concentrated on Galivare; and simultaneously to help Norway and Sweden to give assistance to Finland against the Soviet Union. As Churchill put it to the First Sea Lord, Admiral Sir Dudley Pound, on 11 December: 'It may be that we may find ourselves at war with Russia, and Allies of Sweden, Norway, Finland and Italy.'[7] At the War Cabinet on the same day he expressed himself more carefully but still in terms that indicated a strong shift against the Soviets. He 'thought that it would be to our advantage if the trend of events in Scandinavia brought it about that Norway and Sweden were forced into war with Russia'. If this occurred 'we would then be able to gain a foothold in Scandinavia with the object of helping them, but without having to go to the extent of ourselves declaring war on Russia'.[8] He did not speculate about what attitude the Soviets would have adopted towards such British armed intervention ultimately directed against them. But it seems he no longer greatly cared.

Churchill's renewed bellicosity towards the Soviet Union probably peaked on 20 January 1940 when he made a dramatic radio broadcast. He had now become an enthusiastic supporter of Finland, which was putting up a spirited resistance, and he cheerfully reverted to the anti-Soviet rhetoric of his younger days:

> Only Finland – superb, nay, sublime – in the jaws of peril, shows what free men can do. The service rendered by Finland to mankind is magnificent. They have exposed, for all the world to see, the military incapacity of the Red Army and of the Red Air Force. Many illusions about Soviet Russia have been dispelled in these few fierce weeks of fighting in the Arctic Circle. Everyone can see how Communism rots the soul of a nation, how it makes it hungry and abject in peace, and proves it base and abominable in war.
>
> ... If the light of freedom which still burns so brightly in the frozen North should be finally quenched it might well herald a return to the Dark Ages, when every vestige of human progress during two thousand years would be engulfed.[9]

He then criticised the unheroic European neutral states – obviously having in mind Sweden and Norway which had previously inconsiderately declined to fall in with his plans for a widening of the Scandinavian conflict. But in the end his designs concerning Finland came to nothing. For on 13 March Helsinki simply decided to capitulate to Soviet demands. His plans for intervening in Scandinavia thus had to be revised and eventually took the form of the ill-fated Narvik expedition that in no way involved the Soviet Union.

The only threat to the Soviets now arose out of a French plan to bomb Baku in the Caucasus in an attempt to reduce oil supplies to Germany. This idea also appealed to Churchill. According to the War Cabinet Minutes of 27 March 1940:

> The First Lord of the Admiralty compared the oilfields at Baku with the iron mines at Galivare as regards their economic importance to Germany. Baku could not be bombarded without the goodwill if not the co-operation of the Turks. This project was another reason in favour of the Secretary of State for Foreign Affairs [Halifax] paying a visit to Turkey. It was just posssible that such action might not involve us in war with Russia, but the Turkish Government would realise the danger only too well. With this in view, it was more than ever desirable to get Turkish consent to the passage of submarines into the Black Sea. Two or three submarines would not only interrupt the Russian oil traffic in that sea but would have a terrifying moral effect on the Russians, and would give some protection to Turkey against any combined operations aimed at her northern coast.[10]

In the event, however, the plan to bomb Baku came to nothing following further Anglo-French deliberations.

Why, then, had Churchill as First Lord of the Admiralty swung so strongly against the Soviets over Finland after initially being so sympathetic to Moscow? It is possible that in this period all moves relating to Scandinavia (and later in the Near East) were seen by him as of a tactical character in the central military struggle against Germany. On this interpretation he initially favoured Soviet expansion at Finland's expense in order to weaken Germany's standing in the Baltic, and maybe also in the hope that the Soviets and the Germans would quarrel over Finland. But then he changed his mind when it occurred to him that, if instead the British switched over to giving support to Finland, it might allow them an easy means of intervening in Scandinavia to Germany's disadvantage. As Churchill himself told his War Cabinet colleagues on the day after Finland's capitulation: 'Our real objective was, of course, to secure possession of the Galivare orefields, which would certainly shorten the war and save great bloodshed later on.'[11] And he may likewise have been prepared to see Baku bombed in order simply to deny the Germans oil.

There are, however, two other possible explanations for Churchill's course. One is that he may have briefly flirted with the idea of moving to the right of the majority of his Cabinet colleagues. For at the beginning of 1940 there were rumours that some in high places favoured 'switching the war' from Germany to the Soviet Union; or, alternatively, desired to see Great Britain simultaneously at war with both these countries. The real aim in each case was assumed to be to secure an early compromise peace with Berlin, and maybe eventually with Moscow also. One attracted to the idea of peace, at least with Germany, was Lord Brocket. And, intriguingly, he decided at around the time that Churchill was speaking out on behalf of Finland that the First Lord might become a possible ally. He wrote as follows to the like-minded Arthur Bryant, the 'patriotic historian':

> I feel that we must now redouble our efforts for Peace and I hope you will become a perfect nuisance to Chamberlain, Halifax, [R. A.] Butler [then Under- Secretary at the Foreign Office] and anyone else. What about bearding Winston? Could you knock some sense into his bald head?[12]

The historian Andrew Roberts has commented: 'The idea that Bryant could have lobbied Churchill to negotiate for peace with Germany in January 1940 is an indication of how far removed Bryant and Brocket were from the world of mainstream politics.'[13] But perhaps their instincts about Churchill at this time could have been more widely shared than Roberts imagines. The First Lord, after all, had seemed to be rather uncertain as recently as 1936 about whether Fascism or Communism constituted the greater threat to British interests.

Another and somewhat more plausible explanation for Churchill's reversion to the rhetoric of anti-Sovietism is that he suddenly realised soon after the beginning of the Soviet-Finnish fighting that public opinion in general, and many of his new supporters on the British Left in particular, found Soviet behaviour in this matter much more repugnant than he had anticipated, and certainly much more so than had been the case with the signing of the Molotov–Ribbentrop Pact and the subsequent Soviet seizure of eastern Poland. Hence Churchill, on this reading, found it expedient to shift his ground – using the

Swedish orefields as a convenient justification. That the British public's reaction to the attack on Finland was severe is shown in contemporary gallup polls.[14] And as for the British Left, the sense of betrayal in at least some quarters bordered on the apoplectic. Most notably Clement Attlee and Arthur Greenwood, then Leader and Deputy Leader of the Labour Party respectively, issued in March 1940 a statement in terms that even Churchill at his most anti-Bolshevik would have found it difficult to outbid:

> The Red Czar is now the executor of the traditional imperialism of Czarist Russia. Stalin's men in Great Britain use the freedom which they enjoy to defend War and Tyranny ... They defend tyranny, either because they do not know or those who know refuse to tell, that Fascism and Bolshevism have identical political systems ... Even now, these emissaries of a foreign despotism refuse to see through the disguise of the Red Czar, who has used a new social and political system to invent a new kind of slavery for the Russian people.[15]

Did Churchill perhaps recall when he had been a Liberal in Lloyd George's Coalition but had succeeded in being more anti-Bolshevik than any Conservative? Could he now see a danger that, if he did not support Finland, he in turn would be outflanked by Labour men on the very same issue?

Labour's leaders undoubtedly mattered to Churchill a great deal. For it was obvious that they would be extremely influential if, as in the First World War, a Coalition Government ever had to be formed. And in the event this came to pass within two months of the Finnish capitulation. Having lost the support of a significant number of his followers in a Commons vote on 8 May over the Narvik fiasco, and with Hitler's forces smashing through Allied defences on the Western Front, Chamberlain decided that Labour would have to be brought into an emergency Coalition. He soon discovered that the Labour leadership would not serve under him and he accordingly accepted the need to resign. Labour proved willing, however, to serve under either Churchill or Halifax. The upshot was that Chamberlain advised King George VI to send for Churchill. The latter thus owed everything to Labour's decision not to veto him – a somewhat ironical outcome given his tremendous assaults on both the Labour Party and the trade unions as recently as the 1920s.

Once he had become Prime Minister Churchill was to be heavily dependent on Labour for the remainder of the War. For he knew that many Conservatives disliked him and would gleefully move to replace him if Labour turned against him. So, in considering his wartime approach to the Soviet Union, we have to bear in mind that he could not usually afford to adopt a line that Labour's leaders would not endorse. But in practice Attlee, Greenwood, Bevin and Herbert Morrison caused him very little difficulty – maybe because he gave them a leading role on the domestic front. In his attempts to win left-wing support Churchill did not, however, confine himself to cooperating with Labour's moderate and anti-Communist leadership. He also decided to reach out to the maverick Sir Stafford Cripps – then an independent Socialist MP who had been expelled from the Labour Party in 1939 for sponsoring a Popular Front movement involving British Communists. As recently as March 1937 Churchill had privately insulted Cripps when the latter had asked him, in the interests of free speech, to support a demand that the Trustees of the Albert Hall be asked to reverse a decision not to allow him to hire it. Churchill had replied:

> I cannot feel that the right of free speech is directly involved in the inability of a particular person to procure a particular hall. I do not therefore feel myself impelled to come to your assistance. You are, unless I am misinformed, working in political association with the Communists at the present time, and it has always been their rule whenever they have the power, forcibly to suppress all opinions but their own. This also would make the case you mention by no means a good occasion on which to make a protest to the public. Most people will think that the Communists have a pretty good run over here, certainly much better than they are given by the German Nazis, by whom, if I remember rightly, you declared it would be a good thing if we were conquered.[16]

Now, on 18 May 1940, within days of becoming Prime Minister, Churchill decided that Cripps should be asked to visit Moscow in order to try to improve relations and to forge a trade agreement. Cripps proved so acceptable to the Soviets that he was quickly confirmed as Ambassador in place of Sir William Seeds, in whose time relations had been strained by the Molotov–Ribbentrop Pact and by the Soviet attack on Finland. And when Cripps's name came up in December 1940 as a possible replacement for the recently deceased Lord Lothian (formerly Philip Kerr) as Ambassador to Washington, Churchill's reaction was to say that he was 'a lunatic in a country of lunatics and it would be a pity to move him'.[17]

Cripps's presence in Moscow failed, however, to produce any very considerable change in the Soviet attitude to the Western democracies. Indeed, in June 1940 Stalin risked further alienating them by effectively annexing Latvia, Lithuania and Estonia with German concurrence; and by forcing Romania to cede Bukovina and northern Bessarabia. On the other hand, he did not of course actually welcome Germany's threat to overrun Western Europe. But he was reluctant to make any move that Hitler could find provocative and hence gave little encouragement to Cripps. In any case, by the summer of 1940 London had little to offer to the Soviets. For France and the Low Countries had been overrrun by Germany; Italy had come into the War; and the British were facing a desperate battle in the air to avoid outright defeat. In these circumstances, then, even Churchill had, for a time, little spare energy to devote to matters directly related to the Soviet Union. But on 25 June he did send a message to Stalin that included the following:

> In the past – indeed the recent past – our relations have, it must be admitted, been hampered by mutual suspicions; and last August the Soviet Government decided that the interests of the Soviet Union required that they should break off negotiations with us and enter into a close relation with Germany. Thus Germany became your friend almost at the same moment as she became our enemy.
>
> But since then a new factor has arisen which I venture to think makes it desirable that both our countries should re-establish our previous contact, so that if necessary we may be able to consult as regards those affairs in Europe which must necessarily interest us both. At the present moment the problem before all Europe – our two countries included – is how the States and peoples of Europe are going to react towards the prospect of Germany establishing a hegemony over the Continent ...
>
> The Soviet Union is alone in a position to judge whether Germany's present bid for the hegemony of Europe threatens the interests of the Soviet Union, and if so, how best those interests can be safeguarded.[18]

Churchill cannot have been surprised, however, when Stalin declined in effect to rise to this bait and chose instead to maintain as far as he could cordial and cooperative relations with Berlin during the ensuing months.

It is relevant to our theme to consider here whether Churchill, in the dramatic summer of 1940, was as fanatical and single-minded an opponent of Germany, not only as an expansionist great power but as the embodiment of Nazi tyranny, as popular biographies and histories would lead us to suppose. For if this was actually the case, it might suggest that his anti-Communism to an extent had been definitely superseded by a deeper hatred. Let us, then, begin by noting the words he used to the House of Commons on the occasion of his first intervention there after taking over the Premiership. On 13 May he declared:

> You ask, what is our policy? I will say it is to wage war, by sea, land and air, with all our might and with all the strength that God can give us; to wage war against a monstrous tyranny, never surpassed in the dark, lamentable catalogue of human crime. That is our policy.
>
> You ask, what is our aim? I can answer in one word: It is victory, victory at all costs, victory in spite of all the terror, victory, however long the road may be ...[19]

This was certainly robust language. But the Soviets doubtless noticed that he did not go so far as to say that 'the monstrous tyranny' that was Nazi Germany actually surpassed all others. In short, the Soviet Union might, in his thinking, still be equally 'unsurpassed' in the 'dark catalogue of human crime'.

The other point to note about this speech is that Churchill's emphasis on 'victory at all costs' may not have represented his real expectation. At all events, within two weeks of using these words he was acknowledging in the privacy of the War Cabinet that he was indeed willing in principle to contemplate the possibility of a compromise peace with Nazi Germany. This of course runs completely counter to the myth of his unwavering resolution that prevailed during his lifetime. For example, in the year of Churchill's death, 1965, the historian A. J. P. Taylor wrote:

> The continuance of the war was never formally debated. It was taken for granted. On 28 May Churchill met all ministers of cabinet rank and, after surveying the situation, remarked casually: 'Of course whatever happens at Dunkirk, we shall fight on.' Ministers shouted; 'Well done, prime minister.' Some burst into tears. Others slapped Churchill on the back. This was the nearest approach to a discussion or a decision.[20]

Soon rumours began to spread, however, that the five-man War Cabinet *had* discussed peace negotiations with Germany at the time of Dunkirk. Taylor was accordingly forced to modify his line somewhat. He wrote in 1969:

> Churchill at once defined British war aims, or rather he laid down a single aim: the total defeat of Hitler and the undoing of all Germany's

conquests. When he came to write his account of the war, he implied that his definition was hardly necessary and that the entire nation was united in pursuing total victory or, put the other way round, unconditional surrender by the Germans. It is unlikely that he played such a modest part. Despite Churchill's assertion that negotiations with Hitler were never discussed by the War Cabinet, it is now known that Halifax raised the topic on 27 May. In fact Churchill was showing his usual generosity when he gave the impression that all his associates were as resolute as himself, and his cover for them perhaps appears less surprising, if it is borne in mind that the weaker vessels were Conservatives, members of the party which Churchill led.[21]

But this too has proved to be mistaken. For the War Cabinet archives for 1940, available for inspection in the Public Record Office, reveal that Churchill agreed with his colleagues Halifax and Chamberlain (now Lord President of the Council) that a settlement with Nazi Germany was desirable in principle, provided satisfactory terms could be obtained. The essential point was, in Halifax's words, that 'matters vital to the independence of this country were unaffected'. There was certainly no insistence, as Taylor had supposed, on 'the total defeat of Hitler and the undoing of all Germany's conquests'. On the contrary, Churchill himself made it clear that he would not object in principle to negotiations 'if Herr Hitler was prepared to make peace on the terms of the restoration of German colonies and the overlordship of Eastern Europe'. And at one point he went even further. For, according to the War Cabinet Minutes, he said on 26 May 'that he would be thankful to get out of our present difficulties, provided we retained the essentials of our vital strength, even at the cost of some cession of territory'.[22] That he had in mind cession of British territory is made clear in Chamberlain's diary entry for 27 May, in which he said that the Prime Minister had told his colleagues that 'if we could get out of this jam by giving up Malta and Gibraltar and some African colonies he would jump at it'.[23]

This does not mean, however, that Churchill and Halifax were in complete agreement. But what actually divided them was a rather narrow point: whether and when acceptable peace terms might be on offer. Halifax conceded that the matter was 'probably academic' but he nevertheless favoured accepting and associating Great Britain with a French proposal to invite neutral Italy to try to discover how severe Hitler's terms might be. For the Foreign Secretary was conscious that if the war continued, 'the future of the country turned on whether the enemy's bombs happened to hit our aircraft factories'. According to the War Cabinet Minutes, 'he was prepared to take that risk if our independence was at stake; but if it was not at stake he would think it right to accept an offer which would save the country from avoidable disaster'. Churchill, on the other hand, thought that Germany, with France on the point of collapse, would not at this juncture be willing to make such an offer; and he was concerned that it would have a deplorable effect on national morale if it became known that a fruitless bid for such an offer had been made. Chamberlain then found a formula acceptable to both Halifax and Churchill. According to the War Cabinet Minutes, he said: 'While he thought that an approach to Italy was useless at the present time, it might be that we should take a different view in a short time, possibly even a week hence'. He then proposed framing a reply to the French, 'which while not rejecting their idea altogether, would persuade them that now was the wrong time to make it'.[24]

The French disregarded this advice from London and appealed alone to Mussolini to act as a mediator on their behalf. But he refused, preferring instead to join the war on Germany's side. It must therefore remain a matter for speculation whether, if Mussolini had acted otherwise, Hitler, given that his primary interest had always lain in conquest in the East, would have offered the kind of terms to the two Western Powers that Churchill's Cabinet could have accepted. As it was, the Battle of Britain went ahead. And when its outcome proved sufficiently favourable to the British to allay their worst fears, as expressed by Halifax, the War Cabinet had no difficulty in uniting on the policy of continued unambiguous prosecution of the War.[25]

It must in fairness be stated that some historians have interpreted this record in such a way as to attempt to preserve something of Churchill's former reputation as an inflexible and fanatical opponent of any compromise with Nazi Germany: they simply claim that he did not actually mean what he said to the War Cabinet. For example, John Costello wrote in 1991:

> While Churchill could have carried the majority of the government on his opposition to negotiations, forcing the issue to a vote might have precipitated Halifax's threatened resignation. The urge to appease died hard among those ministers who had made it their article of faith for so many years. History had shown that neither Hitler nor Mussolini could be trusted, but the record shows how Churchill had to battle through that long crisis-filled weekend to forestall Halifax's attempt to resurrect the discredited policies. At the same time he

knew that if he went over the heads of the Foreign Secretary and Lord President, it might have triggered a rancorous parliamentary showdown. If this had erupted during the critical days of the Dunkirk evacuation, it must be doubted whether even Churchill's rhetoric or the support of the opposition parties could have sustained him if the Conservatives in Parliament had turned against his leadership.[26]

More measured, however, in this writer's opinion, is the verdict of David Reynolds:

> there can be little doubt that, contrary to the mythology he himself sedulously cultivated, Churchill succumbed at times to the doubts that plagued British leaders in the summer of 1940 ... The Churchill of myth (and of the war memoirs) is not always the Churchill of history. Scholars working on the 1930s and World War II have long been aware of this discrepancy, but it deserves to be underlined in view of the dogged rearguard action fought by popular biographers and television producers. Contrary to national folklore, Churchill did not stand in complete and heroic antithesis to his pusillanimous, small- minded political colleagues. British leaders in the 1930s and World War II all faced the same basic problem of how to protect their country's extended global interests with insufficient means at their disposal. The various policies they advanced are not to be divided into separate camps – appeasers and the rest – but rather on different points of a single spectrum, with no one as near either extreme as is often believed. This is true of the Chamberlain era; it is also true ... in 1940. In private Churchill often acknowledged that the chances of survival, let alone victory, were slim. He also expressed acceptance, in principle, of the idea of an eventual negotiated settlement, on terms guaranteeing the independence of the British Isles, even if that meant sacrificing parts of the empire and leaving Germany in command of Central Europe ...
>
> This is not in any sense to belittle Churchill's greatness. On the contrary. My contention is that the popular stereotype of almost blind, apolitical pugnacity ignores the complexity of this remarkable man and sets him on an unreal pedestal.[27]

What light, then, does the foregoing summary of the dramatic events of the summer of 1940 and the interpretations of Churchill's approach to them throw on his subsequent attitude towards the Soviet Union? What, above all, are we to conclude from the evidence of his unheroic pliability behind closed doors with respect to the possibility of negotiating with Nazi Germany, which was in such stark contrast to his public rhetoric? It must surely be that we can have no confidence in any contention that Churchill had become, even in 1940, so obsessed with, and fanatical about, the evil that Nazism and Fascism represented that he had essentially ceased to be susceptible, after any immediate national emergency was over, to arguments that the Soviet Union and Communism might after all represent the greater menace – either ideologically or from a balance of power perspective or both. But of course a move in the anti-Soviet direction only became a serious possibilility for a practical politician even in private once the German threat to invade Great Britain had disappeared and was perceived by the general public to have done so.

By the end of 1940 that threat had certainly receded for the immediate future – but it did not disappear entirely from the public mind until at least a further year had elapsed. This fact naturally served to limit Churchill's options *vis-à-vis* the Soviets for a longer period than he might ideally have wished. Meanwhile, however, his general situation had improved considerably in other respects. First, the dying Chamberlain had resigned his governmental and party positions in the autumn and Churchill had been elected in his place as Leader of the Conservative Party – thus giving him a stronger hand as a Coalition Prime Minister than Lloyd George had ever had. Secondly, Churchill had persuaded a reluctant Halifax to take the Washington Embassy – thereby allowing him to restore the Foreign Secretaryship to Eden, whom he probably expected, not altogether correctly, to be able to dominate. Finally, Franklin Roosevelt had secured re-election as US President – a development welcomed by Churchill who saw him as broadly sympathetic to the British cause.

All the same, the outlook remained sombre at the beginning of 1941. For the British were effectively bankrupt and without military allies. The chances were, therefore, that without some major change in the world scene the Anglo-German War (already something not far short of a resumed Phoney War) must eventually peter out. Churchill appears to have thought that a major change in the country's prospects would come from the early entry into the war against Germany of the United States. But he greatly overestimated Roosevelt's ability and perhaps desire to bring this about. Accordingly the first months of 1941 were trying ones for Churchill as the cross-Channel stalemate continued.

Relief of a sort was to come in the spring of 1941, but ironically for Churchill it came from the East rather than the West. For intelligence reports began to reach him indicating that Germany intended to attack the Soviet Union. He was unhesitating in his response: Stalin must be warned. And this, after some misunderstandings involving Cripps, duly happened – but with no discernable consequences. What Churchill did not do was to try to take advantage of the situation by asking his colleagues to consider offering a peace settlement to Germany or responding in any way to what purported to be a German overture delivered by Rudolf Hess. But, given the state of public opinion, this scarcely constitutes proof that Churchill had developed a genuine pro-Soviet outlook. Nor is there any evidence that he actually welcomed or even recognised the prospect that Stalin was about to replace Roosevelt as the powerful long-term ally that Great Britain so desperately needed. Indeed, the likelihood is that at this stage Churchill, for once in his life, greatly underestimated the Soviet Union as a force either for good or ill. Above all, he did not seemingly even contemplate the possibility that the Soviets would be the principal instrument of Germany's defeat. For that role, in his view, was destined to be played by the United States. And it followed therefore that he no longer saw the Soviet Union as a threat to Western Europe, let alone to Great Britain itself. Had he done so, he might have had to relive the mental anguish that had faced him in the early stages of the Spanish Civil War. For he still privately believed that the Soviets were incorrigible barbarians. For example, when Eden offered to visit Moscow in February 1941, just before indications of an impending German attack on the Soviet Union began to emerge, Churchill vetoed the suggestion and added: 'I would hardly trust them for your personal safety or liberty.'[28] The remarkable nature of this suspicion is put in perspective if one recalls that neither Churchill nor anyone else expressed concern for Chamberlain's personal safety at the hands of Hitler when he paid his three visits to Germany in 1938.

How, then, did Churchill react when the German attack on the Soviet Union finally materialised on 22 June? Without consulting the War Cabinet he made a broadcast on the same day containing the following:

> No one has been a more consistent opponent of Communism than I have for the last twenty-five years. I will unsay no word that I have spoken about it, but all this fades away before the spectacle which is now unfolding. The past with its crimes, its follies and its tragedies, flashes away. I see the Russian soldiers standing on the threshold of their native land, guarding their fields which their fathers have tilled from time immemorial ...

We are resolved to destroy Hitler and every vestige of the Nazi regime ... Any man or state who fights on against Nazism will have our aid ... It follows, therefore, that we shall give whatever help we can to Russia and the Russian people ...

It is not for me to speak of the action of the United States of America, but this I will say: if Hitler imagines that his attack on Soviet Russia will cause the slightest division of aims or slackening of effort in the great democracies which are resolved upon his doom, he is woefully mistaken. On the contrary, we shall be fortified and encouraged in our efforts to rescue mankind from his tyrannies. We shall be strengthened and not weakened in determination and in resources.[29]

Ironically, this line was actually more friendly towards Moscow than even Eden had contemplated. But, as in the case of his attitude to Nazi Germany in 1940, Churchill's public rhetoric was misleading. In short, Churchill's approach in private was not so straightforward – as his guests at Chequers on the weekend of the German attack on the Soviet Union had already discovered. True, John Colville, his Private Secretary, recorded in his diary on 21 June:

> The P.M. says a German attack on Russia is certain and Russia will assuredly be defeated. He thinks that Hitler is counting on enlisting capitalist and right-wing sympathies in this country and the U.S. The P.M. says he is wrong: he will go all out to help Russia. [Gilbert] Winant [the US Ambassador in London] asserts that the same will be true in the U.S. After dinner, when I was walking on the lawn with the P.M., he elaborated this and I said that for him, the arch anti-Communist, this was bowing down in the House of Rimmon. He replied that he had only one single purpose – the destruction of Hitler – and his life was much simplified thereby. If Hitler invaded Hell he would at least make a favourable reference to the Devil![30]

When, however, on the next day Ambassador Cripps was invited to luncheon to discuss the news that had just broken Churchill's attitude bore little relation to the solemn words he intended to broadcast to the nation. Colville wrote in his diary: 'At lunch the P.M. trailed his coat for Cripps, castigating Communism and saying that Russians were barbarians. Finally he declared that not even the slenderest thread connected Communists to the very basest type of humanity. Cripps took it all in good part and was amused.'[31] Again, after making his pro-Soviet broadcast, Churchill encouraged a return in private to near-frivolity about Moscow. Colville recorded:

> After the ladies had left the dining room there ensued a vivacious and witty debate between the P.M., supported in spirit but not much in

words by Sir S. Cripps, on the one hand and [Lord] Cranborne and Eden on the other ... Edward Bridges [the Cabinet Secretary] and I sat, fascinated and yet convulsed with laughter. The question at issue was: 'Should there be a debate in the House on Tuesday about Russia?' Eden and Cranborne took the Tory standpoint that if there was it should be confined to the purely military aspect, as politically Russia was as bad as Germany and half the country would object to being associated with her too closely. The P.M.'s view was that Russia was now at war; innocent peasants were being slaughtered; and we should forget about Soviet systems or the Comintern and extend our hand to fellow human beings in distress. The argument was extremely vehement. I have never spent a more enjoyable evening.[32]

How are we to make sense of Churchill's behaviour and to reconcile his private and public utterances during this seminal weekend? Perhaps the most important point is that he believed, as did his military advisers, that the Soviet Union would 'assuredly be defeated'. For on the basis of this assumption he could safely make a broadcast designed mainly to appeal to pro-Soviet opinion at home and hence consolidate his position as a Coalition Prime Minister. And in private he could enjoy himself by good-humouredly teasing his guests with contradictory posturing. Indeed, he may almost have been relishing the likelihood that the Red 'barbarians' were doomed. But if he was so confident that the Germans would defeat the Soviets, how could he be in such a sunny mood? For might not that ultimately prove disastrous for Great Britain? The answer can surely be found in hints given in his broadcast to the effect that the Americans were about to come to the rescue.

Churchill's approach to the Soviets in the first months of their involvement in the War seems indeed to have been entirely based on his initial twin assumptions: that the Soviets would soon leave the War and the Americans would soon join it. He accordingly showed no serious interest in sending British forces to fight alongside the Soviets, and on 19 July he turned down a Soviet request that Great Britain should try to establish a so-called Second Front in Western Europe. Indeed, the British concentrated, as before, on the North African theatre; on bombing Germany; and on attempting to prevent German U-boats gaining mastery in the North Atlantic. True, on 12 July Great Britain and the Soviet Union signed an agreement pledging that neither country would negotiate a separate peace with Germany and providing in vague terms for mutual assistance. In practice, however, this looked like being a phoney alliance to accompany what threatened to become another phase of an almost phoney war for the British until Churchill's ally of choice , the United States, became a full belligerent.

Gradually, however, Churchill was forced to recognise that his trust in the Americans might have been misplaced. Seminal for him were his meetings with Roosevelt from 9 to 12 August 1941 off the coast of Newfoundland in Placienta Bay. Roosevelt naturally made clear his sympathy for the anti-Nazi cause and reaffirmed that vital supplies under the so-called Lend Lease arrangement would continue to come to Great Britain (and now the Soviet Union). And he joined Churchill in signing a high-sounding declaration that became known as the Atlantic Charter. But he gave no hint that he expected to ask for, let alone obtain, Congressional consent to a US declaration of war on Germany. Moreover, after his return to Washington the President went out of his way to stress that the meeting had not brought US entry into the war a day nearer. This was incidentally very much in tune with US domestic opinion – 75 per cent being opposed to war before the meeting and 74 per cent opposed after it.[33] All this led Churchill on 28 August to send a rather pathetic telegram to the President's adviser, Harry Hopkins, in the following terms:

> I ought to tell you that there has been a wave of depression through Cabinet and other informed circles here about the President's many assurances about no commitments and no closer to war &c ... If 1942 opens with Russia knocked out and Britain left again alone, all kinds of dangers may arise. I do not think Hitler will help in any way ... You will know best whether anything more can be done. Should be grateful if you could give me any sort of hope.[34]

No satisfactory reply offering 'hope' was received.

Slowly, then, Churchill was driven to take seriously the option of working more closely with the Soviet Union. For, against his expectations, the Soviets were still in the War by the autumn of 1941 – even though much of their European territory had fallen to the Germans. So Churchill responded positively when Stalin proposed a coordinated invasion and partition of neutral Persia – though, according to Oliver Harvey, Principal Private Secretary to Eden, the moving spirit on the British side was the Foreign Secretary and not the Prime Minister.[35] The joint attack duly began on 25 August. For Churchill there were three advantages: it secured continued British access to Persian oil; it forestalled the possibility of a pro-Nazi regime emerging in Teheran; and it provided a warm-water point of access for supplies destined for the Soviet Union. All the same, this was an act of unprovoked aggression and a clear violation of international law. Hence Churchill was rather uneasy about it and wrote to his son, Randolph, that it was 'questionable as taking a leaf out of the German book'.[36] One wonders whether Churchill recalled in this context that he himself had condemned Chamberlain after Munich for mistreating Czechoslovakia in collaboration with another dictatorship, or that he had warned prophetically that 'this is only the first sip, the first foretaste of a bitter cup, which will be proferred to us year by year'.[37]

Certainly Stalin's bitter cup was soon to be reproferred to Churchill: he was next urged to declare war on Romania, Finland and Hungary, all of which had gone to war with the Soviet Union in the wake of Germany. In the case of the Romanians and the Finns the problem for Churchill was that they were merely seeking to recover territory which had so recently been taken from them during the period of Soviet–German collaboration. Moreover, Romania had actually been given a full-blooded 'guarantee' by Great Britain and France in the spring of 1939 – though this had been disregaraded in June 1940 when the Soviets, with German acquiescence, seized Bukovina and northern Bessarabia, and understandably so given the plight of the Western Allies on the Western Front at that juncture. But it was now extremely unpleasant for Churchill to be asked a little over a year later to declare war on this victim of aggression – even though it had an authoritarian rightist regime moving into Germany's orbit. Finland provided even greater embarrassment for the British in 1941. For it remained a parliamentary democracy and, as has been seen, it had been widely praised in Great Britain, not least by Churchill himself, for resisting the Soviets during the winter of 1939–1940. Nevertheless his own initial reaction to Finland's move against the Soviets, though at this stage not involving contemplation of a formal British declaration of war on Helsinki, was strikingly unsympathetic. He minuted to Eden on 16 July: 'I trust we have already seized all the Finnish ships and subjected the Finns to every inconvenience in our power.'[38] This, incidentally, provoked Churchill's authorised biographer into departing from his almost invariable habit of merely chronicling his subject's deeds (allowing him to 'become his own biographer', as Randolph Churchill had insisted). For Gilbert here permitted himself to make the acid observation: 'This was the same Finland whose resistance against Russia a year and a half earlier had been described by Churchill as "heroic, nay, sublime".'[39]

The Soviets were not, however, satisfied with British economic sanctions being applied to Finland, Romania and Hungary. They became steadily more determined that Great Britain should publicly endorse their position to the extent of formally declaring war. And this Churchill was extremely reluctant to do. But as in the case of Persia the Soviets had a sympathiser in Eden, who repeatedly fought in the War Cabinet for these declarations of war to be made. But Churchill had support in quarters that were surprising to at least some observers. For example, Harvey wrote in his diary on 10 November:

> A.E. [Eden] back from Cabinet very late ... He had had terrible trouble over Russia and declaring war on Finland etc. ... the opposition came from the Labour leaders, Bevin and Greenwood – shocking! They could only see Communists in the Russians and their hatred of Communism blinded them to any other consideration.[40]

But bombarded with angry messages from Moscow and with the United States still a non-belligerent, Churchill gave way to Eden in principle on 21 November. And the declarations of war duly followed on 5 December – just two days before the Japanese attack on the United States. It may well be, then, that Stalin would not have got his way if Pearl Harbor had been bombed a few weeks earlier.

Churchill's approach to sending aid to the Soviet Union during 1941 also needs to be seen in the context of deteriorating confidence in the likelihood of any early US declaration of war on Germany and of increasing respect for Soviet resistance; and, perhaps at least as impor-tant, how all this was perceived by the British public. The Soviets' demands fell into three categories: those for military equipment; those for the British to send forces to fight alongside them on the Eastern Front; and those for British moves to create a Second Front in Western Europe. Churchill, his military advisers and the War Cabinet (with the exception of Beaverbrook) were unanimous in resisting Second Front demands throughout 1941 (and beyond) because it was held to be simply impractical at any early date to reverse the expulsion from the continent that had taken place at Dunkirk in May 1940. But with respect to the other demands Churchill was less dogmatic. He agreed in principle from the outset that whatever equipment could be spared, including tanks and aircraft, should be sent to the Soviets. But when it came to the detailed implications he usually acted as a brake on more enthusiastic colleagues. For example, when, at the end of August, Beaverbrook was appointed to accompany the American Averell Harriman on a misssion to Moscow to examine Soviet requirements,

Churchill minuted to the former: 'Your function will be not only to aid in the forming of the plans to help Russia, but to make sure that we are not bled white in the process.' He added: 'I shall be quite stiff about it here.'[41] All the same, during the course of 1941 many hundreds of British aircraft and tanks did reach the Soviets; and Churchill, aware of mounting domestic disquiet, also urged the Americans to divert some of the military supplies which, under Lend Lease, would otherwise have come to Great Britain.

As for sending British forces to fight alongside the Soviets, Churchill held a basically negative view. At first he maintained that all such forces were required to serve in other theatres, especially North Africa. Then, after the joint invasion of Persia had been completed he offered to place more British troops there in order that Soviet troops could be moved north to fight the Germans – a far too transparently self-serving suggestion to appeal to Stalin. But, finally, in the wake of domestic agitation within and outside Parliament, Churchill wavered: on 25 October he telegraphed to Oliver Lyttelton, then Minister of State in the Middle East, a warning that some troops might have to be moved from the Mediterranean to the Eastern Front. He added: 'I am confronted with Russian demands for a British force to take its place in the line on the Russian left flank at the earliest moment. It will not be possible in the rising temper of the British people against what they consider our inactivity to resist such demands indefinitely.'[42] The timing of this admission is of course significant: for this was when hopes of early belligerency on the part of the United States were fading. But the extent of Churchill's desire to resist giving much help to the Soviets is apparent from an entry in Harvey's diary dated 27 October 1941:

> P.M. is disquieting A. E. [Eden] by giving very evident signs of anti-Bolshevik sentiment. After his first enthusiasm, he is now getting bitter as the Russians become a liability and he says we can't afford the luxury of helping them with men, only with material. No one stands up to him but A.E. – not even the Labour Ministers who are as prejudiced as the P.M. against the Soviets becuase of their hatred and fear of the Communists at home.[43]

Pressure from Stalin, from Ambassador Cripps and from British public opinion had, however, become so great by the end of October that Churchill was driven to consider making a dramatic gesture to disarm his critics. Hence he endorsed the idea of sending Eden to the Soviet Union for a personal encounter with Stalin, who on

25 November agreed to receive him. Stalin made it clear, however, that he would wish to discuss not only matters relating to the immediate conduct of the war but also the terms of a post-war settlement. Churchill's attitude to Eden's visit, never more than half-hearted, now became distinctly negative – even though German forces were perilously near to both Moscow and Leningrad. It was of course too late for him to cancel the visit, which was to last from 16 to 21 December. But he soon made it clear to Eden that no Soviet territorial demands were to be met; he reneged on earlier hints that British troops might be sent to the Eastern Front; and he insisted that no date for the establishment of a Second Front in Western Europe could be given. This left Eden in an unenviable position. For he had been urged by Harvey on 2 December that 'whatever he did he should not go unless and until he has a "full basket"'.[44] But gradually Churchill (and the Chiefs of Staff) had outmanouvred him. So all that Eden in the end could take to Stalin turned out to be a promise of 500 aircraft and 200 tanks; assurances of continuing British endeavours in North Africa; and expressions of goodwill.[45]

Before Eden could reach Moscow, however, the entire global scene had been transformed – thereby for a time making it much easier for the British to stand up to Stalin. For on 7 December 1941 Japan attacked the United States and thus set in train a series of events that not a single statesman or even commentator precisely anticipated. Great Britain at once declared war on Tokyo in solidarity with the Americans. But this did not automatically dispel Churchill's fears about the fate of Europe. For an outbreak of war in the Pacific could paradoxically have meant that Congress would have been even more reluctant to contemplate war with Germany and that military equipment due to be sent to Great Britain and the Soviet Union under Lend Lease would now be diverted to the Americans' own war effort. Churchill, in short, faced the stark possibility that his entire central expectation about the likely course of the European War – based on an early involvement of the United States – would be decisively disappointed. But his reputation for foresight was to be in large measure vindicated, at least among the masses, as a result of entirely unexpected news from Berlin. For on 11 December Hitler, for reasons never satisfactorily explained, gratuitously declared war on the United States. Churchill on the following day telegraphed triumphantly to Eden (then *en route* to Moscow): 'The accession of the United States makes amends for all, and with time and patience will give certain victory.'[46] One wonders, however, whether the shade of Neville Chamberlain did not wish to whisper in his ear: 'By God, you were lucky!'

NOTES

1 Patrick Cosgrave, *Churchill at War: Vol. I: Alone, 1939–40*, London, 1974, p. 63, quoting CAB 66/2, PRO.
2 *The Times*, 2 October 1939.
3 P. M. H. Bell, *John Bull and the Bear: British Public Opinion, Foreign Policy and the Soviet Union*, London, 1990, p. 34.
4 War Cabinet Minutes, 16 November 1939, CAB 65/2, PRO. See also Churchill's unsent draft Cabinet Memorandum, 27 October 1939, Churchill Papers, in Gilbert, *Finest Hour*, pp. 99–100.
5 War Cabinet Minutes, 30 November 1939, CAB 65/2, PRO.
6 Churchill Note, 5 December 1939, ADM 199/1929, PRO, in Gilbert, *Finest Hour*, pp. 101–2.
7 Churchill to Pound, 11 December 1939, ADM 199/1929, PRO, in Ponting, *Churchill*, p. 417.
8 War Cabinet Minutes, 11 December 1939, CAB 65/2, PRO.
9 *The Times*, 22 January 1940.
10 War Cabinet Minutes, 27 March 1940, CAB 65/6, PRO.
11 *Ibid.*, 14 March 1940, CAB 65/12, PRO.
12 Quoted in Andrew Roberts, *Eminent Churchillians*, London, 1994, p. 309.
13 *Ibid.*, pp. 309–10.
14 Bell, *John Bull and the Bear*, p. 34.
15 *Ibid.*, p. 32.
16 Churchill to Cripps, 12 March 1937, Churchill Papers, Gilbert, *Churchill: V, Companion, The Coming of War*, p. 596.
17 John Colville, *The Fringes of Power: Downing Street Diaries, 1939–1955*, London, 1985, p. 309.
18 Churchill to Stalin, 25 June 1940, in Llewellyn Woodward, *British Foreign Policy in the Second World War*, 5 vols, London, 1970–6, vol. I, pp. 466–7.
19 *Hansard*, 13 May 1940, vol. 360, cols 1501–2.
20 Taylor, *English History*, p. 489.
21 A. J. P. Taylor *et al.*, *Churchill: Four Faces and the Man*, London, 1969, p. 36. Cf. Churchill, *The Second World War*, II, p. 88.
22 War Cabinet Minutes, 26, 27 and 28 May 1940, CAB 65/13, PRO.
23 Neville Chamberlain Diary, 26 May 1940, in Clive Ponting, *1940: Myth and Reality*, London, 1990, p. 107.
24 War Cabinet Minutes, 28 May 1940, CAB 65/13, PRO.
25 The preceding analysis draws on David Carlton, 'Churchill in 1940: Myth and Reality', *World Affairs*, CLVI, 1993–94, pp. 97–103.
26 John Costello, *Ten Days That Saved the West*, London, 1991, p. 252.
27 David Reynolds, 'Churchill and the British "Decision" to Fight On in 1940', in Richard Langhorne (ed.), *Diplomacy and Intelligence during the Second World War*, Cambridge, 1985, pp. 165–6. See also Andrew Roberts, *'The Holy Fox': A Biography of Lord Halifax*, London, 1991, pp. 215–27. Roberts

compared the Churchill of popular legend to a heroic Toby Jug and asserted that Halifax saw his occasional outbursts of 'exuberence and childlike enthusiasm' as reminiscent of Toad of Toad Hall.

28 PREM 3/396/16, PRO, in Elisabeth Barker, *Churchill and Eden at War*, London, 1978, p. 226.
29 *The Times*, 23 June 1941.
30 Colville, *The Fringes of Power*, p. 404. Nearly ten years later Colville claimed to recall that Churchill had been much less pessimistic than others in his entourage about the Soviets' prospects but the published version of his contemporary diary does not confirm this. See Gilbert, *'Never Despair'*, p. 550.
31 Colville, *The Fringes of Power*, p. 405.
32 *Ibid.*, pp. 405–6.
33 Robin Edmonds, *The Big Three: Churchill, Roosevelt and Stalin in Peace and War*, New York, 1991, p. 223.
34 Churchill to Hopkins, 29 August 1941, PREM 3/224/2, PRO.
35 John Harvey (ed.), *The War Diaries of Oliver Harvey, 1941–1945*, London, 1978, p. 39.
36 Churchill to Randolph Churchill, 29 August 1941, Churchill Papers, in Gilbert, *Finest Hour*, p. 1177. See also Harvey (ed.), *War Diaries*, p. 36.
37 *Hansard*, 5 October 1938, vol. 309, col. 374.
38 Churchill Minute, 16 July 1941, Churchill Papers, in Gilbert, *Finest Hour*, p. 1137.
39 *Ibid.*; and Randolph S. Churchill, *Winston S. Churchill: Vol. I: Youth, 1874–1900*, London, 1966, p. xx.
40 Harvey (ed.), *War Diaries*, pp. 62–3.
41 Churchill Minute, 30 August 1941, Churchill Papers, in Gilbert, *Finest Hour*, p. 1178.
42 Churchill to Lyttelton, 25 October 1941, Churchill Papers, in *ibid.*, p. 1223.
43 Harvey (ed.), *War Diaries*, p. 57.
44 *Ibid.*, p. 68.
45 *Ibid.*, p. 69.
46 Churchill to Eden, 12 December 1941, Churchill Papers, in Gilbert, *Finest Hour*, p. 1274.

5

ALLIED
WITH HELL

1942–1945

IMMEDIATELY after Pearl Harbor Churchill's first wish was to hasten to Washington for a meeting with Roosevelt. But he was given no clear encouragement until after Germany had declared war on the United States.[1] Then, and only then, did he receive the firm invitation he craved. Once in Washington, apart from giving public performances which culminated in an address to a joint session of Congress on 26 December, Churchill was naturally mainly interested in securing an undertaking from Roosevelt to give priority to the European theatre. And this he obtained – but only in vague terms. In fact, the United States, in the ensuing months and years, continued to devote much attention and manpower to the Pacific theatre and as a result Churchill was gradually forced to recognise that the defeat of Hitler would be a more protracted affair than he had anticipated. On 30 August 1941, for example, he had privately expressed the view that the United States 'alone could bring the war to an end – her belligerency might mean victory in 1943'.[2] But this was based on the expectation that in a US–German war the Japanese would remain neutral – something Churchill hinted to the War Cabinet on 12 November 1941 was in Great Britain's best interest.[3]

How, then, did Churchill see Moscow's likely contribution to the defeat of Germany in the first months of American involvement in the unanticipated two-front war? At first, being slow to realise how many resources Roosevelt would devote to the Pacific theatre, he was inclined to minimise the Soviets' importance and accordingly was even less disposed than before to make concessions to them. But he soon showed signs of wavering and then, during 1943 and 1944, moved very far towards accepting the unavoidable necessity of treating Stalin as an indispensible partner, whose every wish, however repugnant, had to be taken with extreme seriousness. This evolution in Churchill's approach to Moscow was also probably greatly influenced by Eden, who emerged much earlier than his chief as a powerful advocate of far-reaching appeasement of Moscow.

The explanation for this divergence is open to more than one interpretation. It is possible to see the two men by 1941 as already more rivals than allies and hence to contend that all their arguments about policy issues have to be seen in this light. Certainly they were never remotely on the kind of terms that Winant, the American Ambassador in London between 1941 and 1946, saw fit to describe in his memoirs:

> The personal relationship between the Prime Minister and Anthony Eden was as close and real as President Roosevelt's friendship with Harry Hopkins. Roosevelt and Churchill, each a great leader, single-minded in serving his country, understood that most men who crossed their doorsteps wanted something. Eden and Hopkins wanted nothing beyond being loyal to a leader and cause.[4]

Equally misleading was Morrison who claimed in his memoirs that the two had an almost 'father-and-son' relationship.[5] Their contrasting experiences during the 1930s made that quite unlikely. For while Churchill had been in the wilderness, Eden had prospered. A protégé of Baldwin, Churchill's *bête noire*, Eden had risen to become Foreign Secretary in December 1935. He held the post until February 1938, when he surprisingly resigned not over the Chamberlain's efforts to conciliate Hitler but over the appeasement of Mussolini, whom he had evidently come to loath. By contrast, Italian Fascism came low on Churchill's list of concerns – far behind both Nazism and Communism as a threat to European stability. Hence there is no reason to take at all seriously Churchill's later claim in his war memoirs that on the night of Eden's resignation he had been so troubled that sleep had deserted him. More revealing are the facts – not revealed in his war memoirs – that he had written in 1935 that Eden's appointment as Foreign Secretary did not fill him with confidence and that in 1936 he had considered him to be a lightweight.[6] And it is also significant that in the aftermath of his resignation Eden had little to do with Churchill. In fact the two men established rival groups of followers – with Eden's

30 MPs (the so-called 'glamour boys') being around five times more numerous than those associated with Churchill. Thus, many observers in the aftermath of the Munich Conference saw Eden as the more likely successor to Chamberlain if the appeasement policy should be decisively discredited. In the event, however, Churchill overtook Eden in the race for Number Ten – but probably only because in September 1939 Chamberlain invited the former but not the latter to serve in his War Cabinet. In the 1940s, therefore, Eden had no particular reason to show unwavering loyalty or deference to Churchill – and that this was actually the case was obvious to insiders. But though the two argued bitterly and even tempestuously over many matters, for example with respect to policy towards General Charles de Gaulle and the Free French, there was a particular edge to their differences over Soviet-related matters. This arose in part, no doubt, because Churchill was never able for long to forget his searing experiences with the early Bolshevik regime. But it was also due to Eden's tendency to adopt a remarkably sympathetic approach, for a supposed Conservative, towards the Soviet Union. Eden, for example, had visited Moscow in 1935 and formed a favourable impression of Stalin. As he recorded in his memoirs: 'Though I knew the man to be without mercy, I respected the quality of his mind and even felt a sympathy which I have never been able entirely to analyse.'[7] As for the Marxist–Leninist ideology, he does not appear to have taken it at all seriously as an important determinant of Soviet conduct in world affairs. Once back in the Foreign Office at the end of 1941, moreover, Eden saw fit to reappoint as his Principal Private Secretary Harvey, who, judging by his diaries, was an extreme left-wing sympathiser of the Soviet experiment. For example, when he and Eden visited the Soviet Union in December 1941, he saw from his train seat without pity evidence of the 'Gulag Archipeligo' and held that the ruthlessness involved was the price that had to be paid for the modernisation of the Soviet Union.[8] Eden himself was, of course, by no means a Communist fellow-traveller. But it is not without importance that he appears to have had no difficulty about tolerating as the head of his Private Office one who, in this period at least, came near to fitting this description. And it seems clear that Eden was now only nominally a Conservative. For example, Harvey wrote in his diary on 25 August 1942:

> He [Eden] had ... had a most useful dinner with Bobbety [Lord Cranborne] who was most sympathetic to his ideas. He too spoke of the importance of drawing the younger men together as a nucleus for

a future party ... he thought they should work with Labour (Bevin and Co.) and leave the opposition to the Communists. This is also an idea of A.E.'s [Eden's].[9]

Thus the differences between Churchill and Eden over Soviet-related issues were all too likely to arise as the war took its course.[10]

A major early divergence between Churchill and Eden over Soviet policy surfaced even while the former was still in the United States in the aftermath of Pearl Harbor. For Eden, during the course of his visit to Moscow in December 1941, had reached the conclusion that Stalin would go far to forgiving the British for not doing more to assist the immediate Soviet war effort, provided only that they gave undertakings to recognise postwar Soviet frontier demands. On his return to London, therefore, Eden telegraphed to Churchill, urging that he raise with the Americans the case for the Soviets' 1941 frontiers being immediately acknowledged. But Churchill was unpersuaded and replied as follows:

> Your telegram surprised me ... We have never recognized the 1941 frontiers of Russia except *de facto*. They were acquired by acts of aggression in shameful collusion with Hitler. The transfer of the peoples of the Baltic States to Soviet Russia against their will would be contrary to all the principles for which we are fighting this war and would dishonour our cause. This also applies to Bessarabia and to Northern Bukovina, and in a lesser degree to Finland, which I gather it is not intended wholly to subjugate and absorb ...
>
> You suggest that the 'acid test of our sincerity' depends upon our recognizing the acquisition of these territories by the Soviet Union irrespective of the wishes of their peoples. I, on the contrary, regard our sincerity involved in the maintenance of the principles of the Atlantic Charter to which Stalin has subscribed ...
>
> When you say ... that 'nothing we and the US can do or say will affect the situation at the end of the war' you are making a very large assumption about the conditions which will then prevail. No one can foresee how the balance of power will lie, or where the winning armies will stand. It seems probable however that the US and the British Empire, far from being exhausted, will be the most powerfully armed and economic bloc the world has ever seen, and that the Soviet Union will need our aid for reconstruction far more than we shall need theirs.
>
> ... there must be no mistake about the opinion of any British Government of which I am the head: namely, that it adheres to the principles of freedom and democracy set forth in the Atlantic Charter, and that these principles must become especially active whenever any

question of transferring territory is raised. I conceive, therefore, that our answer should be that all questions of territorial frontiers must be left to the decision of the Peace Conference.[11]

Once back in London, however, Churchill was soon in retreat. For public opinion was showing strong sympathy for the Soviets who, contrary to most earlier expectations, were clearly going to survive the winter. And Eden was ready to press their demands with his colleagues, resting his case for appeasement on this logic: 'On the assumption that Germany is defeated and German military strength is destroyed and that France remains, for a long time at least, a weak power, there will be no counterweight to Russia in Europe ... Russia's position on the European continent will be unassailable.'[12] The War Cabinet, meeting on 6 February, turned out to be dramatically split about this matter, with Beaverbrook threatening to resign if Eden's policy was not approved and Attlee threatening to do so if it was.[13] Churchill, perhaps already beginning to come to terms with the horrific possibility that the Soviets and not the Americans might be the principal victors in Europe, now emerged with an acceptable compromise: the Americans should be asked whether they favoured the British yielding to all the Soviets' territorial demands or whether it would be enough merely to offer them effective control over the Baltic States. But Roosevelt approved neither idea and indicated that he would try to work matters out in bilateral dealings with Stalin.

This did not greatly appeal to Churchill. Moreover, his own authority at home had clearly weakened, with military setbacks in North Africa having been followed by the loss of Singapore to the Japanese. Accordingly, on 26 March he allowed Eden to carry the War Cabinet for a policy of entering into negotiations with Moscow about frontiers notwithstanding American opposition. The upshot was that in May Molotov arrived in London to conduct the bargaining.

Meanwhile, however, rumours about an impending British sell-out of Finland, Romania, Poland and the Baltic States were circulating in London and many private protests began to reach Churchill. Church leaders were prominent, including the Bishop of Gloucester who was inconsiderate enough to inform the Prime Minister that during 1941 the Soviets had, for example, 'tortured the Inspector of the Latvian police till he went mad' and that 'a former Latvian Cabinet Minister had sharp needles driven between his nails'.[14] Even more serious for Churchill was that numerous politicians, who had been variously supporters and opponents of the appeasement policies pursued during the 1930s, began to rebel. For example, Duff Cooper, who had resigned from the Cabinet over Munich, held that 'German interference in Czecho-Slovakia ... and with Poland were far more excusable than that of Russia against the Baltic States'.[15] And Lord Simon, now Lord Chancellor, who as Chancellor of the Exchequer had supported Munich, did not see how he could defend this new and presumably worse form of appeasement.

Churchill's response to this agitation was to perform another volte-face: Eden was now given the unenviable task of trying to dissuade Molotov from publicly insisting that the favourable British hints about frontiers that had already been made to Moscow should not be turned into treaty form. Luckily for both Churchill and Eden, Molotov proved amenable and agreed instead to the signing of a twenty-year Anglo-Soviet Treaty of Friendship which made no reference to frontiers. This was not, however, a case of Soviet magnanimity. What made the difference was that Molotov was about to travel on from London to Washington, where he was desperate to obtain concrete American backing for the Soviets' immediate war needs, and he had been informed by Ambassador Winant how strongly Roosevelt felt about the undesirability of any bilateral Anglo-Soviet treaty dealing with post-war frontiers. For Churchill, therefore, this entire episode must have left him with mixed feelings. On the one hand, he had at one stage seemed unable to avoid taking further unwelcome sips or even gulps from the Soviets' bitter cup. On the other hand, Roosevelt had at the last minute moved against Moscow and hence the Soviets had had to yield.

For a time Churchill no doubt was confirmed in his earlier belief that if the Soviets avoided defeat at the hands of Germany they could hope for no more than to find themselves at the end of the War dependent on the goodwill of the Western Powers. But the remainder of 1942 can have provided little evidence to reinforce this conviction. For it became clear that Germany and its allies in North Africa and the Mediterranean theatre generally would not rapidly capitulate even though the Americans were now concentrating manpower and supplies there. And the British and the Americans had to take the decision in the summer that no Second Front in Western Europe would be possible until 1943 at the earliest. Ironically, it was Churchill himself who held the strongest convictions about the military inevitability of this step – but he could not avoid the corollary that the Soviets had thereby gained a possible free hand in determining the future of much of Europe if the Germans suddenly buckled in the great military showdown on the Eastern Front that was now imminent. Churchill's private preference in these circumstances was for the Western Powers to concentrate on what he called 'the Soft Under-belly of the Axis' – moving from North Africa into Italy, then into the Balkans, and finally up into the heart of Europe from the South. It can never be known, however, whether this approach, if endorsed wholeheartedly by the United States, would have effectively checked Soviet expansion. For in the event the Americans refused to go beyond attacking the Axis in North Africa and Italy and insisted thereafter on preparations being made for rather belated major landings in Western Europe. It would probably be a mistake, however, to suppose that essentially ideologically-driven calculations about how best physically to block Soviet ambitions in Eastern Europe were Churchill's highest priority. For it may be that, by 1942, even he had been driven by practical necessity to recognise the merit from Great Britain's point of view in Baldwin's aforementioned dictum from 1936 that 'if there is any fighting in Europe to be done, I should like to see the Bolshies and the Nazis doing it'. At all events, by emphasising the Mediterranean theatre Churchill was instrumental in delaying the cross-Channel operation until 1944, and hence he minimised the risk that British forces would be subjected to mass slaughter such as they had so frequently endured during the First World War – not least at Gallipoli for which he had had much responsiblity. But if avoiding recklessness with British lives was his overriding concern there was likely to be a high price to be paid: if Germany lost the War largely as a result of Soviet efforts, then Moscow would expect to have a major say in shaping the postwar settlement. The Prime Minister was not, however, ready to face up to the full implications of this until 1944.

An immediate consequence for Churchill of the Anglo-American decision not to attempt to create an early Second Front in Western Europe was that he had to recognise that once it became known, there would probably be a great increase in agitation at home and abroad from those who believed that the Soviets were being deliberately let down. He therefore judged it necessary to try to minimise as far as possible Stalin's suspicions that the capitalist allies were fundamentally insincere. This led him to take the courageous decision to invite himself to Moscow.

For Churchill it must have been a moment of considerable emotion and perhaps apprehension when, on 12 August 1942, his aircraft landed in the capital of 'this sullen, sinister Bolshevik State' (as he himself put it in his War Memoirs).[16] What followed has been extensively described – by Churchill himself; by Harriman (who was present as Roosevelt's representative); and by several members of the British party including Cadogan, Alan Brooke (the Chief of the Imperial General Staff), Sir Archibald Clark Kerr (who had succeeded Cripps as British Ambassador in Moscow and who later became Lord Inverchapel), Air Marshal Sir Arthur Tedder and Sir Charles Wilson (who was the Prime Minister's doctor and who later became Lord Moran).[17] Yet historians cannot be sure what Churchill and Stalin really made of each other or whether the visit was an overall success. For amid much feasting and drinking there were moments of conviviality as well as angry exchanges between the two men – and all conducted through interpreters who may not in every case have been particularly competent. Churchill himself also appears to have been astonishingly unprofessional in disregarding the posssibility that his private remarks to his aides might be picked up by hidden devices. Tedder, for example, was shocked when the Prime Minister spoke of Stalin 'as just a peasant, whom he, Winston, knew exactly how to tackle'. This led Tedder to send the Prime Minister a note on which he scribbled 'Méfiez-vous'.[18] And Clark Kerr came upon Churchill in his private quarters denouncing Stalin in 'ponderous Gibbonesque prose' and on another occasion 'declaring that he would not leave the Kremlin until he had Stalin in his pocket'.[19] But perhaps the most remarkable moment came when, having been cautioned not for the first time about possible hidden microphones, Churchill replied: 'We will soon deal with that. The Russians, I have been told, are not human beings at all. They are lower in the scale of nature than the orang-utang. Now then, let them take that down and translate it into Russian.'[20] Probably some of these indiscretions were caused by excessive consumption of alcohol and the Soviets, assuming they were able to replay them, may have made allowance for this. Even so, Churchill's choice of words seems in retrospect to be remarkable. And, given that less than two years earlier he had opposed a visit to Moscow by Eden, as has been seen, on the grounds that he 'would hardly trust them [the Soviets] for your personal safety and liberty', it is as if he almost relished provoking those he still clearly considered to be barbarians. It is perhaps not surprising, therefore, that in a more reflective moment he mused in his doctor's presence: 'We're a long way from home ... And the journey is not without danger.'[21]

Churchill's first meeting with Stalin took place on the evening of 12 August. The Prime Minister came straight to the point: the British and the Americans had agreed that there would be no Second Front in Western Europe during 1942. Stalin's reaction was one of disappointment but not initially one of rage. And this encouraged Churchill to break to him the good news that an Anglo-American invasion of North Africa would certainly take place before the end of the year. Stalin for his part appeared to accept that, if successful, *Torch* as it was to be codenamed would have various positive benefits for all Hitler's enemies. Thus the two leaders ended their first encounter on good terms and they agreed to meet again on the following evening.

The second meeting was, however, to be of a very different character. Stalin, having had time to reflect on the matter, coldly presented Churchill with a formal memorandum accusing the British and the Americans of breaking promises concerning a Second Front made to Molotov in the previous May and demanding that they be fulfilled. This placed the Prime Minister in a difficult position. For promises of a sort had indeed been made – though more categorically by the Americans than by the British. But Churchill stood his ground and insisted that minds had been made up and that *Torch* would definitely be going ahead. Stalin next became extremely abusive and, if clumsy translations were to be believed, accused the British of lacking the courage to take on Germany. Churchill naturally gave as good as he got. The upshot was that the evening ended with the British party returning to its *dacha* in a mood of near-despair.

During much of 14 August Churchill seemed to his entourage to be on the verge of terminating his visit without a further meeting with Stalin, whom he denounced ceaselessly. But in the evening he duly attended a banquet at the Kremlin. He found Stalin in a more conciliatory frame of mind and for a time a relatively friendly atmosphere prevailed. But late in the proceedings, perhaps as a result of excessive alcohol consumption, Churchill's own mood changed and he bade his host goodnight with a minimum of warmth.

On the following day, his last in Moscow, Churchill again denounced Stalin to his entourage. For example, he told Clark Kerr that he could hardly bring himself to shake Stalin's hand and added: 'Did he not realize who he was speaking to? The representative of the most powerful empire the world has ever seen.'[22] Now the question was whether the Prime Minister would attend a final brief meeting with Stalin but once again he decided, after some hesitation, to do so.

This turned out to be a relatively successful encounter and lasted much longer than planned. Apart from reaching agreement on an appropriate communiqué, the two leaders dealt with little of substance. But they reminisced cordially and eventually Churchill was invited into Stalin's private quarters in the Kremlin, where he he met Svetlana, the latter's daughter, and was then offered an unscheduled dinner. The visit thus ended on a satisfactory note.

Churchill subsequently proclaimed in Parliament, in the War Cabinet and sometimes even in private his belief that he had succeeded in achieving a personal rapport with Stalin. For example, he told the Commons on 8 September 1942:

> It was an experience of great interest to me to meet Premier Stalin. The main object of my visit was to establish the same relations of easy confidence and of perfect openness which I have built up with President Roosevelt. I think that, in spite of the accident of the Tower of Babel which persists as a very serious barrier in numerous spheres, I have succeeded to a considerable extent. It is very fortunate for Russia in her agony to have this great rugged war chief at her head. He is a man of massive outstanding personality, suited to the sombre and stormy times in which his life has been cast; a man of inexhaustible courage and will-power and a man direct and even blunt in speech ... Above all, he is a man with that saving sense of humour which is of high importance to all men and all nations, but particularly to great men and great nations. Stalin also left upon me the impression of a deep, cool wisdom and a complete absence of illusions of any kind. I believe I made him feel that we were good and faithful comrades in this war – but that, after all, is a matter which deeds not words will prove.[23]

In fact we now know that Stalin formed no very favourable impression of the Prime Minister. Milovan Djilas, the prominent Yugoslav Communist, recorded that Churchill was seen by the Soviet leaders as 'a farsighted and dangerous "bourgeois statesman"' and that 'they did not like him'.[24] And, within two months of Churchill's visit, Stalin was to send to Maisky a telegram in which he said that everyone in Moscow had 'the impression that Churchill is holding a course heading for the defeat of the USSR, in order thereafter to reach agreement with the Germany of Hitler or [Heinrich] Brüning [Germany's Chancellor in the later stages of the Weimar Republic] at expense of our country'.[25]

As for Churchill, he seems intermittently to have persuaded himself that Stalin was someone he could influence and he had heard enough in Moscow to dispel fears that the Soviets were likely to open early negotiations with Germany for a separate peace. But none of this meant that he was looking forward to forging a post-war partnership with the Soviet Union. When, for example, in October 1942 Eden urged the adoption of a Four Power Plan for the running of the post-war world by Great Britain, the United States, the Soviet Union and China, Churchill was aghast. He minuted to the Foreign Secretary:

> It sounds very simple to pick out these four Big Powers. We cannot, however, tell what sort of Russia and what kind of Russian demands we shall have to face ... It would be a measureless disaster if Russian barbarism overlaid the culture and independence of the ancient States of Europe ... I look forward to a United States of Europe ... I hope to see the economy of Europe studied as a whole. I hope to see a Council consisting of perhaps ten units, including the former Great Powers, with several confederations – Scandinavian, Danubian, Balkan etc. – which would possess an international police force and be charged with keeping Prussia disarmed.[26]

Clearly Churchill still hoped that the Soviet Union would be in effect locked out of this future Europe. A post-war Soviet historian, belatedly aware of the existence of this evidence of Churchill's hostility, drew this conclusion:

> How he must have hated the Soviet people and their country to have written these words when the Battle of Stalingrad was being fought. They bring to mind other words, namely: 'If [Bolshevik] methods succeed ... European culture ... would be superseded by the most frightful barbarism of all times.' Similar as they are they were written by different people. The latter extract is from a statement made by Adolf Hitler at the National-Socialist Party Congress in Nuremberg in 1936.[27]

Churchill's plans for the postwar future, however, soon began decisively to unravel. For by the summer of 1943 it had become obvious that the Soviets would triumph on the Eastern Front. Indeed, their great victories at Stalingrad and Kursk, as Churchill readily grasped, could have no other meaning. Indeed, he was soon reflecting sadly on the implications for his own long-term reputation. His son, Randolph, recalled:

> Harold Macmillan, in 1962, told the author the following pregnant anecdote. He described how in Cairo in 1943 Churchill suddenly said to him late one night: '[Oliver] Cromwell was a great man, wasn't he?' 'Yes, sir, a very great man.' 'Ah,' he said, 'but he made one

terrible mistake. Obsessed in his youth by fear of the power of Spain, he failed to observe the rise of France. Will that be said of me?' He was of course thinking of Germany and Russia.[28]

With the Soviets doing so well on the battlefields the only hope of preventing their domination of the Peace Settlement in Eastern Europe and the Balkans, and maybe even in Europe as a whole, had clearly come to depend on one of two possibilities. The first would be for the Western Powers to make a deal with Germany provided Hitler was removed. Whether Churchill speculated about this is not known. But he would surely have had little hope of carrying his War Cabinet or Parliament or British public opinion if he had seriously attempted anything of this kind. Moreover, he found Roosevelt moving in entirely the opposite direction. For as early as January 1943 at the Anglo-American summit held in Casablanca the President insisted on a joint declaration calling for unconditional German (and Japanese) surrender. This of course effectively precluded any kind of bargaining with anti-Hitlerian elements in Germany. A second possibility was that the United States would effectively confront the Soviets and deny them control over any part of Europe that had not been in their hands in 1938. At first sight this might have seemed equally impractical as matters stood in military terms in the summer of 1943. But glimmers of hope emerged as Mussolini was ousted from power in Rome and his successors joined the Anglo-American camp. And in August 1943 Churchill and Roosevelt, meeting at the latter's home in Hyde Park, New York, reviewed the encouraging progress that was being made on the project designed to produce an atomic bomb – and, most importantly, Roosevelt agreed that the Soviets should not be invited to participate in or even be informed about it. All the same, Churchill still had little about which to be optimistic in the autumn of 1943. For he was increasingly realising that Roosevelt was becoming rather sympathetic to the Soviets and evidently did not intend to insist to breaking point on self-determination for the nations of Eastern Europe. All this, as will be seen, culminated in a humiliation for Churchill at the three-power Summit held at Teheran in November and December 1943.

Meanwhile, however, Churchill had had to face a particularly dispiriting incident in Anglo-Soviet relations. This arose as a result of the Polish Government-in-Exile being based in London and hence supposedly subject to broad guidance as to their conduct from the British Government as their hosts. The issue that placed Churchill in an acute dilemma related to the fate of around 10,000 Polish officers who had surrendered to the Soviets in 1939. The Polish Government-in-Exile, after resuming diplomatic relations with the Soviet Union at British insistence in 1941, repeatedly sought information concerning the whereabouts of these prisoners and Churchill himself raised the matter with Stalin. They met only with Soviet evasions. But on 13 April 1943 the Germans, now in possession of Eastern Poland, formerly under Soviet control, claimed to have discovered mass graves at Katyn near Smolensk. They said that evidence found on the bodies showed the victims to be the missing Polish officers and that they had been shot in the back of the neck in 1940 when the Soviets were the occupiers. The London Poles were immediately convinced that for once Nazi Germany was telling the truth. And Churchill privately undoubtedly shared their view. For example, he told the Polish leaders Wladyslaw Sikorski and Eduard Raczynski on 15 April: 'Alas, the German revelations are probably true. The Bolsheviks can be very cruel.'[29] But the Prime Minister was embarrassed when the Poles then publicly demanded, like Germany, that an International Red Cross Inquiry be held. For Stalin at once denied Soviet responsibility, blamed Germany for the killings and suspended diplomatic relations with the Polish Government-in-Exile. Churchill's response was to line up not with the victims but with those he believed to be the murderers and war criminals. He required the Polish Government-in-Exile to drop their charges against the Soviet Government and he introduced rigorous censorship to ensure that Polish-language newspapers in London did not endorse the German claims. And he even discouraged the Foreign Office from seeking more detailed information about the matter, minuting to Eden on 28 April: 'There is no use prowling morbidly round the three-year graves of Smolensk.'[30] In putting it this way, however, he was signalling that he had no doubt about the identity of the guilty party. For three years earlier Smolensk had been in Soviet hands. Then in the Commons on 4 May Eden, with Churchill's approval, stated that 'His Majesty's Government have no wish to attribute blame for these events to anyone except the common enemy.'[31]

Why, then, had Churchill again drunk so deeply from the bitter cup of appeasement? The truth was surely that he had to play out the hand he had dealt himself. He himself had said in 1941 that 'if Hitler invaded Hell he would at least make a favourable reference to the Devil'. And by 1943 much of British public opinion, fed on a media diet of adulation for 'our gallant allies', thought of the Soviets in much friendlier terms than that. Moreover, Churchill had a particular reason for wanting to avoid Anglo-Soviet recriminations over Katyn: he feared that the Soviets would now be tempted to organise and recognise a puppet regime designed for imposition on postwar Poland – the country for which Great Britain had so nobly gone to war in 1939. And he judged that the best hope of avoiding this humiliation would be to persuade Stalin to forgive the London Poles and restore diplomatic relations with them. In an attempt to bring this about he accordingly decided to intervene on their behalf with what was perhaps the most grovelling message ever sent by a British Prime Minister to a foreign leader. On 28 April the self-styled 'representative of the greatest empire the world has ever seen' telegraphed to Stalin: 'Eden and I have pointed out to the Polish Government that no resumption of friendly or working relations with Soviet Russia is possible while they make charges of an insulting character against the Soviet Government and thus seem to countenance the atrocious Nazi propaganda.' He then appealed for a resumption of Soviet diplomatic relations with the London Poles and asked that Polish forces be allowed to leave the Soviet Union. He went on: 'We earnestly hope that ... you will consider this matter in a spirit of magnanimity.'[32]

Two sequels may be briefly recorded here. First, the Soviets never did resume relations with the Polish Government-in-Exile and in due course installed in Warsaw a regime dominated by Communists and their fellow travellers, to which Churchill's Government accorded formal diplomatic recognition on 5 July 1945. Secondly, the Soviet Government, then headed by Mikhail Gorbachev, formally admitted on 14 April 1990 that the Soviets and not the Germans had killed the Polish officers found at Katyn.[33]

Churchill's increasing propensity to appease Moscow was to be decisively reinforced at the Teheran Summit Conference which opened on 28 November 1943. For Roosevelt, now in weakening health and increasingly under the influence of his pro-Soviet adviser Hopkins, made it unmistakably clear that he was not willing to fall in with the Prime Minister's wish to have separate discussions in order that the Western Democracies could present the Soviets with a common front. But the President was prepared to have an early meeting with Stalin from which Churchill was pointedly excluded. This led the latter's doctor to record in his diary on the second day of the Conference:

Until he came here, the P.M. could not bring himself to believe that, face to face with Stalin, the democracies would take different courses. Now he sees he cannot rely on the President's support. What matters more, he realizes that the Russians see this too. It would be useless to try to take a firm line with Stalin. He will be able to do as he pleases.[34]

In the four-day Conference Roosevelt repeatedly made it clear, to Stalin's apparent pleasure, that the United States and Great Britain would invade France in May 1944 and that Mediterranean/Balkans military distractions were in practice to be given a low priority. And he also indicated a private inclination to acquiesce in Soviet frontier demands. Churchill evidently felt that in these circumstances he had to avoid isolation and he accordingly said nothing to contradict Roosevelt. Indeed, he even went out of his way to offer to try to persuade the London Poles to accept revised frontiers acceptable to Moscow. And he and Eden even thought it wise to take the initiative in attempting to get informal agreement about the form these frontiers would take – given that Roosevelt could hardly do so with a Presidential Election less than a year away and hence with a large Polish-American vote to consider. The British minutes of a meeting held on 28 November give a flavour of what followed:

> PRIME MINISTER said he had no power from Parliament, nor he believed had the President, to define any frontier lines. He suggested that they might now, in Teheran, see if the Heads of Government, working in agreement, could form some sort of policy which might be pressed upon the Poles and which we could recommend to the Poles, and advise them to accept.
> MARSHALL STALIN said we could have a look.
> THE PRIME MINISTER said we should be lucky if we could.
> MARSHALL STALIN asked whether it would be without Polish participation.
> THE PRIME MINISTER replied in the affirmative and said that this was all informally between themselves, and they could go to the Poles later.
> MARSHALL STALIN agreed ...
> MR EDEN said what Poland lost in the east she might gain in the west.
> MARSHALL STALIN said possibly they might, but he did not know.
> THE PRIME MINISTER demonstrated with the help of three matches his idea of moving Poland westwards, which pleased Marshal Stalin.

Three days later, on 1 December, the three Heads of Government and their Foreign Ministers returned to the Polish issue; by now the Soviets appeared ready to agree in principle to moving Poland westward as far as the River Oder at Germany's expense in return for acceptance of Soviet ownership of the Polish territory transferred to them under the Molotov–Ribbentrop agreement of 1939, which the Soviets claimed was essentially the same as what Curzon had proposed for them in 1919. Eden maintained, however, in line with Polish thinking, that the city of Lvov had been intended in 1919 to belong to Poland even though it had been given to the Soviets in 1939. But when this was disputed by Molotov, Churchill proved unwilling to support Eden (and the Poles) on what he probably saw as a trivial matter. And hence he rather capriciously announced that 'he was not prepared to make a great squawk about Lvov'.[35] As will be seen, this concession to the Soviets was later to assume great importance and may possibly have made a decisive difference to the chances of the London Poles playing any part in the post-war affairs of Poland.

Whether or not he had been careless with respect to Lvov, however, the main point about Teheran was that Churchill had shown himself to be a rapid learner. For in a matter of days he had fully digested the lesson that Roosevelt had given him and he was henceforth ready to deal with the Soviets on the assumption that they had effectively neutralised the United States as any kind of barrier to their ambitions in Eastern Europe. But he was also aware as he entered 1944 that the President was facing a re-election battle in the following November and hence would be unwilling for some time to commit himself to any formal acceptance of Soviet hegemony in that region. He accordingly decided, in a spirit of ruthless opportunism, to offer Stalin apparently generous concessions there, going far beyond anything Roosevelt could openly endorse. It is of course certain that Churchill was privately in deep despair at Roosevelt's attitude and that he was the most reluctant of appeasers. But he had concluded, with great speed and decisiveness, that British weakness was such that he must now positively go out of his way to gain Stalin's goodwill and if possible, to wring a few concessions out of him while US forces were still in Europe. The historian Richard Lamb has argued that this approach constituted nothing less than treachery on Churchill's part – not least towards Poland: 'Thus at Teheran Churchill sacrificed the hard-won Polish victory of 1920 and betrayed the ally for whom Britian had gone to war. War is the art of the possible, but in negotiations with a thug like Stalin only iron firmness produces results.'[36] But Lamb does not explain how 'iron firmness' in negotiations can be sustained without the military means to back it up.

Churchill clearly confirmed his new course in a minute to Eden sent on 16 January 1944. After referring, not very plausibly, to 'the new confidence which has grown in our hearts towards Stalin', the Prime Minister indicated that he no longer wished to maintain that East European territorial issues raised by the Soviets in 1941 and 1942 should be left for settlement at a post-war peace conference. On the contrary: 'We are now about to attempt the settlement of the eastern frontiers of Poland, and we cannot be unconscious of the fact that the Baltic States, and the questions of Bukovina and Bessarabia, have very largely settled themselves through the victories of the Russian armies.'[37] In fact Eden, so keen on meeting Soviet wishes in 1942, now had difficulty in keeping up with his chief's desire for all-out courting of Moscow. But during the course of 1944 the two men gradually forged a partnership that did much, for good or ill, to determine the shape of post-war Europe.

Churchill's new strategy of seeking a far-reaching understanding with Moscow could not at first be pursued too openly. For slow-thinking colleagues in the War Cabinet and anti-Soviet die-hards in Parliament were unlikely to approve any sudden volte-face in declaratory policy. And Roosevelt was to prove extremely reluctant to endorse any Anglo-Soviet indulgence in the 'old diplomacy' of carving up Europe into spheres of influence. So Churchill found it necessary to wait until October 1944 before finally risking the forging of a direct bilateral bargain with Stalin.

Meanwhile, however, he began to send friendly signals to Moscow. One of these related to Yugoslavia. For most of 1943 the British Government had been troubled by the fact that two rival guerrilla groups, ostensibly established to resist German and Italian occupation, had been squandering British-supplied arms in fighting one another. The question at issue was whether the Right-wing Chetniks, led by Dragolub Mihailovic, or the Communist Partisans, led by Josip Broz Tito, had the greater responsibility for this state of affairs. It was probably not by chance that within days of the end of the Teheran Conference Churchill finally decided in favour of the Partisans. In arguing for this he even claimed to believe the Communist claim that Mihailovic was in effect a stooge of Axis forces. Eden, in line with Foreign Office thinking, disagreed. He telegraphed to Churchill:

> it would be a mistake to promise Tito to break with Mihailovic. If we
> have a public and spectacular breach with Mihailovic our case against
> him for treachery must be unanswerable ... I am still without
> evidence of this. Breach with Mihailovic whenever it comes will

certainly attract a great deal of attention both here and in America and I should have liked to have moved in step with Russians and Americans if we could.[38]

Later Eden urged that at very least Tito's exclusive role as British-approved insurgent leader in Yugoslavia should be recognised only after he had agreed to co-operate with the London-based King Peter. But when Tito in effect refused to do this, Churchill overcame his Foreign Secretary's reluctance and the British Government duly broke off relations with Mihailovic (who was eventually to be executed by his Communist enemies). And King Peter was persuaded to do likewise. The Soviets, who were kept informed of developments, were naturally supportive of Churchill's actions. On the other hand, Roosevelt initially disapproved and for many months refused to break off contact with Mihailovic. But in this theatre British support counted for most and hence Yugoslavia, thanks in large measure to Churchill, was set firmly on course for a post-war Communist dictatorship under Tito.[39]

On Poland, too, Churchill sought during 1944 to appease Moscow. On returning from Teheran he set out to persuade the Polish Government-in-Exile that they must now accept the so-called Curzon Line (or, in other words, the Molotov–Ribbentrop Line of 1939 in large measure) as their eastern frontier with the Soviet Union. In three meetings with Prime Minister Stanislaw Mikolajczyk and two of his colleagues, on 20 January and on 6 and 16 February, Churchill did not attempt to conceal his unwillingness to quarrel with Stalin about Polish frontiers: he thought the best he could do for Poland as compensation for loss of its pre-war territory was to secure great power agreement to its western borders being extended to the River Oder at the expense of Germany. His main concern, however, was that if the London Poles did not rapidly accept this idea as a basis for discussion, the Soviets would refuse to have any further dealings with them. This would mean that the Soviets would not only shape Poland's borders as they thought fit but would also be able to instal a puppet government. But Mikolajczyk and his colleagues, still reeling from the Katyn affair and the Soviets subsequent decision to break off diplomatic relations with them, did not believe that Churchill would be able to achieve any kind of compromise with Moscow and hence they were extremely reluctant to make any concessions.

Desperation now led Churchill, at the third meeting, frankly to acknowledge to the Poles that British weakness and American indifference underlay his approach to Moscow and he was even led partially to face up to the comparison with Munich:

> The Poles might say they did not trust the Russians. If the Russians did in fact prove untrustworthy it would indeed be a bad prospect for all the world but worst of all for the Poles. Britain would always do her best against tyranny in whatever form it showed itself. But Britain, though better situated, was not much bigger than Poland. We would do our best, but this would not save Poland. The Prime Minister had heard talk of of a second Munich. No Pole should say this because the Poles had participated in the pillage of Czechoslovakia ...
>
> Poland had no chance of getting out of the German grip without the Russians. British and American strength was mainly in the sea and in financial and other resources. He doubted whether the United States would be ready to go on fighting in Europe for several years to liberate Warsaw. It was no use expecting us to do more than we could ...
>
> His heart bled for them, but the brutal facts could not be overlooked. He could no more stop the Russian advance than stop the tide coming in. It was no use saying something which would only make the Russians more angry and drive them to the solution of a puppet Government in Warsaw.[40]

Seemingly Churchill was near to confessing that he had arrived, millions of East European deaths later, at the same realistic view about the limits of British power as Chamberlain had held in 1938. His words could even be said to constitute the nearest he ever came to acknowledging the underlying futility and even bankruptcy of the policies that had brought him to the Premiership in 1940. At all events, his dramatic appeal evidently impressed the London Poles. For by 20 February they were ready to agree to Churchill sending a lengthy telegram to Stalin that effectively gave their consent to the Soviets having the substance of what they wanted with respect to frontiers, provided no public statement had to be made until a later date. Churchill asked in return only that the Soviets should 'facilitate the return of the Polish Government to the territory of liberated Poland at the earliest possible time'.[41] But Stalin now showed no interest in any immediate deal with the London Poles or even in a resumption of diplomatic relations with them. What he now apparently wanted was for the London Poles publicly to accept the Curzon Line forthwith and, more importantly, to reconstruct their Government along lines that would be acceptable to him. This was of course something that even Churchill did not at this stage have the effrontery to ask Mikolajczyk to do. And so events had to be left to take their course: by July the Soviets had driven the Germans out of enough Polish territory to make it possible for them to establish at Lublin an administration of their own choosing known as the Polish Committee of National Liberation. Stalin frankly acknowledged that it might in due course 'serve as a nucleus for the formation of a Provisional Polish Government out of democratic forces'.[42] It is a measure of the extent to which Churchill was still basically set on the appeasement of Stalin over Poland that he solemnly told the War Cabinet on 24 July that the Lublin Poles were 'neither Quislings nor Communists'.[43] Needless to say, this judgment was not to be vindicated. All the same, as will be seen, Churchill's Government in due course granted the Lublin Poles the full diplomatic recognition that Stalin desired.

This necessity to engage in sustained appeasement of the Soviets was of course wholly repugnant to Churchill and at times during the first half of 1944 he gave private indications to this effect. For example, on 1 April he wrote to Eden: 'Although I have tried in every way to put myself in sympathy with these Communist leaders, I cannot feel the slightest trust or confidence in them. Force and facts are their only realities.'[44] Then on 8 May he minuted: 'I fear that very great evil will come upon the world. This time at any rate we and the Americans will be heavily armed. The Russians are drunk with victory and there are no lengths they may not go.'[45] But in the absence of any firm evidence that Roosevelt shared his apprehensions Churchill saw no alternative to pursuing the broad course he had adopted after the Teheran conference.

During the summer of 1944 Churchill had to endure the beginnings of a new humiliation. This related to prisoners-of-war who increasingly fell into British hands following the successful D-Day landings in Normandy on 6 June. Many thousands turned out to be Soviet citizens who had earlier been captured by the Germans and had either volunteered to or been forced to fight on the Axis side. There were also to be some prisoners-of-war who, while Russian in origin, denied that they had ever been Soviet citizens. For Churchill's Cabinet all these men were to prove a great embarrassment. For large numbers sought asylum in the West. And it was generally assumed – and rightly – that execution or a long term in a labour camp would be the probable fate of those returning to the Soviet Union. Naturally, however, the Soviets made it clear that they would regard it as an unfriendly act if the Britsh saw fit to adopt a policy of granting asylum to these men. For it would clearly constitute a blatant declaration that the British saw their Soviet allies as inhumane and/or had no confidence in their system of justice.

In these circumstances Eden, backed by his officials, became convinced that the bulk of the Soviet prisoners must if necessary be forcibly repatriated and he got the War Cabinet, with Churchill in the chair, to accept this on 17 July. By the 26th, however, the matter had been reopened as a result of Churchill receiving a letter of protest from Lord Selborne, a relatively junior minister responsible for the Special Operations Executive. The Prime Minister now decided that 'we dealt rather summarily with this at Cabinet' and urged Eden to reconsider.[46] But on 4 September the War Cabinet, which had before it an unrepentant memorandum by Eden, reaffirmed the original decision in favour of forcible repatriation.The upshot was that by November 1944 the Americans had decided to follow the British lead and in the ensuing thirty months more than two million people were forcibly handed over to the Soviets. Frequently these handovers took place amid harrowing protests from the victims at the inhumanity involved. Indeed, it is doubtful whether British and American forces had ever before been systematically asked to be a party to anything of this kind. But, like their Nazi German and Soviet counterparts in similar situations, they docilely obeyed their superiors. As for the victims, they are thought almost invariably to have met with a grisly fate. Among them were numerous *émigrés* who had fought for Churchill's beloved Whites in the Russian Civil War.[47]

Churchill's acquiescence in this policy has to be seen, of course, in the broader context of his belief, tenaciously held throughout 1944, that his all-out appeasement of Stalin would at some point produce a dividend for Great Britain. In particular, he was acutely aware that, with Germany on the verge of collapse, the entire future of the Balkans and the Eastern Mediterranean was at stake. Most alarming perhaps was that pro-Communist guerrillas appeared to be capable of seizing power in Greece – even though no Soviet forces were likely to be present when the Germans initially withdrew. On 4 May Churchill had accordingly asked Eden the rhetorical question: 'Are we going to acquiesce in the communization of the Balkans and perhaps of Italy?' His answer to his own question was: 'I am of opinion on the whole that we ought to come to a definite conclusion about it and that, if our conclusion is that we resist the communist infusion and invasion, we should put it to them pretty plainly at the best moment that military

events permit.' But then he realistically added: 'We should of course
have to consult the United States first.'[48] And, although he did not say
so on this occasion, both he and Eden already knew by now that the
Americans would give the British no encouragement to offer any kind
of military resistance to the Soviets. Churchill was thus driven to
favour proposing to Stalin a spheres-of-influence deal in the hope of
securing a free hand to keep Communists out of power at least in
Greece, whose strategic position in the Eastern Mediterranean was of
great importance given its proximity to the route which brought Middle
Eastern oil to Great Britain via the Suez Canal. So, on the following
day, 5 May, Eden told the Soviet Ambassador, now F. T. Gusev, that
the British believed that the Soviet Union should take the lead in an
attempt to get Romania out of the War. On the other hand, as Greece
was in the British theatre of command, 'we felt entitled to ask for
Soviet support for our policy there in return for the support we were
giving to Soviet policy with regard to Romania'.[49]

Most surprisingly the Soviet reply on 18 May was positive – but
linked to an embarrassing question about whether the Americans had
been consulted. Eden had no other alternative than to tell Gusev that
the Americans had not been consulted but he added implausibly that
he had no doubt about their agreement. In fact the seemingly high-
minded US State Department did not agree because they feared – not
incorrectly – that this was the beginning of a spheres-of-influence
agreement to which they had consistently claimed to be opposed. This
forced Churchill on 31 May to appeal to Roosevelt, saying that the
proposed Anglo-Soviet arrangement applied only to war conditions
and was not an attempt to carve up the Balkans into spheres of
influence ahead of a peace settlement. Roosevelt was unimpressed and
on 11 June held that the result would be 'the division of the Balkan
region into spheres of influence despite the declared intention to limit
the arrangement to military matters'.[50] Churchill then urged the
President to consent to the arrangement being given a three-month
trial. And on the 13th Roosevelt rather weakly gave way, despite State
Department objections. This turned out to be a decision of great
importance. For it ultimately enabled the devious Churchill, as will be
seen, to save Greece from Communism. The President seemed close to
having second thoughts, however, when on 22 June he telegraphed
Churchill, rebuking the British for originally having proposed the deal
to the Soviets without prior consultation with Washington –
something he had only just discovered. Churchill was furious and even

contemplated threatening to resign over what he later characterised as the 'pedantic interference of the United States'.[51] But he succeeded in keeping his temper and the three-month trial seems tacitly to have limped into an unexciting and informal existence.

The importance of the tacit trial, however, was that when it was due to end Churchill felt emboldened into trying to covert it into something much more meaningful – just as the Americans had feared. And this time he decided to deal directly with Stalin and to keep Roosevelt in a considerable degree of ignorance as to what was afoot. His first move, on 27 September, was to ask Stalin to receive him and Eden in Moscow in the following month. Churchill did not inform Roosevelt of his intentions, however, until two days later. Furthermore, he deliberately misled the President about his priorities, stressing that the Pacific War and Poland were the 'two objects' he and Eden had in mind but then added that 'there were other points too concerning Yugoslavia and Greece which we could also discuss'.[52] Roosevelt was uneasy about the proposed visit but, owing to the proximity of the US Presidential Election, could not possibly go to Moscow himself in order to keep an eye on his two allies. He insisted, however, that he saw Moscow as a mere preliminary to a later three-power meeting. He also appointed Harriman, now US Ambassador in Moscow, to be a US 'observer' at the Anglo-Soviet Summit – though in the event Harriman was not invited to attend the most crucial meetings. Stalin meanwhile, on 2 October, had cordially accepted Churchill's suggestion. Accordingly the Prime Minister and his Foreign Secretary, with almost indecent haste, arrived in Moscow on 9 October and stayed until the 18th.

For one historian, Warren F. Kimball, this Conference was 'not Churchill's finest hour'.[53] But perhaps it would be fairer to say that it was not Great Britain's finest hour. For the truth seems to be that at a time of great national weakness Churchill, without a single decent card in his hand, effectively bluffed Stalin into giving him a free hand in Greece. In so doing he demonstrated, just as Chamberlain had done at Munich, that even brutal dictators can at times find it difficult to resist flattery and an overwhelming show of goodwill when offered by a front-rank representative of the world elite. And in Churchill's case, a degree of ruthless dishonesty also played a part. For he gave Stalin to understand that he was speaking not only for himself but in a certain sense also for Roosevelt.

The extraordinary way in which Churchill played his hand *vis-à-vis*

Stalin is to be seen in the following passage from the 'unofficial' minutes of their first meeting which have survived in Clark Kerr's Papers:

> Prime Minister then produced what he called a 'naughty document' showing a list of Balkan countries and the proportion of interest in them of the Great Powers. He said that the Americans would be shocked if they saw how crudely he had put it. Marshal Stalin was a realist. He himself was not sentimental while Mr Eden was a bad man. He had not consulted his cabinet or Parliament.[54]

The figures on the 'naughty document' (or on 'a rather dirty and clumsy document' as the Soviets records have it[55]) were as follows:

Romania	
Russia	90%
The others	10%
Greece	
Great Britain (in accord with USA)	90%
Russia	10%
Yugoslavia	50–50%
Hungary	50–50%
Bulgaria	
Russia	75%
The others	25%

Stalin, according to Churchill, 'took his blue pencil and made a large tick upon it, and passed it back to us'.[56] Despite some subsequent and indecisive haggling between Molotov and Eden about the precise percentages appropriate for Bulgaria and Hungary, a clear if informal deal had been done on the point that mattered most to Churchill: he had Stalin's consent to handle Greece as he saw fit.

True, Stalin got in return a free hand from Great Britain in Romania and Bulgaria. But this was actually an extremely uneven bargain, in that the Soviets were in any case in the process of taking physical control of these countries and hence stood in no real need of British blessing; whereas the British could not in practice have massively interfered in the internal affairs of post-liberation Greece without Soviet acquiescence. Why, then, had Stalin lost out to Churchill? Possibly he was simply taken in by Churchill's pretence that he was speaking for Roosevelt as well as for himself and hence was afraid that the Soviet Union would find itself isolated. But he may also have wanted to acknowledge his gratitude to Churchill for all the appeasing gestures that had come his way in the preceding months and to signal that he was not actually averse to a degree of continuing co-operation with London in the post-war world. However that may be, we can be reasonably sure that the 'percentages deal' would never have come about if Churchill had either drifted vaguely along in the wake of the seemingly high-minded Roosevelt or, alternatively, if he had antagonised Stalin over matters like the repatriation of Soviet prisoners-of-war or the demands of the London Poles. In short, Churchill's adoption of Chamberlain's brand of positive appeasement opened the way for Greece to be saved from Communism.

The other main issue to which Churchill and Stalin devoted attention in Moscow concerned Poland – which was not of course mentioned in the 'naughty document'. For both leaders realised that this was a particularly sensitive matter for Roosevelt on the eve of an election – given the the large number of Polish-American electors. They therefore in effect agreed to leave this subject for definitive resolution until an American President could join them in a post-election Summit. But Churchill at least went through the motions of trying to promote a reconciliation between Stalin and the London Poles. He accordingly summoned Mikolajczyk from London to Moscow. But little progress at first proved possible. For Mikolajczyk had no authority from those he represented to make any concessions to Stalin. Eventually, however, under great and even bullying pressure from Churchill, he indicated that he would try to obtain unequivocal support from his colleagues in London for the Soviet demand for recognition of the Curzon Line as the basis for establishing Poland's eastern frontier. But without any acknowledgement that this would lead to the inclusion of the city of Lvov in Poland – which the Soviets, perhaps encouraged by Churchill's concession on the point at Teheran, unequivocally refused to concede had been intended by Curzon to be Polish – Mikolajczyk knew that he had little hope in that direction. He also undertook to present a Stalin–Churchill suggestion that the Lublin and London Poles should aim at creating a provisional government on a 50–50 basis. The upshot was that, on his return to London, Mikolajczyk was unable to win over his colleagues and he accordingly resigned. He was replaced by an uncompromising anti-Communist Socialist, Tomasz Arciszewski.

Churchill maintained that the London Poles had turned out to be their own worst enemies. Yet can he have been in any doubt about Stalin's malign intentions towards them – even if they had been willing to accept Mikolajczyk's approach? For just prior to Churchill's visit to Warsaw he had watched with impotent fury as the Soviets refused to give any assistance to the pro-Western Polish underground's uprising against the German occupiers of Warsaw. But he had felt unable to intervene militarily with a British airlift in the absence of Soviet consent. Nor did he publicly condemn the Soviets and, indeed, duplicitously told Stalin in Moscow that he 'absolutely' accepted that the Soviets could not have done anything to bring help to those taking part in the uprising.[57] But this was no doubt because, as he put it in his memoirs, 'terrible and even humbling submissions must at times be made to the general aim'.[58] It seems likely, then, that Churchill did not really fail to understand the attitude of the London Poles and did not genuinely consider Mikolajczyk to be guilty of the 'cowardice' of which he openly accused him in Moscow.[59] Nor can he have seriously believed that a satisfactory solution could have been achieved if the London Poles had all been as 'statesmanlike' as Mikolajczyk eventually proved willing to become. But this did not stop Churchill from using the alleged stubbornness of the London Poles as some kind of lame public explanation for the failure of his efforts on their behalf. In a speech in the Commons on 15 December 1944, for example, he said that Mikolajczyk and his supporters were 'the only light which burns for Poland in the immediate future' and he condemned 'the obstinate and inflexible resistance' of those who now ran the Polish Government-in-Exile.[60]

In these circumstances it came as no surprise when, on 31 December, the Soviets granted recognition to the Lublin Poles as the new Provisional Government of Poland. There was now, as indeed had been the case for many months past, only one rather remote possibility of saving Poland from Soviet domination. This would have been for the United States to intervene in an extremely vigorous fashion. Churchill, for his part, hoped, against all the evidence, that this might indeed occur at the three-power Summit which eventually convened at Yalta on 3 February 1945. But, as will be seen, he had to face yet another disappointment.

In the meantime, however, Churchill had taken the fullest possible advantage of the only major concession he had won from Stalin on his Moscow visit, namely his free hand in Greece. Faced with mounting evidence that pro-Communist guerrillas intended to seize power in recently-liberated Athens, Churchill decided on 4 December to use British troops to crush them. Deliberately ignoring the United States and even members of his own War Cabinet apart from Eden, he sent the following dramatic telegram to General Ronald Scobie: 'We have to hold and dominate Athens. It would be a great thing for you to succeed in this without bloodshed if possible, but also with bloodshed if necessary.'[61] A Foreign Office official, Pierson Dixon, recorded in his diary how the Prime Minister set about dictating this and other related messages to a secretary, Elizabeth Layton, 'who did not bat an eyelid at the many blasphemies with which the old man interspersed his official phrases'. 'He was,' wrote Dixon, 'in a bloodthirsty mood, and did not take kindly to suggestions that we should avoid bloodshed if possible.'[62] One historian, Warren F. Kimball, has found it 'difficult to explain why Churchill was so obsessed with events in Greece'. He wrote:

> Whatever his dedication to 'constitutional liberties' and a British-style rule of law, his percentages agreement with Stalin conceded that those values would not prevail in the Baltic states, Romania, and Bulgaria. Why then his all-out commitment to Greece? Perhaps it was a geopolitical view generated by the events of two wars, each of which found Greece a linchpin in the control of the eastern Mediterranean. Perhaps Churchill's image of Greece as the 'cradle of democracy' inspired a romantic desire to protect that society from bolshevism. Perhaps Churchill was right when he equated an EAM triumph with a Communist takeover. A massacre 'would have ensued,' he told Roosevelt, 'followed by a ruthless terror in the name of a purge. I am sure you would not like us to abandon this thankless task now and withdraw our troops and let things crash.' But these reasons were window dressing. Churchill got tough over Greece because he concluded that Britain's Great Power status had to be tested, and Greece was where it could pass that test. Stalin had agreed that Greece should be a British sphere of influence, and British military power seemed sufficient for the situation. Even without Soviet aid, the Greek Communists (the label Churchill applied to all those opposed to a 'British solution') posed a challenge to what the prime minister wanted. If Britain could not control events in a small part of the world, how could it play the role of a Great Power? Greece was important more as an expression of Britain's place in the world than as a place where freedom had to be defended.[63]

But this writer is not persuaded that 'a romantic desire to protect [Greece] from bolshevism' was mere 'window dressing'. For there is a flavour in Dixon's account of the genuine relish with which Churchill was able, after so many months of enforced dissimulation, to indulge to the full in the particular case of Greece his unchanging anti-Communist appetites.

However this may be, Scobie's actions proved successful in decisively checking the Greek Communists. But unfortunately for Churchill the terms of his robust telegram leaked into the press and provoked a storm among Labour MPs at home. More seriously, the United States publicly criticised what they saw as unwarranted interference in Greece's internal affairs. But Churchill was able to disregard his critics. For he was given the tacit support of the Soviet Union! He was never to forget this remarkable event. For example, in retirement in 1956 he told an American journalist, C. L. Sulzberger:

> Stalin never broke his word to me. We agreed on the Balkans. I said he could have Rumania and Bulgaria; and he said we could have Greece (of course, only in our sphere, you know). He signed a slip of paper. And he never broke his word. We saved Greece that way. When we went in in 1944 Stalin didn't interfere. You Americans didn't help, you know.[64]

For his part Churchill took pains to make Stalin believe that he also was a man of his word. As a result he sent a minute to Eden on 19 January 1945 that must surely rank among the harshest and most brutal ever written by any British Prime Minister. The background to it was that the Soviets, now in control in Romania, were in the process of abducting large numbers of Romanian citizens (some of whom were and are German-speaking) for transportation to the Soviet Union. There they were treated as slaves and forced to work in Soviet coal-mines. Learning of this, some British diplomats in Bucharest protested to their Soviet counterparts. But Churchill objected:

> We seem to be taking a very active line against the deportation of the Austrians, Saxons and other German or quasi-German elements from Roumania to Russia for labour purposes. Considering all that Russia has suffered, and the wanton atttacks made upon her by Roumania, and the vast armies the Russians are using at the front at the present time, and the terrible condition of the people in many parts of Europe, I cannot see that the Russians are wrong in making 100 or 150 thousand of these people work their passage. Also we must bear in mind what we promised about leaving Roumania's fate to a large extent in Russian hands. I cannot myself consider that it is wrong of the Russians to take Roumanians of any origin they like to work in the Russian coal-fields in view of all that has passed.[65]

The severity of these remarks is surely difficult to understand or excuse. For Romania's 'wanton attacks' on the Soviet Union can only be understood in the context of the latter's initial seizure of Romanian territory, in 1940, in collusion with Germany. And the apparent endorsement of the Soviets' moral right to turn Romanian citizens into slaves is nothing less than astonishing. Possibly pressure of work led Churchill to write here in terms that on mature reflection he would have regretted. More easily comprehended, for example, is another minute he wrote to Eden a day earlier:

> Why are we making a fuss about the Russian deportations in Roumania of Saxons and others? It is understood that the Russians were to work their will in this sphere. Anyhow we cannot prevent them.[66]

This last sentence is perhaps the key to understanding Churchill's enthusiasm at the time and later for the Moscow deal involving Romania/Bulgaria and Greece: he had outwitted the Soviets in that he could in any case have done nothing for Romania and Bulgaria, whereas Stalin, by lining up with Roosevelt, could surely have stopped the British from forestalling the impending Communist coup in Athens.

Less easy for Churchill to justify, however, was the policy of continuing forcibly to return prisoners-of-war to the Soviet Union. For here at least he could not say that it was literally beyond his powers to prevent it. But he seems to have remained convinced that it was right to sacrifice them – presumably another 'terrible and even humbling submission' that 'must at times be made to the general aim'. And given Churchill's triumph with respect to Greece this is an extremely forceful argument. All the same, there is something especially repugnant about one particular exchange of minutes between Sir Hastings Ismay of the War Cabinet staff and the Prime Minister over this matter. On 1 January 1945 Ismay consulted Churchill about arrangements for his journey to the Yalta Summit with Stalin and Roosevelt and proposed that the SS Franconia, a substantial liner, be used for this purpose. He added:

> Marshal Stalin is pressing for the repatriation of Soviet Nationals taken prisoner by us on the Western Front, and it is proposed to put one or two thousand of these into the Franconia, if you approve. I am assured that they can be completely segregated from our Party, and that they will be reasonably sanitary. They will, of course, be disembarked directly we get to our destination so that they will in any case not be in your way.

To this chillingly Churchill replied: 'I see no harm in this provided the place can be properly be cleared up after they have left.'[67] In the event, however, his travel plans were changed for reasons unconnected with the Soviet prisoners-of-war; he was to go to the Crimea via Malta entirely by air. This was a stroke of good fortune for Churchill. For if he had actually made the journey to Yalta in the manner proposed by Ismay the damage to his subsequent reputation would surely have been substantial. As it is, his penning of an incredibly callous minute on the matter, though recorded without comment by his authorised biographer, has so far failed to make any impact on posterity's view of Churchill.

If Churchill was an appeaser of Stalin in the run-up to the Yalta Conference with respect to repatriation of prisoners-of war and much else, he had an exactly contrary approach when it came to meeting Soviet wishes concerning the future of the right-wing dictatorship in Spain. For this at least was so unambiguously in Great Britain's sphere of geographic influence that Churchill was for once strong enough not even to have to bargain about it in the Moscow Conference of October 1944. In this matter his problems lay more with his own anti-Fascist compatriots and to some extent also with their American sympath-isers. But Churchill fought determinedly and almost single-handedly to ensure that the Spanish Left did not come to power in the post-war era. For he believed such people would turn out to be pro-Communist and pro-Soviet. This meant that in practice his goal was to ensure that Franco's regime would endure. He never of course expressly stated this. But he repeatedly said that he opposed a re-opening of the Civil War and any interference by foreign powers in Spain's internal affairs – which amounted to the same thing.

He made his first move during the course of a wide-ranging speech in the House of Commons on 24 May 1944. It was, incident-ally, a speech which was only belatedly seen by the Foreign Office, whose Permanent Under-Secretary, Cadogan, recorded in his diary on the same day:

> A good madhouse in A's [Eden's] room at 10.30. A., and 16 other people, fluttering pages of the P.M.'s draft speech (for this morning!) looking over each other's shoulders and all talking at once. Towards the end when asked my opinion, I said that if I could have a chance to read the damned thing I might express one. From the smell of it, I didn't see anything wrong (it's rather a good speech).[68]

Churchill was thus not prevented from slipping in some gracious passages about Spain's and Franco's helpful attitude when Allied landings in North Africa had first taken place in 1942. He continued:

'As I am here to-day speaking kindly words about Spain, let me add that I hope she will be a strong influence for the peace of the Mediterranean after the war.' And the Prime minister added: 'Internal problems of Spain are a matter for Spaniards themselves. It is not for us – that is the Government – to meddle in such affairs.' He had nothing critical to say about Franco's earlier friendship with Nazi Germany and Fascist Italy – symbolised by the fact that on his desk in the Pardo Palace he had ostentatiously kept photographs of Hitler and Mussolini alongside one of the Pope. Nor did Churchill mention that Spain had had forces, the so-called Blue Division, fighting with the Germans against the Soviets on the Eastern Front until 1943. A back-bench Labour MP, Haden Guest, intervened to ask: 'Is not a Fascist Government anywhere, a preparation for an attack?' But the Prime Minister evaded by replying: 'I presume we do not include in our pro-gramme of world renovation any forcible action against any Govern-ment whose internal form of administration does not come up to our own ideas.'[69] Further criticism at home soon came from the Trades Union Congress and in the United States from a variety of news-papers. But Churchill was unrepentant and telegraphed to Roosevelt: 'I do not care about Franco but I do not wish to have the Iberian peninsula hostile to the British after the war … We should not be able to agree here in attacking countries which have not molested us because we disliked their totalitarian form of government.'[70]

Later in 1944, however, Churchill had to face severe difficulties concerning Franco's future from his War Cabinet colleagues, Eden and Attlee. A central role was also for a time played by Lord Templewood, formerly Sir Samuel Hoare, who had served under Baldwin as Foreign Secretary and under Chamberlain as Home Secretary. Templewood had been Churchill's choice to be Ambassador in Madrid during the perilous period when Franco was being tempted to enter the war on Germany's side. As a well-known appeaser he had seemed an inspired choice to deal with the anti-Soviet Spanish Government. And he did indeed serve Churchill well until the autumn of 1944. He had, for example, warmly welcomed Churchill's speech of 24 May 1944 and had noted with approval how well it had been received in Madrid. But then, for no obvious reason, he effectively turned against Franco just before he was due to return to retirement in London. For he recom-mended in a memorandum dated 16 October 1944 that the British, the Americans and the Soviets send a warning to Madrid that Spain must reform its internal regime or face economic sanctions. Eden found this approach broadly attractive and, to Churchill's fury, wished to raise the matter in the War Cabinet.

Meanwhile Attlee also decided to intervene by submitting on 4 November a memorandum to the War Cabinet. It was one of the few moves he ever made in the field of international affairs during the lifetime of the Coalition Government that was seriously unwelcome to Churchill and that seemed certain to please Moscow. Presumably Attlee felt under pressure from his own followers. He feared, he stated, that Great Britain was in danger of being regarded as the Franco regime's sole external supporter among the victors and he accordingly urged a change of direction: 'We should use whatever methods are available to assist in bringing about its downfall. We should, especially in the economic field, work with the United States and France to deny facilities to the present regime.'[71] Selborne, as Minister of Economic Warfare, strongly objected, however, to the possibility of economic sanctions being applied to Spain. And in a Cabinet memorandum of his own, dated 14 November, he boldly argued:

> Whatever we may think of 'the incompetence, corruption and oppression' of the Franco regime [Attlee's words], there is plenty of evidence that they are less than under the regime it displaced, and also that the Franco atrocities are fewer and less horrible than those that preceded them. Nor is there any reason to believe that Franco is more authoritarian or more severe to his political opponents than our Allies Stalin and [Antonio] Salazar [of Portugal].[72]

Churchill was meanwhile privately confronting Eden. The Prime Minister had, above all, been dismayed by a Foreign Office draft intended to be sent to the US Government which had argued that 'if the present unsatisfactory position [in Spain] is allowed to crystallize we may therefore eventually be faced with a new Spanish civil war as the only means of getting rid of the present regime'.[73] This seemed to Churchill to amount to the promotion of Communism. He accordingly drafted a candid minute for his Foreign Secretary, dated 10 November, that surprisingly finds no place in his authorised biography. It certainly tells us something of his contempt for the Foreign Office and perhaps for Eden personally. And it also tells us much about the extent of his fear of Europe-wide Communism at this stage of the war and how central in that context the future of Spain seemed to him to be (and thereby, incidentally, justifying the space devoted to Spain in the present work). First, he stated: 'I am no more in agreement with the internal government of Russia than I am with that of Spain, but I

certainly would rather live in Spain than Russia.' It may seem odd to
some analysts that he should have begun with this plainly-stated
personal preference rather than with assertions about balance of
power considerations and narrow British interests. But the probability
is that his long-standing ideological and practical hatred of Communism was once again at the forefront of his mind when he contemplated
the future of any European country – and certainly so when it was
within his power to shape events as was to be the case with respect to
Spain (and, as has been argued here, with respect also to Greece in the
same period). In his minute to Eden of 10 November he went on to
argue that economic sanctions would not lead to a benign transtition
to a more liberal order in Spain. He wrote of Franco:

> He and all those associated with him will never consent to be
> butchered by the Republicans, which is what would happen. It is a
> matter of life or death in Spain and I do not think we should, without
> more careful consideration, make ourselves responsible for starting
> another blood-bath. What you are proposing to do is little less than
> stirring up a revolution in Spain. You begin with oil [sanctions]; you
> will quickly end in blood.

Churchill also set the issue in the wider European context:

> if we now lay our hands on Spain I am of the opinion that we shall be
> making needless trouble for ourselves and very definitely taking
> sides in ideological matters. Should the Communists become masters
> of Spain we must expect the infection to spread very fast through
> Italy and France. This surely requires consideration. I certainly was
> not aware that the Foreign Office nursed such sentiments. It would
> be far better to allow these Spanish tendencies to work themselves
> out instead of precipitating a renewal of the civil war, which is what
> you will do if you press this matter. At this time every country that is
> liberated or converted by our victories is seething with Communism.
> All are linked together and only our influence with Russia prevents
> their actively stimulating this movement, deadly as I conceive it to
> peace and also to the freedom of mankind.
> I can well believe that such a policy as you outline would be hailed
> with delight by our Left Wing forces, who would be very glad to see
> Great Britain in the Left Wing of a doctrinal war. I doubt very much,
> however, whether the Conservative Party would agree once the case
> was put before them, and personally I should not be able to seek a
> fleeting popularity by such paths. I should of course be very glad to
> see a Monarchical and Democratic restoration, but once we have
> identified ourselves with the Communist side in Spain which, what-
> ever you say, would be the effect of your policy, all our influence

would be gone for a middle course. A river of blood flows between the two sides in Spain, and there is hardly a family which does not nurse a blood feud.

Might I venture to beg you to consider the three principal tenets to which I hold: opposition to Communism, non-intervention in the domestic affairs of countries which have not molested us, and no special engagements in Europe requiring the maintenance of a large British Army, but rather the effective development of a World Peace Organisation thoroughly armed.[74]

Here, then, is clear evidence that 'opposition to Communism' *per se* and not mere balance of power calculations inspired Churchill's international policy in 1944. This minute also deserves to be analysed in the context of the British domestic scene. For maybe the Prime Minister intended this minute to be understood by Eden as being the preliminary to a resignation threat. For it should not be forgotten that at this time the House of Commons still had a clear majority of Conservative and even perhaps Chamberlainite MPs. Was not Eden, in short, being pointedly reminded that it was in fact the same House of Commons that had been elected in 1935 and that had shown so little sympathy in the late 1930s for the Left in the Spanish Civil War?

Eden, however, was defiant and made clear his resentment at Churchill's charging the Foreign Office with having Communist sympathies. In an unusually pompous minute dated 17 November the Foreign Secretary wrote:

It was certainly not my desire to provoke or to precipitate a revolution in Spain. Nor indeed is this at all likely at the present stage ... My fear is that if we do not give General Franco a straight warning now, the moderate forces in Spain, which are well represented in the army, will lose all influence. Another civil war will then become inevitable sooner or later, probably sooner ...

You also raised in your minute the general question of opposition to Communism. I hope I have satisfied you that it is far from Foreign Office intention to foster Communism in Spain. I think I ought to add that Foreign Office policy has never tended towards fostering Communism anywhere else. In Western Europe we have worked closely with Dr. Salazar and we are now working closely with French, Belgian, Dutch and Norwegian elements which are anything but Communist. In both Yugoslavia and Greece we have consistently drawn attention to the dangers of support for the Communist elements in those countries and in Poland and other Eastern European countries we favour moderate peasant and similar elements, who are likely to form the strongest bulwark against Communism.[75]

With extremely maladroit timing Franco himself now took a hand. He saw fit on 21 November to have delivered to the Foreign Office a dramatic letter to Churchill which urged improving Anglo-Spanish relations on grounds that were no doubt intended to appeal to the Prime Minister personally but were assuredly not welcome to the War Cabinet as a whole. His letter included the following:

> Since we cannot believe in the good faith of Communist Russia, and since we know the insidious power of Bolshevism, we must take account of the fact that the weakening or destruction of her neighbours will greatly increase Russia's ambition and powers, making necessary more than ever an intelligent and understanding attitude on the part of the Western countries. The events in liberated Italy, and the serious situation in France, where the government orders are ignored and the *maquis* groups impudently proclaim their aim of setting up a Soviet Republic – for which they claim to have the support of the USSR –, speak for themselves ...
> ... once Germany is destroyed, England will have only one country left in Europe towards which she can turn her eyes – Spain. The French and Italian defeats, and the internal decomposition of these countries, will probably not allow anything solid to be built upon them for many years to come ... What we deduce from this is clear – reciprocal friendship between England and Spain is desirable.[76]

This was in fact the first anti-Communist clarion call by anyone who was to be a national leader in the postwar world – predating Churchill's own Fulton speech by well over a year. But to Churchill it was quite unwelcome at the time because it allowed Eden to insist that the Prime Minister must send a hostile reply.

All these matters came to a head at a War Cabinet meeting on 27 November 1944. The upshot was that Churchill had to give some ground on the margins but was successful in ensuring that Franco (and hence, as the Prime Minister saw it, anti-Communist interests throughout Western Europe) did not suffer any really damaging long-term blows. First, Attlee, though encouraged by Eden, was evidently reluctant to confront Churchill. In short, tabling a memorandum seems to have sufficiently served his purposes. At all events, the Cabinet Minutes record him as having 'expressed his entire agreement with the action proposed by the Prime Minister', which did not of course include any economic sanctions against Spain. Then Templewood's plea for threats to be made to Franco was in effect obfuscated. But what could not be avoided was the need for Churchill to send some reply to Franco's letter. And on this point the War Cabinet was not willing to leave it to the Prime Minister's judgement – though he offered to send a 'rough' message to Madrid. On the contrary, he was to be somewhat humiliated by being invited to sign a reply which Eden would initially draft.[77]

Churchill's reaction was to begin another determined duel with Eden and, above all, to engage in blatant procrastination. Hence no reply was to be despatched to Franco until 15 January 1945. One happy consequence of this delay for Churchill was that Templewood, who was eager to deliver the reply in person at his farewell interview, was to be frustrated. And, more important, Churchill eventually persuaded Eden that the United States should merely be informed of the contents of the letter but not definitely encouraged to take simultaneous action in Madrid. But in the end Churchill had to put his signature to what he called an 'insulting' message.[78] This stressed that Spain had sent a division 'to help our German enemies against our Russian allies'. And it indicated that Spain would not be allowed to participate in the peace negotiations or join the new world organisation (later named the United Nations). Finally, Franco was curtly informed that the British Government would not consider joining 'any grouping of Powers in Western Europe or elsewhere on a basis of hostility towards or the alleged necessity of defence against our Russian allies'.[79] None of this was good news for Franco. But it could have been much worse. For the fact is that Churchill had almost single-handedly thwarted those in London who were pressing for economic sanctions and who wanted, in his words, to 'make suggestions to the [US] State Department to beat up the Spaniards'.[80]

The Yalta Conference lasted from 3 to 11 February 1945. It was to be dominated, so far as Churchill was concerned, by the quest to persuade Stalin to show a reasonable degree of restraint in his handling of Poland. But unfortunately for the Prime Minister Roosevelt had other priorities, namely to secure Soviet promises to join the war against Japan after the defeat of Germany and to sponsor a new world body, the United Nations, in a fashion that would be acceptable to US opinion. Churchill claimed to have believed at the time and later that if Roosevelt had joined him in giving first priority to Poland and had been willing to threaten a public quarrel with the Soviets on the issue, Stalin would have capitulated. This is impossible to disprove. But the fact is that the Soviets had physical possession of Poland and knew that there would be negligible support in either the United States or

Great Britain at this time for the use of armed force to evict them –
even if this had been militarily feasible at a point when, it must be
remembered, Roosevelt could have had no certainty about when, if
ever, an arsenal of atomic bombs would be available to him. It is not
therefore surprising that the President decided to avoid an immediate
confrontation with Stalin over Poland – concentrating instead, and
with success, on obtaining Soviet cooperation concerning Japan and
the United Nations. Roosevelt further assured Stalin, perhaps as a
quid pro quo, that US forces would soon withdraw from Europe once
Germany had been defeated.

Poland was not of course ignored at Yalta. Instead, an ambiguous
package was constructed by the Soviets and the Americans – and
Churchill had no alternative in the end other than to give it his formal
approval. First, the Soviets unsurpisingly secured acceptance of
Poland's eastern frontier in the form on which they had long insisted.
Secondly, they got the better of the bargaining with respect to the
composition of the future provisional Polish government: the Lublin
Poles were in effect to form its nucleus but discussions were to take
place in Moscow between Molotov and the US and British Ambassadors about the extent to which places in it could also be found for
further personalities currently based in London or Warsaw. Thirdly, it
was agreed that elections would eventually take place in Poland –
though British and American offers to play a supervisory role to
ensure fairness were ominously rejected by Stalin. It seems, then, that
neither Churchill nor Roosevelt could have had any real illusions that,
under these arrangements, Poland could count on full independence.
But the agreements reached were not, at least on paper, so wholly one-
sided as to preclude them from proclaiming their satisfaction.

It is in this context that Roosevelt's final move at Yalta has to be
evaluated: he proposed that the three leaders should sign a Declaration
on Liberated Europe. This appeared to commit the victors to promote
'self government' and 'free elections' among 'liberated peoples'. Stalin
cheerfully agreed to this proposal and it was accordingly given wide
publicity and contributed greatly to the media in the United States and
Great Britain taking an optimistic view of the future prospects for
cooperation among what had come to be known as 'the Big Three'. But
what did Roosevelt really think of the Declaration he had persuaded
Stalin and Churchill to sign? He cannot have seriously believed that
Stalin intended to allow free elections in the Western sense to take
place in every liberated country: for, despite his deteriorating health,

he was well aware of what was happening in Romania and Bulgaria and he was far from optimistic about the portents for Poland. So why did he promote so misleading a document as the Declaration on Liberated Europe? One view is that he merely wished to use it as window-dressing to enable him to grab short-term plaudits from the US media and from Congress – and this presumably is what Stalin believed at the time. But on another interpretation Roosevelt may have been deliberately setting a trap for the Soviets – with the intention of putting them in the dock about anticipated misconduct in Eastern Europe once they were no longer needed against Germany and Japan. It will probably never be known which of these aims was uppermost in Roosevelt's mind. But there can be little doubt that Churchill for his part soon decided that Stalin had indeed blundered badly in signing the Declaration and that once the immediate euphoria over Yalta had evaporated he would attempt ruthlessly to exploit this fact.

On returning to London Churchill's initial line both in the War Cabinet and in Parliament was greatly to exaggerate the importance of the Declaration and the other agreements reached; and to pretend to believe in Stalin's reliability. To his colleagues in the War Cabinet he stated on 19 February that he was 'quite sure' that Stalin 'meant well to the world and to Poland'. He was 'a person of great power, in whom he had every confidence'.[81] Two days later he told them that 'his own feeling was that the Russians would honour the declaration that had been made'.[82] Then, on 27 February, he addressed the Commons, where a minority of backbenchers, Labour as well as Conservative, was uneasy or even indignant about the treatment Poland had received at Yalta. The Prime Minister sought to reassure the critics: 'Most solemn declarations have been made by Marshal Stalin and the Soviet State.' He continued:

> The impression I brought back from the Crimea, and from all my other contacts, is that Marshal Stalin and the Soviet leaders wish to live in honourable friendship and equality with the Western democracies. I feel also that their word is their bond. I know of no Government which stands to its obligations, even in its own despite, more solidly than the Russian Soviet Government. I decline absolutely to embark here on a discussion about Russian good faith.[83]

Was Churchill, then, in this phase deliberately overstating the case in favour of the Soviets' essential benevolence in order to be able later to claim that they had gone back on 'most solemn declarations'?

The suspicion must be that this was indeed his intention. At all events, Churchill was never again to speak so warmly about Stalin. And within a week of making his Commons speech on Yalta he was clearly signalling to his War Cabinet colleagues and to Roosevelt that he thought the time had come to confront rather than conciliate Moscow. In its way this was as sudden an abandonment of appeasement as that perpetrated by Chamberlain in March 1939 when he so unexpectedly accepted the need to 'guarantee' Poland against a possible German attack. In Churchill's case, however, his volte-face was evidently not against his better judgment and was certainly not the result of pressure on him by Cabinet colleagues. Yet perhaps even he could not have foreseen the dramatic anti-Communist language he would be employing just one year later at Fulton, Missouri.

NOTES

1   Ponting, *Churchill*, p. 553.
2   Colville, *The Fringes of Power*, p. 434.
3   War Cabinet Minutes, 12 November 1941, CAB 65/24, PRO.
4   John G. Winant, *A Letter from Grosvenor Square*, London, 1947, p. 66.
5   Lord Morrison, *An Autobiography*, London, 1960, p. 200.
6   Churchill, *The Second World War*, I, p. 201; and Gilbert, *Prophet of Truth*, pp. 694, 696.
7   The Earl of Avon, *The Eden Memoirs: Facing the Dictators*, London, 1962, p. 153.
8   Harvey (ed.), *War Diaries, passim*; and David Carlton, *Anthony Eden: A Biography*, London, 1981, pp. 184–5.
9   Harvey (ed.), *War Diaries*, p. 152.
10   For a fuller treatment of the Churchill–Eden relationship during the period of their wartime 'partnership' see, Carlton, *Anthony Eden*, ch. VII; and Barker, *Churchill and Eden at War*. For their relationship generally see also David Carlton, 'Churchill and Eden: An Uneasy Partnership', *The Listener*, 6 August 1981.
11   PREM 3/399/7, PRO, in Carlton, *Anthony Eden*, pp. 192–3.
12   WP 48(42), CAB 66/21, PRO, in *ibid.*, p. 193.
13   War Cabinet Minutes, 6 February 1942, CAB 65/29, PRO; and Kenneth Young, *Churchill and Beaverbrook: A Study in Politics and Friendship*, London, 1966, p. 235.
14   PREM 4/43/9, PRO, in Carlton, *Anthony Eden*, pp. 195–6.
15   Cooper to Eden, 22 April 1942, FO 954/25, PRO, in *ibid.*, p. 197.
16   Churchill, *The Second World War*, IV, p. 428.
17   *Ibid.*, IV, chs 27, 28; W. Averell Harriman and Elie Abel, *Special Envoy to Churchill and Stalin, 1941–1946*, New York, 1975; Dilks (ed.), *Cadogan*; Arthur Bryant, *The Turn of the Tide: A Study Based on the Diaries and Autobiographical Notes of Field-Marshal The Viscount Alanbrooke*, London, 1957; Inverchapel Papers, PRO; Lord Tedder, *With Prejudice*, London, 1966;

and Lord Moran, *Winston Churchill: The Struggle for Survival*, London, 1966.

18   Tedder, *With Prejudice*, p. 330.

19   Martin Kitchen, *British Policy towards the Soviet Union during the Second World War*, New York, 1986, pp. 135, 137.

20   Dilks (ed.), *Cadogan*, p. 471.

21   Moran, *Winston Churchill*, p. 58.

22   *Ibid.*, p. 62.

23   *Hansard*, 8 September 1942, vol. 383, col. 95.

24   Milovan Djilas, *Conversations with Stalin*, New York, 1962, p. 106.

25   Edmonds, *The Big Three*, p. 304.

26   Churchill to Eden, 21 October 1942, PREM 4/100/7, PRO.

27   V. Trukhanovsky, *British Foreign Policy during the Second World War*, Moscow, 1970, p. 307.

28   Randolph S. Churchill, *Winston S. Churchill: Vol. II: Young Statesman, 1901–1914*, London, 1967, p. 283. It is perhaps as well that Randolph Churchill added the last sentence quoted. For otherwise some historians, for example Alan Clark or John Charmley, might subsequently have been tempted to speculate whether he might have been thinking not of Russia but of the United States as the equivalent of seventeenth-century France!

29   Dilks (ed.), *Cadogan*, p. 521.

30   Churchill to Eden, 28 April 1943, PREM 3/354/8, PRO.

31   *Hansard*, 4 May 1943, vol. 389, col. 31.

32   Churchill to Stalin, 28 April 1943, PREM 3/354/8, PRO.

33   Edmonds, *The Big Three*, p. 321.

34   Moran, *Winston Churchill*, pp. 140–1.

35   Teheran Conference Records, 28 November, 1 December 1943, CAB 120/113, PRO. On the Teheran Conference see also Keith Sainsbury, *The Turning Point: Roosevelt, Stalin, Churchill, and Chiang-Kai-Shek, 1943: The Moscow, Cairo and Teheran Conferences*, Oxford, 1985, ch. 8.

36   Richard Lamb, *Churchill as War Leader: Right or Wrong?*, London 1991, p. 247.

37   Churchill to Eden, 16 January 1944, PREM 3/399/6, PRO.

38   Eden to Churchill, 1 January 1944, in Lamb, *Churchill as War Leader*, p. 261.

39   According to some analysts the British move to support Tito was greatly influenced by a nest of Communist agents serving with the Special Operations Executive in Cairo. See *ibid.*, ch. 19; David Martin, *The Web of Disinformation: Churchill's Yugoslav Blunder*, New York, 1988; and Michael Lees, *The Rape of Serbia: The British Role in Tito's Grab for Power, 1943–1944*, San Diego, 1990. For a more sceptical assessment see Stafford, *Churchill and the Secret Service*, pp. 253–5.

40   FO 954/20, PRO, in Gilbert, *Road to Victory*, pp. 682–4.

41   Churchill to Stalin, 20 February 1944, Churchill Papers, in *ibid.*, p. 686.

42   Woodward, *British Foreign Policy in the Second World War*, III, p. 195.

43   War Cabinet Minutes, 24 July, 1944, CAB 65/47, PRO.

44   Churchill to Eden, 1 April 1944, PREM 3/396/14, PRO.

45   Churchill to Eden, 8 May 1944, FO 954/20, PRO, in Gilbert, *Road to Victory*, p. 761.

46   Churchill to Eden, 26 July 1944, PREM 3/364/8, PRO.

47   See Nikolai Tolstoy, *Victims of Yalta*, London, 1977, *passim*. See also

Nicholas Bethell, *The Last Secret: Forcible Repatriation to Russia, 1944–7*, London, 1974.

48 Churchill to Eden, 4 May 1944, FO 371/43636, PRO.
49 Woodward, *British Foreign Policy*, III, p. 116.
50 *Ibid.*, p. 118.
51 Barker, *Churchill and Eden*, p. 381; and Churchill minute, 9 July 1944, PREM 3/66/7, PRO, in Fraser J. Harbutt, *The Iron Curtain: Churchill, America and the Origins of the Cold War*, Oxford, 1986, p. 69.
52 Woodward, *British Foreign Policy*, III, p. 149.
53 Warren F. Kimball, 'Naked Reverse Right: Roosevelt, Churchill, and Eastern Europe from TOLSTOY to Yalta – and a Little Beyond', *Diplomatic History*, IX, 1985, p. 6.
54 Inverchapel Papers, FO 800/302, PRO.
55 Trukhanovsky, *British Foreign Policy*, p. 408.
56 Churchill, *The Second World War*, VI, pp. 196–7.
57 Harbutt, *The Iron Curtain*, p. 75.
58 Churchill, *The Second World War*, VI, p. 124.
59 Charmley, *Churchill: The End of Glory*, p. 591.
60 *Hansard*, 15 December 1944, vol. 406, col. 1482.
61 Churchill to Scobie, 5 December 1944, FO 371/43736, PRO.
62 Dixon Diary, 4 December 1944, quoted in Carlton, *Anthony Eden*, p. 249.
63 Warren F. Kimball, *Forged in War: Churchill, Roosevelt and the Second World War*, London, 1997, p. 297; and Churchill to Hopkins, 11 December 1944, in Warren F. Kimball (ed.), *Churchill and Roosevelt: The Complete Correspondence*, 3 vols, Princeton, New Jersey, 1984, vol. III, enclosure to C-850/1.
64 C. L. Sulzberger, *The Last of the Giants*, New York, 1970, p. 304.
65 Churchill to Eden, 19 January 1945, FO 954/20, PRO, in Carlton, *Anthony Eden*, pp. 253–4. Gilbert (*Road to Victory*, p. 1154) later also printed this minute in his authorised biography of Churchill but he offered no comment.
66 Churchill to Eden, 18 January 1945, FO 954/23, PRO, in Gilbert, *Road to Victory*, p. 1154.
67 Ismay Minute, 1 January 1945 and Churchill Minute, 2 January 1945, CAB 120/170, PRO, in *ibid*, p. 1159.
68 Dilks (ed.), *Cadogan*, p. 630.
69 *Hansard*, 24 May 1944, vol. 400, cols 769–72.
70 Churchill to Roosevelt, 4 June 1944, PREM 3/472, PRO.
71 Attlee Memorandum, 4 November 1944, WP (44) 622, CAB 66/57, PRO.
72 Selborne Memorandum, 14 November 1944, WP (44) 651, CAB 66/58, PRO.
73 Draft telegram, 9 November 1944, FO 371/39671/C15949, PRO.
74 Churchill Minute no. M 1101/4 to Eden, 10 November 1944, FO 371/39671/C16068, PRO. A summary of this Minute, omitting Churchill's attack on the Foreign Office for allegedly being pro-Communist, appears in Woodward, *British Foreign Policy*, IV, pp. 31–2.
75 Eden to Churchill, 17 November 1944, FO 371/39761/C16068, PRO.
76 Brian Crozier, *Franco: A Biographical History*, London, 1967, pp. 400–1.
77 War Cabinet Minutes, 27 November 1944, CAB 65/48, PRO.
78 Churchill to Eden, 2 December 1944, in Barker, *Churchill and Eden at War*, p. 161.
79 Woodward, *British Foreign Policy*, IV, p. 35.

80 Churchill Minute no. M1254/4 to Eden, 31 December 1944, PREM 8/106, PRO.
81 War Cabinet Minutes, 19 February 1945, CAB 65/51, PRO.
82 *Ibid.*, 21 February 1945, CAB 65/51, PRO.
83 *Hansard*, 27 February 1945, vol. 408, cols 1283–4.

6

PREACHING CONFRONTATION

1945–1949

O N 6 MARCH 1945 Churchill gave the War Cabinet the first clear sign that he was no longer ready to abandon Poland to its fate without at least getting it on the record that he was appalled at Soviet behaviour and that he had done all in his power to persuade the United States to react appropriately. Seizing on news from Moscow that Molotov was unwilling to see a serious broadening of the Communist-dominated Polish Government, Churchill told his colleagues that the British Government 'had been fully entitled to take the line we had in the debate [in the House of Commons] on the Crimea [Yalta] Conference, since we were bound to assume the good faith of an Ally in the execution of an Agreement so recently signed'. He would now, however, have to seek 'the full support of the USA ... for we could do no more to help the Poles than the United States would help us to'. He foresaw, moreover, that if the Soviets did not modify their attitude 'we should have to explain the position to Parliament and admit with great regret that the Yalta Agreement had failed'.[1] Churchill's tone of surprise and indignation suggests insincere posturing on his part. For only a week earlier he had spoken very differently in private to Harold Nicolson when under criticism in the Commons for failure to do more for Poland at Yalta. Nicolson had written in his diary:

> He is really very sensible. He says he does not see what else we could possibly do. 'Not only are the Russians very powerful, but they are on the spot; even the massed majesty of the British Empire would not avail to turn them off that spot.' ... Winston is as amused as I am that

the warmongers of the Munich period have now become the appeasers, while the appeasers have become the warmongers.[2]

Churchill was not, however, content with performing a volte-face in the War Cabinet. Two days later, on 8 March, he despatched a telegram to Roosevelt that was clearly intended to cause him the maximum embarrassment:

> The news from Moscow about Poland is also most disappointing ... I have based myself in Parliament on the assumption that the words of the Yalta declaration will be carried out in the letter and the spirit. Once it is seen that we have been deceived and that the well-known communist technique is being applied behind closed doors in Poland, either directly by the Russians or through their Lublin puppets, a very grave situation in British public opinion will be reached.
>
> As to the upshot of all this, if we do not get things right now, it will soon be seen by the world that you and I by putting our signatures to the Crimea settlement have under-written a fraudulent prospectus ...
>
> I feel that this is the test case between us and the Russians in the meaning which is to be attached to such terms as Democracy, Sovereignty, Independence, Representative Government and free and unfettered elections.

Anticipating that Roosevelt might ask why Poland, rather than Romania and Bulgaria, should be made a test case, Churchill even had the effrontery to plead in the same telegram that the deal he had made with Stalin in Moscow in October 1944 over Greece to some extent tied his hands.[3] His hope thus appeared to be that the Americans would give a lead in denouncing the Soviets for breaking with the Yalta Declaration with respect to Romania, Bulgaria and Poland and that Great Britain would give voluble support only on the issue of Poland.

Roosevelt by now was in extremely poor health. But he was clear-headed enough not to allow himself to be 'bounced' into any early quarrel with Moscow. He accordingly sent a vague and mollifying reply on 12 March. This only led, however, to Churchill issuing to the President on the following day a threat that almost smacks of blackmail:

> At Yalta also we agreed to take the Russian view of the frontier line. Poland has lost her frontier. Is she now to lose her freedom? That is the question which will undoubtedly have to fought out in Parliament and in public here.

I do not wish to reveal a divergence between the British and United States Governments, but it would certainly be necessary for me to make it clear that we are in presence of a great failure and an utter breakdown of what was settled at Yalta, but that we Britons have not the military strength to carry the matter further and that the limits of our capacity to act have been reached.[4]

The upshot was that Roosevelt and his advisers decided in effect to call what they presumed to be Churchill's bluff by simply declining to denounce the Soviets. Indeed, on 12 April the President sent a telegram to Churchill concerning Poland that the latter must have seen as a clear rebuff:

I would minimize the general Soviet problem as much as possible because these problems, in one form or another, seem to arise every day and most of them straighten out ...

We must be firm, however, and our course thus far is correct.[5]

Whether or not Churchill would have proceeded to publicise his divergence from the President can never be known with certainty. For he was to learn, only hours after receiving this unsatisfactory telegram, that Roosevelt had suddenly died.

The swearing in of the new President, Harry Truman, appeared to give an immediate boost to Churchill's hopes of persuading the United States to inaugurate a crusade against Soviet expansionism in Eastern Europe. For Truman was on the record as an anti-Communist in striking contrast to his predecessor. In particular, he had said in June 1941, when the United States was still neutral but Germany was already at war with the Soviet Union: 'If we see that Germany is winning, we ought to help Russia and if Russia is winning we ought to help Germany and that way let them kill as many as possible.'[6] Then, on 23 April 1945, Truman was to rebuke Molotov in person for the Soviets' failure 'to stick to their agreements' with respect to the Yalta Declaration and Poland. Molotov is said to have 'turned white at the dressing down'. 'I have never been spoken to like that in my life', he said. 'Carry out your engagements, 'replied Truman, 'and you won't get talked to like that.'[7]

Churchill must, therefore, have been greatly encouraged when Truman, within a week of becoming President, agreed to send to Stalin a joint *démarche* about Poland. And it was decided that with the German surrender would come the abrupt American termination of Lend Lease assistance to Moscow. Gradually, however, Truman began to realise that his predecessor's conduct at Yalta had amounted to a degree of acquiescence in Soviet control over Poland. And he seems belatedly to have grasped that he was being manipulated by the Prime Minister. For he wrote to Eleanor Roosevelt on 10 May that 'the difficulties with Churchill are very nearly as exasperating as they are with the Russians'.[8] The upshot was that the President soon began to back away from any immediate confrontation with Moscow.

Churchill's first realisation that Truman was going to be no consistent 'hawk' came as Germany's military collapse accelerated. The Prime Minister was eager, as he had already told Roosevelt, to see Anglo-American forces engage in a race with the Soviets to secure as much of Central Europe as possible. He had hopes, for example, of securing Vienna, Prague and even Berlin. And he wanted to occupy as much as possible of what was already, under the terms of a three-power agreement made in 1944, intended to be the future Soviet Occupation Zone of Germany. Churchill's wish, as he explained to Eden on 4 May 1945, was to see the withdrawal of Anglo-American troops only as part of a general settlement with the Soviets in which the latter would be expected to give satisfaction 'about Poland, and also about the temporary character of the Russian occupation of Germany and the conditions to be established in the Russianised or Russian-controlled countries in the Danube valley, particularly Austria and Czechoslovakia and the Balkans'.[9] But the Supreme Commander, General Dwight Eisenhower, was not eager to provoke the Soviets unduly, clearly fearing that fighting might result; and he accordingly, much to Churchill's disgust, did not engage in any overt 'race' with the Soviets. Churchill for his part seemed willing to run any risk and even contemplated arming surrendering Germans if the necessity for a military showdown with the Soviets arose. He accordingly instructed his military advisers to draw up detailed contingency plans for an early Anglo-American war against the Soviet Union. Truman, however, inclined to Eisenhower's view about not 'racing' the Soviets. And he did not favour retaining as bargaining counters such parts of the intended Soviet Zone of Germany as had naturally fallen under Western control by 8 May, the date of the unconditional German surrender. Hence the President attempted, gradually and with a remarkable degree of diplomacy, to allow Churchill to come to terms with this disappointment. But eventually, on 12 June, in the face of much insensitive persistence from Churchill, Truman informed him bluntly that Western forces must withdraw unconditionally and immediately from any part of Germany already promised to the

Soviets. Churchill replied sourly: 'Obviously we are obliged to conform to your decision, and the necessary instuctions will be issued.' But he added pointedly: 'I hope that your action will in the long run make for a lasting peace in Europe.'[10] On this matter Harriman was eventually to reflect perceptively :

> It is important to remember that we still had a war to win in the Pacific; our military plans called for a massive reployment of American troops from Europe to the Far East. I am not persuaded that by refusing to withdraw from the Elbe we could in fact have forced the Russians to allow free elections, and the establishment of freely elected governments, in Eastern Europe ...
>
> There was no way we could have prevented these events in Eastern Europe without going to war against the Russians ... But I cannot believe that the American people would have stood for it, even if the President had been willing, which he was not.[11]

Nor was Churchill to obtain more than temporary encouragement from Truman with respect to Poland. For once he had realised that solidarity with Churchill would mean a public break with the Soviets, the President soon showed a willingness to conciliate Stalin. To this end he decided to send the pro-Soviet Hopkins to Moscow at the end of May with the mission of 'solving' the Polish issue. This Hopkins was cheerfully able to achieve by accepting the overwhelming domination of the Polish Cabinet by Lublin nominees – with only a token addition of a handful of others, none of whom was to be unacceptable to Stalin. Truman pretended that this was satisfactory and hence came back into line with what had been the main thrust of Roosevelt's policy with respect to Eastern Europe.

Churchill had meanwhile found himself confronted, on the night of 26–27 May, by an extremely unfriendly emissary from Truman. This was Joseph E. Davies, who had been a fellow-travelling US Ambassador to Moscow in the late 1930s. He unfolded a plan for Truman and Stalin to hold a Summit Meeting to whose latter stages Churchill would be invited. The Prime Minister indignantly rejected the idea and indicated that he would not attend at all on such a basis. The two men proceeded to discuss acrimoniously what Churchill depicted as the Communist threat to Europe and the unreliability of Soviet promises. According to one who has consulted Davies's notes:

> He [Davies] accused Churchill of having 'confessed that Hitler was right' about Russia, 'and now that we had jointly defeated Hitler, the Russians could not be trusted in the execution of the "Grand Design"

of preserving the Peace we had won'. 'He pulled no punches,' added the ex-Ambassador, 'neither did I.' The scene may be imagined.[12]

Thereafter Churchill naturally felt the greatest dislike for Davies and said to associates that 'he needed a bath in order to get rid of the ooze and slime'.[13]

In the event Churchill was soon able to persuade Truman that he should be a full participant in the forthcoming summit – which duly opened at Potsdam, near Berlin, on 17 July. But he could not so easily overcome the difficulty embodied in the result of Hopkins's visit to Moscow, namely that the United States now definitely did not intend to confront the Soviets over the future of those parts of Europe already under Soviet occupation. In March – as has been seen – Churchill had threatened a public break from Roosevelt over Poland in particular – though even this may have been mere bluff. By early June, however, it would surely have been political suicide for Churchill to say anything of an extreme nature in public about the United States or even about the Soviet Union. For on 21 May Attlee had informed him that the Labour Party insisted on a General Election taking place before the defeat of Japan and accordingly polling day had been fixed for 5 July. In these circumstances, then, Churchill could only express himself against Truman's policy in private. This he did in late May in a dramatic draft telegram intended initially for Truman's eyes but also, presumably, in the long run, for the 'bar of history'. He wrote:

> It must be remembered that Britain and the United States are united at this time upon the same ideologies, namely, freedom, and the principles set out in the American Constitution and reproduced with modern variations in the Atlantic Charter. The Soviet Government have a different philosophy, namely Communism, and use to the full the methods of police government, which they are applying in every State which has fallen victim to their liberating arms. The Prime Minister cannot readily bring himself to accept the idea that the position of the United States is that Britain and Soviet Russia are just two foreign Powers, six of one and half a dozen of the other, with whom the troubles of the late war have to be adjusted. Except in so far as force is concerned there is not equality between right and wrong. The great cause and principles for which Britain and the United States have suffered and triumphed are not mere matters of the balance of power. They in fact involve the salvation of the world.[14]

In the event, however, Churchill had second thoughts about sending these harsh words to the President. Instead, on 4 June, he sent him a much shorter note in effect accepting the 'deal' Hopkins had struck with Stalin over Poland. Churchill wrote:

> I agree with you that Hopkins' devoted efforts have produced a breaking of the deadlock … I will therefore join with you, either jointly or separately, in a message to Stalin accepting the best that Hopkins can get, providing of course that our Ambassadors are not debarred from pressing for further improvements.[15]

Given the essentially resigned tone of this message, it is scarcely surprising that on 5 July the Churchill Government, in one of their last acts before the Labour Party took office, decided, in concert with the United States, to grant full recognition to the new Soviet-dominated Polish Government.

Churchill's first effort to promote Western confrontation with the Soviets had thus ended in failure. But what had been his motives for appearing in the spring of 1945 to move so far away from the spheres-of-influence approach that had marked his conduct at Moscow in October 1944? They were certainly a mystery to an indignant Stalin. They probably also baffled those Americans, like for example Harriman, who had some conception of what had led up to the 'percentages' agreement. And even historians, with the benefit of hindsight, may never quite fathom what led Churchill into executing this particular volte-face.

For one historian, Warren F. Kimball, 'domestic politics seem to have been a major factor'. He refers in this connection to the fact that 'a general election was in the offing'. He also alludes to 'mending some political fences at home'. In this connection it is of interest that Beaverbrook wrote to Hopkins on 1 March 1945:

> over Poland the opposition is strong. It is led by a powerful Tory group who are the erstwhile champions of Munich. These followers of Chamberlain make the undercover case that Churchill beat them up in 1938 for selling the Czechs down the river, and now has done to the Poles at Yalta exactly what Chamberlain did to the Czechs at Munich.

And it is fair to add that some Labour backbenchers joined the Chamberlainites in expressing unease at the fate of Poland during the debate in the Commons on Yalta. Kimball concludes that Churchill's 'public image, not Soviet expansion, was the real problem'.[16] There is some plausibility in this explanation. Yet, unlike Chamberlain in 1939, Churchill faced no serious revolt in the quarter that mattered, namely the War Cabinet. And by June 1945 it is likely that the Prime Minister would have lost rather than gained votes if he had publicly condemned Hopkins's concessions to the Soviets on the issue of Poland.

Another possibility is that Churchill was not wholly serious in his private attempts to push first Roosevelt and then Truman into a confrontation with the Soviets. Maybe he realised all along that they were quite unlikely to do as he suggested. But, if so, what was the point of risking annoying them – and the Soviets – in this fashion? The answer may lie in his desire to stand well at the 'bar of history'. He had of course written extensively about his experiences during the First World War – causing critics to say that he had written a book about himself and called it *The World Crisis*. And he frequently boasted to his friends that history would vindicate his role with respect to the origins and course of the Second World War because he intended to write it himself. So it is possible that the fusilade of lengthy telegrams with which he bombarded two US Presidents between March and June 1945 were drafted by Churchill, perhaps half-expecting to lose office in the near future, with at least one eye on postwar publication – which is of course precisely what happened to many of these telegrams.[17]

Yet there is another explanation that deserves consideration. It is that he was still at heart the same fanatical enemy of Marxism–Leninism that he had been when the Soviet Union was created and that he once again allowed this to some degree to become evident in the months after Yalta. The timing, on this interpretation, can be explained along the following lines. First, Germany's early defeat was now at hand and hence Soviet military support was no longer so important to Great Britain. Secondly, he may have been stirred to protest at the drift of American policy by Roosevelt's unexpectedly explicit indication at Yalta that the United States was intending, if possible, to withdraw its troops from Europe, within two years of the collapse of Nazi Germany. Thirdly, he may have become increasingly aware that the West would probably soon have a monopoly on atomic weaponry – though admittedly there appears to be no hard evidence that this was influencing his thinking at the time of his volte-face in March 1945. Fourthly, he was undoubtedly given encouragement to pursue his new course with increased vigour during April and May as a result of the change in the US Presidency. For not only was Truman inexperienced and hence possibly vulnerable to manipulation but he actually made some early anti-Soviet moves of his own without prompting from Churchill. And, finally, the Prime Minister was surely conscious by March 1945 that Communist prospects in Greece had been decisively checked and that in this matter he therefore no longer needed Stalin's goodwill to the same extent that had applied earlier.

It is the matter of Greece, above all, that merits attention here. For, as has been seen, Churchill, in order to secure a free hand there, had been willing to go to great lengths to persuade Stalin that, far from being a committed enemy of the Soviets, he was now just a hard-headed realist, ready to recognise crude spheres of influence. His conduct in Moscow in October 1944 had indeed been so unsentimental that it is at least superficially difficult to believe that it was the same person who later elected to make so much fuss about the fate of Poland in the aftermath of Yalta (though, interestingly, not to the same extent at Yalta itself). As Kimball has put it: 'if Soviet control in eastern Europe was acceptable in November 1944, why was that not so in March 1945? If Churchill chose to compromise in the autumn, why did spring bring confrontation, especially when that confrontation would not change the political realities?'[18] The answer may simply be that Churchill felt no ethical obligation to honour the spirit of his 'percentages' bargain once Greece had been secured – provided only that it could be made to appear that the Americans were taking the lead in condemning Soviet conduct. As he put it to the War Cabinet on 6 March: 'It would be for consideration whether the Yalta Declaration on liberated territories could be construed as superseding previous arrangements such as that in respect of Rumania and Greece which had been made at a time when we could not rely on United States assistance.'[19] As the historian Fraser Harbutt has commented: 'So much for fidelity to agreements!'[20] Yet, ironically, Churchill was to pay tribute in later years to Stalin's own good faith over Greece: 'He signed a slip of paper. And he never broke his word.'[21] Presumably Churchill felt that his own conduct, though in this respect apparently less honourable than Stalin's, was amply justified by the fact that he was, after all, only attempting to cheat the leader of a murderous tyranny.

Whatever Churchill's motives for his volte-face of March 1945 may have been, he had no alternative but to retreat for a time after Truman had given full support to Hopkins's definitive surrender to Stalin over Poland. Hence at the Potsdam Conference he was compelled to fall in with the largely collaborative mood engendered by

Truman and Stalin. Churchill was of course in an exceptionally weak position, as was symbolised by the presence there from the outset of Attlee, now Leader of the Opposition. All concerned knew that the two men would travel to London on the ninth day of the Conference, 25 July, to hear the delayed British General Election results and that only one of them would return. If that leader had been Churchill he would of course have had renewed authority. And, according to his own account, he would have demanded improved Soviet conduct in Eastern Europe. In particular, he would seemingly have publicly resisted the transfer to Poland of at least some of the German territory that was eventually handed to it by the Red Army.[22] But in the event Attlee and his Foreign Secretary, Bevin, were the ones who returned and they put up little effective resistance. Would Churchill really have behaved so differently? It seems unlikely. For without reliably robust support from Truman, which was not on offer, no British leader could even have hoped to deny the Soviets control of that part of Europe which they occupied. And Churchill's own conduct at Potsdam in the days before his return to London was by no means such as to lead observers to suppose that he was positioning himself for a public break with both Stalin and Truman. For example, Eden disapprovingly wrote in his diary on 17 July: 'he [Churchill] is again under Stalin's spell. He kept repeating "I like that man [Stalin]"'[23] The fact is that Churchill, by the summer of 1945, already knew that the shape of the post-war world now depended almost entirely on the ways in which both Stalin and Truman conducted themselves. And at Potsdam Churchill apparently had hopes that either or both might not entirely disappoint him. So far as Stalin was concerned Churchill spoke to Moran at one point in terms that are scarcely compatible with any feelings of total despair:

> Stalin gave me his word there will be free elections in the countries set free by his armies. You are sceptical, Charles? I don't see why. We must listen to these Russians. They mobilized twelve million men, and nearly half of them were killed or missing ... 'I think,' he said, 'that Stalin is trying to be as helpful as it in him to be.'[24]

Perhaps, as in the middle of 1936, he had not quite abandoned hope that Stalin might be trying, in the face of resistance from 'orthodox Communists', to move the Soviet Union to the Right.[25]

As for Truman, Churchill was immensely encouraged by his demeanour once it became known that an atomic bomb had been successfully tested. On this the diary entry of 22 July of Henry Stimson, Truman's Secretary of War, is revealing:

> [Churchill] told me that he had noticed at the meeting of the Three yesterday that Truman was evidently much fortified by something that had happened and that he stood up to the Russians in a most emphatic and decisive manner, telling them as to certain demands that they absolutely could not have [them] and that the United States was entirely against them. He said, 'Now I know what happened to Truman yesterday. I couldn't understand it. When he got to the meeting after having read this report [on the atomic bomb test] he was a changed man. He told the Russians just where they got on and off and generally bossed the whole meeting.' Churchill said he now understood how this pepping up had taken place and that he felt the same way.[26]

Sir Alan Brooke, the Chief of the Imperial General Staff, also noticed that the atomic bomb test helped Churchill to face the future with a degree of optimism. He recalled:

> It was now no longer necessary [according to Churchill] for the Russians to come into the Japanese war; the new explosive alone was sufficient to settle the matter. Furthermore, we now had something in our hands which would redress the balance with the Russians. The secret of this explosive and the power to use it would completely alter the diplomatic equilibrium which was adrift since the defeat of Germany. Now we had a new value which redressed our position (pushing out his chin and scowling); now we could say, 'If you insist on doing this or that, well ... And then where are the Russians!' ...
>
> It is interesting to note Winston's reactions and my counter-reactions to the Atomic Bomb news. Winston's appreciation of its value in the future international balance of power was far more accurate than mine. But what was worrying me was that, with his usual enthusiasm for anything new, he was letting himself be carried away by the very first and rather scanty reports of the first atomic explosion. He was already seeing himself capable of eliminating all the Russian centres of industry and population without taking into account any of the connected problems, such as the delivery of the bomb, production of the bombs, possibility of Russians also possessing such bombs etc. He had at once painted a wonderful picture of himself as the sole possessor of these bombs and capable of dumping them where he wished, thus all-powerful and capable of dictating to Stalin![27]

This kind of fantasising did nothing in practice to strengthen Churchill's hand at Potsdam. For it was obvious that it would be the

Americans and not the British who would physically possess the few atomic weapons that would actually be in existence in the immediate postwar years. And though Churchill undoubtedly favoured the use of atomic bombs on Japan in the absence of unconditional surrender, this controversial policy was only adopted because Truman himself favoured it over the alternative, which would have been to try to induce the Japanese to capitulate rapidly on the basis of the Emperor being allowed to remain on his throne. In practice therefore, Churchill could do little at Potsdam other than engage in a limited degree of robust private posturing and otherwise leave it to Stalin and Truman to settle matters. Only in one respect does he seem to have played a really decisive role at Potsdam on a matter of fundamental importance. And this concerned not Eastern Europe but Spain. Not unexpectedly, the Soviets suggested formally that the Big Three break off all relations with Franco's Government and give support to the 'democratic forces' in Spain and thus enable the Spanish people to 'establish such a regime as will respond to their will'. Truman and Attlee, representing left-wing parties in the West, evidently felt that they were in no position to fight for the cause of a Fascist dictator, given all the emotions that had been stirred by the Spanish Civil War. But Churchill's approach at Potsdam was consistent with the line he had taken with his War Cabinet colleagues during 1944; and his vociferous resistance to Stalin ensured that the issue was effectively postponed for consideration into the postwar era.[28] This meant that Franco's regime survived – something in the Cold War context that all US Presidents and even most British leaders came round in effect to approving. For example, both Attlee and Bevin were consistently to ignore left-wing protests on the matter throughout their terms in office. How much did all this matter – other than to the people of Spain? Certainly in the late 1940s, to put it at its lowest, the existence of an anti-Muscovite regime in Spain did nothing to add to the troubles of governments in France and Italy that were at times hard pressed to prevent Communist takeovers. And in the early 1970s, when pro-Soviet forces in parts of the West were having something of an Indian Summer in the aftermath of the Vietnam War, the Franco regime was possibly of decisive importance in 'encouraging' some anti-Soviet elements in Portugal to just sufficient an extent to prevent Marxist–Leninist extremists triumphing in Lisbon as the right-wing authoritarian regime there collapsed. In these respects Churchill's contribution to the post-war scene in Western Europe may have been of exceptional importance, and one hitherto underrated by writers who may sense that it might not be 'politically correct' to do other than simply piously regret the post-war survival of right-wing dictatorships in the Iberian Peninsula.

In most accounts, Churchill's principal contribution to the anti-Communist cause in the aftermath of VE Day is said of course to be his rallying of American opinion in his famous speech at Fulton, Missouri, delivered on 5 March 1946. But this evaluation is open to challenge. For by early 1946 large numbers of influential Americans had already come to believe that a confrontation of some kind with the Soviets was unavoidable. For example, James Forrestal, the US Navy Secretary, was expressing private views of an extreme anti-Communist character from the very beginning of the Truman Administration. And as moderate an observer as George Kennan, then based in the US Embassy in Moscow, had despatched his influential anti-Soviet 'Long Telegram' to Washington before Churchill had even arrived in Fulton. And as for Truman himself, he had, according to his own account, told his Secretary of State, James Byrnes, on 5 January 1946 that he was tired of 'babying the Soviets' and that 'unless Russia is faced with an iron fist and strong language another war is in the making'.[29] Churchill naturally fell in eagerly with this new mood when addressing the students at Westminster College, Fulton, in the presence of Truman (who took the chair). He spoke, as is well known, of an iron curtain having descended across Europe from Stettin to Trieste; and of Communist Parties on the eastern side 'seeking everywhere to obtain totalitarian control' and of the fear of the 'policeman's knock'. He also drew attention to the fact that 'in a great number of countries far from the Russian frontiers and throughout the world, the Communist fifth columns are established and work in complete unity and absolute obedience to the directions they receive from the Communist centre'. The remedy, according to Churchill, was 'a special relationship between the British Empire and the United States', enabling the two countries 'to walk forward in sedate strength'.[30] All this was quite sensational less than a year after the Big Three had defeated Nazi Germany – particularly given Truman's presence. But it is important to recognise that the invitation to Churchill to speak at Fulton had been issued as early as 3 October 1945. And Truman had at that stage agreed to chair the meeting solely as a consequence of his political roots lying in the state of Missouri. It seems safe to conclude, therefore, that neither Churchill nor Truman had any notion in October 1945 that this speech would take the stridently anti-Soviet form that it did. But it had not at that point become fully apparent, for example, how far brutal Soviet interference in Bulgaria and Romania would go.

What is true, however, is that Churchill, Truman and Byrnes conspired immediately before the speech was delivered to ensure that it became a major rallying call to the West. But if Churchill had been unable or unwilling to play the part of inaugurating an all-out war of words against Moscow, it is surely not to be doubted that Truman would not for long have been frustrated in this respect. Churchill did of course act as a useful lightning conductor in that, when some initial American media comment was critical, Truman was able to pretend that he had no foreknowledge of what he intended to say. But by the summer of 1946 the public mood in the United States had changed to such an extent that the President risked falling behind rather than getting too far in front of it. For example, a Gallup Poll of June 1946 revealed that 36 per cent of respondents wanted American Communists to be killed or imprisoned; and a month later 60 per cent believed that 'Russia is trying to build herself up to be the ruling power of the world'.[31] By March 1947 Truman was thus fully ready to carry forward Churchill's war-of-words with the enunciation of the so-called Truman Doctrine to a joint session of Congress. It was, if anything, a move on the President's part that was overdue. He could have made it months before without much domestic risk. And this would probably have been true with or without Churchill's intervention at Fulton. For the fact is that there was never any chance that the establishment of several Communist police states in Eastern Europe, on which Stalin seems to have been unalterably set, could have occurred without alienating the high-minded American people. Alienation and indignation do not, however, necessarily imply an appetite for ultimatums and/or war. And certainly in this case Truman and his nation never unambiguously demanded that the Soviets leave any part of Eastern Europe or face war. Indeed, even Churchill did not make such a call in precise terms on any public platform. On the contrary, at Fulton and elsewhere he usually urged no more than that preparations be made for joint Anglo-American resistance by a variety of means but only seemingly with a view to preventing the spread of Communism beyond the areas explicitly or tacitly allocated to Stalin at the Conferences in Moscow, Yalta and Potsdam during 1944 and 1945.

Churchill's public line enunciated at Fulton was thus fully compatible with the emerging drift of US policy: namely pained acquiesence in Soviet control over Eastern Europe accompanied by an increasing determination to contain Soviet and/or Communist expansion into other areas such as Western and Southern Europe, Iran and East Asia. The rhetoric was, however, rather in advance of what most British politicians were yet ready to endorse in public. Bevin, for example, did not favour public name-calling *vis-à-vis* Moscow and was tempted to denounce Churchill's Fulton speech – a step which would have greatly appealed to most Labour backbenchers, including future Prime Minister James Callaghan. True, Attlee was more cautious and in the end the Labour Front Bench decided to pretend that a speech by the Leader of the Opposition was like that of a private person and therefore did not call for comment. At the same time, Churchill's Conservative colleagues, including his heir apparent and Foreign Affairs spokesman, Eden, were annoyed at the lack of consult-ation and were privately sympathetic to Attlee and Bevin with their unsensationalist approach to alleged Soviet misdeeds. For example, Lord Cranborne feared that Labour backbencers would so object to Churchill's extreme tone as to make it more difficult for Bevin to express his more measured criticisms of Moscow. And as soon as he had heard of the Fulton speech Eden privately expressed the hope that Churchill would prove 'less interrested in leading a parliamentrary opposition than an anti-Russian crusade independently of the Conservative Party'. Churchill, however, took no notice of his Con-servative colleagues – contemptuously dismissing all attempts to persuade him to step down as Leader of the Opposition.[32] And he not only repeated his Fulton arguments frequently as Soviet-American tensions increased in the ensuing years but even deliberately courted unpopularity by repeatedly coming to the aid of the beleaguered Franco regime in Spain. As early as 5 June 1946 he was, for example, telling the House of Commons that it had been 'very unwise of the French Government, under Communist impulsion, to take such an aggressive line against Spain' [in encouraging an abortive uprising on the other side of the Pyrennes]. He of course took the precaution of saying that 'none of us likes the Franco regime'. But then he greatly blunted the impact of this pious declaration by adding: 'personally, I like it as little as the present British administration' – a judgment of moral equivalence that must have delighted Franco as much as it appalled Attlee. Churchill then went on to denounce Poland's attempt to persuade the United Nations to urge all member states to break off diplomatic relations with Spain:

> Everyone knows where their [the Poles'] impulse comes from. Let us
> discard cant and humbug. I believe it is a fact, to put it mildly, that
> there is as much freedom in Spain under General Franco's reaction-
> ary regime – and actually a good deal more security and happiness for
> ordinary folk – as there is in Poland at the present time.[33]

Few Western liberals, even those who were already becoming critical
of the Soviet Union and its new satellites, were ready in 1946 to
endorse this kind of assertion of ultimate preference between different
types of authoritarianism. And even in our own day many would
demur. For example, Paul Preston, the author of a recent extremely
critical biography of Franco, comments on Churchill's assessment:

> the comparison of life in Spain with the lot of the citizens of Poland
> after successive Nazi and Soviet invasions and occupations was
> hardly a fair one. In the light of Franco's own boasts about the peace
> and prosperity which he had bestowed upon neutral Spain, the scale
> of hunger and repression in the country remained startling.[34]

But Churchill returned to the Spanish theme repeatedly as the Cold
War unfolded. On 10 December 1948 he called for Spain's admission
to the United Nations and asserted provocatively: 'I say there is far
more liberty in Spain under General Franco than in any of the
countries behind the iron curtain.'[35] And on 17 November 1949,
speaking in the House of Commons, he deplored the then British
policy of conforming with a United Nations resolution of December
1946 that had called for the withdrawal of ambassadors from Spain:

> Fancy having an ambassador in Moscow, but not having one in
> Madrid. The individual Spaniard has a much happier and freer life
> than the individual Russian – [HON MEMBERS: "Oh"] – or Pole or
> Czechoslovak. I do not suppose that there are ten hon. Members in
> this House who, if it was actually put before them as a decision which
> they must take tomorrow morning, whether they would rather live
> the next five years in Franco's Spain or in Soviet Russia, would not
> book their ticket for the south.[36]

This kind of rhetoric, which served to remind liberal critics of
Churchill's pro-Mussolini record during the interwar period, was
most unwelcome to most Conservative moderates. Gradually, however, Soviet conduct in the Cold War tended to diminish the gap
between Churchill and uneasy colleagues like Eden and Macmillan.

Churchill's general Fulton line, in some distinction from his
attitude to Spain, was of course rather rapidly held to have been
vindicated – even by most of his fellow MPs in the three principal

political parties. For the US and British Governments soon drew together in their hostility to the Soviet Union once it became clear that the latter's East European sphere of influence was not to be the only or even the main issue causing severe tension. Early in 1947, for example, both the British and American leaders came to the conclusion that the pro-Western governments of Greece and Turkey faced a serious threat of internal subversion and that only strong American financial support could sustain them. Similar though less acute shared fears existed with respect to France and Italy. The upshot was that, in May 1947, the United States produced the Marshall Plan – whose purpose was to use US economic strength to bolster what became known as the containment policy. Even more potentially dramatic was the breakdown of negotiations concerning the future of Germany in general and of Berlin in particular. Gradually it became apparent that the three Western occupying powers, the United States, Great Britain and France, would be driven into forging a liberal capitalist-type German state and that the Soviets would create a Communist version in their occupation zone to the East. But the future of Berlin, divided into four sectors and buried deep in the Soviet Occupation Zone, became the most dramatic issue in the international politics of 1948–1949.

All this increasing tension served to make Churchill's Fulton speech look increasingly prophetic and its author once more the greatest statesman of the hour. The ironic truth is, however, that he was by no means in full agreement with his own supposed line. He did not in fact think, as his Fulton audience might have gathered, that Anglo-American solidarity in support of containment of the Soviets would necessarily suffice to deter war and he did not accept that the West had now no alternative but to avoid a decisive confrontation over, say, Poland. In short, in private he was much more extreme. His real opinion was that a 'showdown' with the Soviets was sooner or later inevitable and that the West's best chance of prevailing was during a period when it had a monopoly of atomic weapons. He accordingly held that an ultimatum should be sent to Moscow, demanding a general settlement on terms that would would bring about an opportunity, if the Soviets did not simply capitulate, for the West to wage a preventive war that would leave their cities in atomic ruins. That Churchill's ideal ultimatum would have required Soviet withdrawal from Eastern Europe and East Germany is not to be doubted. It must in fairness be added, however, that he usually presented his arguments in such a fashion as to imply that the Soviets would surely accept totally humiliating conditions, provided that the Western ultimatum was delivered before the Americans lost their atomic monopoly. But he neglected to explain in any detail why he expected the alleged fanatics in the Kremlin to behave in such an unheroic way – given the small number of atomic bombs in the American arsenal in the late 1940s and given the large Soviet preponderance in conventional strength in the European theatre. Hence it seems safe to conclude that Churchill was, in his own mind, by no means ruling out that a preventive war would have to be fought as well as merely threatened if the Soviet menace was to be effectively countered.

It scarely needs stating that no leading personality in any Western Government appears to have sympathised in the least with Churchill's extraordinarily 'hawkish' approach – which would also surely have been unacceptable to public opinion everywhere in the Western world with the possible exception of some parts of the United States. The leaders of the United States, Great Britain and Canada were all privately regaled with Churchill's remarkable thesis, especially during 1947 and 1948, and all reacted with an absolute unwillingness to support his central argument. True, those concerned treated him with great respect and patience. But in terms of influence he was again in a certain sense as much in the wilderness as he had been during the 1930s. That this was the case was not, however, widely known among the general public in the West. And nor is it how matters have usually been presented by historians. For example, Churchill's authorised biographer, Gilbert, has not depicted him as an isolated 'hawk' at any stage. Indeed, he wrote in 1997 in terms that suggested statesmanlike consistency from Yalta to final retirement:

> On 6 April [1955] Churchill resigned. A decade of seeking amelioration with the Soviet Union, and a summit to set in train a wider negotiated detente, was over. It had been his last, his most sustained, and least successful foray into international affairs.[37]

There are two explanations why Gilbert and others who take this line have not hitherto been subject to much vigorous challenge. One is that Churchill had the good sense to avoid persistent public crusading in favour of his policy during the late 1940s – though he occasionally spoke in a relatively muted way about the merits of a 'showdown'. A second reason is that American, British and Canadian leaders were seemingly too honourable to engage in the systematic 'leaking' to the media of private communications that has become commonplace in the later twentieth century.

One historian who has recognised that Churchill was a critic of the mainstream containment strategy of the West during the late 1940s, however, is Henry Kissinger. He in fact has discerned four different schools of thought among the critics of containment. On one extreme were those who agreed with Henry Wallace, the former American Vice-President, who argued that the West was morally equivalent to the Soviet Union and hence should simply passively acquiesce in the Soviets' control over that part of Europe which they had liberated from Nazi domination. Then, according to Kissinger, there were those who agreed with the distinguished journalist Walter Lippmann, who believed that a global containment policy was too reactive in that it allowed the Soviet Union to select the points of dispute and thus invariably have the initiative and the advantage. Lippmann urged, largely in vain, that American foreign policy be guided by a 'case-by-case analysis' of American interests and not by universalist general principles. Another school of critics of containment which gradually emerged was that represented by John Foster Dulles and his followers in the Republican Party. According to Kissinger:

> They were the conservatives who accepted the premises of containment but questioned the absence of urgency with which it was being pursued. Even if containment did in the end succeed in undermining Soviet society ... it would take too long and cost too much. Whatever containment might accomplish, a strategy of liberation would surely accelerate.

Finally, according to Kissinger, there was Churchill who objected to 'the postponement of negotiations' with the Soviet leaders since he believed that 'the West's position would never again be as strong as it was at the beginning of what came to be known as the Cold War, and that its relative bargaining position could therefore only deteriorate'. But it seems to this writer that Churchill in the late 1940s was not in favour of negotiations at all – at any rate not as this word is normally understood. And Kissinger himself half-acknowledged this when he wrote that 'Churchill's public statements strongly suggest that he envisaged some kind of diplomatic ultimatum by the Western democracies'.[38] In short, was not this much the same as what Dulles encouraged people to think would be involved in the adoption of a 'liberation' or 'roll-back' strategy? Ironically, however, Churchill and

Dulles were not destined to be warm collaborators when both held positions of responsibility during the early 1950s. But by then both had seemingly undergone a surprising metamorphosis: Dulles had shifted to an essentially cautious but firm and reserved approach towards the Soviet Union barely distinguishable from that of the Truman Administration; and Churchill had adopted an emollient public line in favour of 'easement' of relations with Moscow that seemed to some of his 'hawkish' critics in London and Washington not to be too far removed in some respects from the thinking of Wallace.

Some further details concerning Churchill's moves during the late 1940s in favour of an early 'showdown' with the Soviets would, however, at this point seem to be appropriate. We have already noted the bloodthirsty relish with which, according to Brooke, he reacted to news of the first American atomic test in July 1945. Then, during 1946 his private views moved increasingly towards predicting an all-out war between the West and the Soviet Union – in some contrast to the public line he took at Fulton about an alliance between the United States and Great Britain, enabling the two countries 'to walk forward in sedate strength'. For example, in May he met Mackenzie King, the Prime Minister of Canada, and according to the latter's diary, announced that there would be a war with the Soviets within eight years – by which time the Soviets would, he seems to have expected, have atomic bombs of their own. He foresaw 'the greatest war – the most terrible war which may mean the end of our civilization'. But oddly, again to some extent revisiting the optimistic evaluation he had made about him in the middle of 1936, Churchill opined that Stalin represented the world's best hope: 'He was the one man in Russia to-day who could save a situation and might save it.' It may be, however, that only a sense of prudence caused him not to take the line with King that a 'showdown' probably would and certainly should be precipitated by the West before the Soviets themselves obtained atomic bombs. What he actually said to King, according to the latter's account, was:

> We are in the same position as we were with Hitler. The last war might have been prevented if we had dealt with Hitler at once and in the right way. Did not allow him to go to the lengths that he should not have been permitted to go. It is the same with the Russians. If we let them have their way and bit by bit crush on the free world as they are doing, there is no doubt we will pay a greater penalty than any that the world has thus far paid to dictators. He spoke of the regime in Russia as being a terrible regime – a regime of terror.[39]

That preventive war may already have been in Churchill's mind is suggested by his remarks to Brooke in 1945. And certainly by the autumn of 1946 he was talking privately along such lines to Moran with whom he was of course on more intimate terms than with King. To his doctor Churchill said on 8 August :

> We ought not to wait until Russia is ready. I believe it will be eight years before she has these [atomic] bombs. America knows that fifty-two per cent. of Russia's motor industry is in Moscow and could be wiped out by a single bomb. It might mean wiping out three million people, but they [the Soviets] would think nothing of that.

As for the timing of the desired 'showdown' Churchill was somewhat unsure. But on 24 October 1946 he told Moran that there might even be a very early war with the Soviets – 'perhaps this winter'.[40]

As 1947 drew to a close, with the Cold War intensifying, Churchill began insistently to urge on other world leaders the case for, in effect, initiating a preventive war against Moscow. On 25 November 1947, for example, he had a further meeting with King. And on this occasion, according to the latter's diary, he went so far as to say: 'What the Russians should be told … is that the nations that have fought the last war for freedom have had enough of this war of nerves and intimidation. We do not intend to have this sort of thing continue indefinitely.' He wanted an ultimatum put to the Soviets. If they rejected it, 'we will attack Moscow and … other cities and destroy them with atomic bombs from the air'. The precise nature of the ultimatum that Churchill had in view is not wholly clear from King's somewhat confusing diary. For at one point Churchill is reported as having proclaimed: 'We will not allow tyranny to be continued.' But King also recorded: 'He [Churchill] thought America would, as indeed she should, tell the Russians just what the United States and the United Kingdom were prepared to do in meeting them in the matter of poitical boundaries, seaports, etc., but let them understand that if they were not prepared to accept this, their cities would be bombed within a certain number of days. He said if they were told this plainly enough, he thought they would retreat.' King added:

> Churchill admitted we did not know how great their [Russia's] power was. He thought the difficulty in dealing with the forthcoming war was greater than that of the one with Hitler in that the Russian ideology had made a religion of the issue. Hitler did not have that side. Churchill's statements being made in the presence of [J. C.] Smuts [the Prime Minister of South Africa] and myself as well as Sir

John Anderson and Harold Macmillan made them much more significant.

Maybe, then, Churchill meant only that the Soviets should be required to agree not to extend their system into Western Europe; or maybe he wanted them to consent to abandoning Communist tyranny in general. But what is apparent is that, if Churchill had had his way, the Soviets would have had to accept a public humiliation or face all-out war. King also noted Churchill's demeanour as he warmed to his anti-Soviet theme:

> his eyes seemed to be bulging out of his head, so much so that one could see the greater part of the white of the eyes as well as the pupils, which looked as though they would come out of his head altogether. When he turned and looked and spoke as he firmly did, to me direct, his look was an earnest beseeching one. The gleam in his eyes was like fire. There was something in his whole appearance and delivery which gave me the impression of a sort of volcano at work in his .brain.[41]

Then, on 17 April 1948, Churchill spoke candidly to the American Ambassador in London, Lewis Douglas, who duly reported to Robert Lovett in Washington in the following terms:

> You probably know his view, that when the Soviet develop the atomic bomb, war will become a certainty, even though by then Western Europe may have become again the seat of authority and a stable political part of the world. He believes that now is the time, promptly, to tell the Soviet that if they do not retire from Berlin and abandon Eastern Germany, withdrawing to the Polish frontier, we will raze their cities. It is further his view that we cannot appease, conciliate, or provoke the Soviets; that the only vocabulary they understand is the vocabulary of force; and that if, therefore, we took this position, they would yield.[42]

By 27 July, by which date the Soviet blockade of West Berlin had come into effect, Churchill was minded to impose an even greater humiliation on the Soviets. He wrote to Eisenhower urging that the West should use its possession of overwhelming force to compel them not merely to quit Berlin and all Germany but to retire entirely to within their own borders. Failure to do this would make a third world war inevitable.[43]

Truman and his advisers rejected this advice and sought to withstand the siege of West Berlin by means of the well-known airlift. Churchill was not particularly impressed by this moderation. But he was apparently in two minds whether 1948 or 1949 was the better year for a 'showdown'. In September, for example, he gave his not entirely consistent private view to two Conservative colleagues. Boothby recorded him as saying:

'I would have it out with them now. If we do not, war might come. I would say to them, quite politely: "The day we quit Berlin, you will have to quit Moscow." I would not think it necessary to explain why. I am told that they are absolutely certain that we shall behave decently, and honourably, and do the right thing – according to their ideas of our own standards – in all circumstances. With me around, they would not be quite so sure'.[44]

And to Eden Churchill wrote on 12 September:

I have felt misgivings and bewilderment which is latent but general in thoughtful circles about the policy of delaying a real showdown with the Kremlin till we are quite sure they have got the atomic bomb. Once that happens nothing can stop the greatest of all world catastrophes. On the other hand it must be borne in mind that the American Air Force will be nearly double as strong this time next year ... Therefore while we should not surrender to Soviet aggression or quit Berlin, it may well be that we and the Americans will be much stronger this time next year ... I am not therefore inclined to demand an immediate showdown, although it will certainly have to be made next year. None of this argument is fit for public use.[45]

When 1949 came, however, the United States did not seek a 'showdown' with the Soviets. Instead, they persisted with the Berlin airlift until the Soviet blockade was lifted in May; and they forged the North Atlantic Treaty with Canada and ten West European states. Deterrence, not preventive war or a contrived 'showdown', was to be Truman's policy. True, he did publicly acknowledge that the use of atomic bombs was possible – but only in the event that the fate of the Western democracies was at stake. He clearly did not, in contrast to Churchill, favour attempting to use atomic threats to 'roll back' Soviet power from East Germany and Eastern Europe. Churchill's rather disingenuous response was to write to the President on 29 July 1949 to congratulate him merely on his publicly-stated willingness to use atomic bombs.[46] He implied that Truman had thus taken his advice. But this was misleading. For there was a vital difference between the two men – as Truman certainly realised. In short, Churchill believed in threatening a preventive war given that an even worse war was sure to result once the Soviets acquired atomic bombs; whereas Truman held that a world war was not inevitable and that mutual nuclear deterrence, once it arrived, was likely both to contain Soviet expansionism and to prevent all-out war. Perhaps recognition of this divergence explains why Truman pulled out of a public commitment to attend a speech by Churchill at the Massachusetts Institute of Technology on 31 March 1949.

In public Churchill was more reticent about urging a 'showdown' with Moscow – an argument that he at one point, as has been seen, told Eden was 'not fit for public use'. But there were just two or possibly three occasions when he did give an indication to this effect. The first came on 23 January 1948 when he told the House of Commons:

> The best chance of avoiding war [is], in accord with the other Western democracies, to bring matters to a head with the Soviet Government, and, by formal diplomatc processes, with all their privacy and gravity, to arrrive at a lasting settlement ... I believe it would give the best chance of preventing it [war], and that, if it came, we should have the best chance of coming out of it alive.[47]

Later in the same year, on 9 October, Churchill was rather more forthright in a speech to the Conservative Party. He declared that 'the Western nations would be far more likely to reach a lasting settlement, without bloodshed, if they formulated their just demands while they had the atomic power and before the Russians had it too'. 'We ought,' he proclaimed, 'to bring matters to a head and make a final settlement.' He added: 'We ought not to go jogging along improvident, incompetent, waiting for something to turn up, by which I mean waiting for something bad for us to turn up.'[48] Much of the British media and general public may not have grasped that this amounted to a call for a threatened immediate military 'showdown'. But *The Times* at least saw the point and did not minimise the risks involved. Its editorial contained the following passage:

> it is extremely unlikely that just the threat of the bomb would make Russia consent to a settlement on western terms. No great and proud nation will negotiate under duress; Britain and the United States have rightly refused to do so in the case of Berlin. It is unreasonable to suppose that Russia will willingly negotiate on the division of the world under threat of nuclear bombardment.[49]

As for the Soviets, they too were quick to react unfavourably. An editorial in *Pravda* read:

> Churchill demands neither more nor less than the abolition of the People's Democracies in the East European countries; the withdrawal

of the Soviet occupation forces from Germany and Austria; the self-disbandment of the communist movements in all countries, and at the same time of the liberation movements in the colonies and semi-colonies; finally opening the way for the international monopolies to the exploitation of the 'vast spaces' of the USSR, that is, in the final analysis, the revival in the Soviet Union of the capitalist order and renunciation of its independence.[50]

After this Churchill showed even greater restraint in public. But on 25 March 1949 when visiting New York City, he stated:

The only way to 'deal' with a Communist is by having superior force on your side on the matter in question – and they must also be convinced that you will use – you will not hesitate to use – these forces if necessary, in the most ruthless manner. You have not only to convince the Soviet Government that you have superior force ... but that you are not restrained by any moral consideration if the case arose from using that force with complete material ruthlessness. And that is the greatest chance of peace, the surest road to peace. Then the Communists will make a bargain.[51]

This was not quite the same thing, however, as urging a preventive war and it was not so interpreted by the general public in the West.

More striking in this New York City speech perhaps was Churchill's decision explicitly to declare Communism a greater threat than Nazism – something he had never previously done in war or peace. He stated:

We are now confronted with something which is quite as wicked but much more formidable than Hitler, because Hitler had only the Herrenvolk stuff and anti-Semitism. Well, somebody said about that – a good starter, but a bad stayer. That's all he had. He had no theme. But these fourteen men in the Kremlin have their hierarchy and a church of Communist adepts whose missionaries are in every country as a fifth column.[52]

Churchill made no mention of Neville Chamberlain in this connection – but it was the Chamberlainite line all the same. It is perhaps notable therefore that these remarks have been seen by his authorised biographer as 'his most outspoken denunciation of Communism since his warnings in 1919 and 1920'.[53] It was, however, a public approach Churchill was soon to abandon. For yet another apparent volte-face was at hand.

NOTES

1   War Cabinet Minutes, 6 March 1945, CAB 65/51, PRO.
2   Nigel Nicolson (ed.), *Harold Nicolson: Diaries and Letters, 1939–1945*, London, 1967, p. 437.
3   Churchill to Roosevelt, 8 March 1945, in Kimball, 'Naked Reverse Right', p. 19.
4   Churchill to Roosevelt, 13 March 1945, in *ibid.*, p. 20.
5   Roosevelt to Churchill, 12 April 1945, in *ibid.*, p. 23.
6   *New York Times*, 24, June 1941, quoted in Hugh Thomas, *Armed Truce: the Beginnings of the Cold War, 1945–46*, London, 1986, p. 187.
7   Quoted in Daniel Yergin, *Shattered Peace: The Origins of the Cold War*, London, 1978, pp. 82–3.
8   Truman to Eleanor Roosevelt, 10 May 1945, in Harbutt, *The Iron Curtain*, p. 306, n. 61.
9   Churchill to Eden, 4 May 1945, Avon Papers, FO 954/20. PRO.
10   Churchill, *The Second World War*, VI, pp. 525–6.
11   Harriman and Abel, *Special Envoy*, p. 479.
12   Roy Douglas, *From War to Cold War, 1942–48*, London, 1981, p. 93. See also William Leahy, *I Was There*, London, 1950, pp. 441–5.
13   Kenneth Young (ed.), *The Diaries of Sir Robert Bruce Lockhart, 1939–1965*, London, 1980, p. 443.
14   Woodward, *British Foreign Policy*, III, p. 583n. This account appears to be more reliable than that in Churchill, *The Second World War*, VI, pp. 502–5.
15   Churchill, *The Second World War*, VI, p. 506.
16   Kimball, 'Naked Reverse Right', p. 18; and Warren Kimball, 'Churchill, Roosevelt and Post-war Europe', in Parker (ed.), *Winston Churchill*, p. 147.
17   See Churchill, *The Second World War*, VI, *passim*.
18   Kimball, 'Naked Reverse Right', p. 24.
19   War Cabinet Minutes, 6 March 1945, CAB 65/51, PRO.
20   Harbutt, *The Iron Curtain*, p. 94.
21   Sulzberger, *The Last of the Giants*, p. 304. See also Churchill to Eisenhower, 16 April 1956, in Gilbert, *'Never Despair'*, p. 1192.
22   Churchill, *The Second World War*, VI, p. 581.
23   The Earl of Avon, *The Eden Memoirs: The Reckoning*, London, 1965, p. 545.
24   Moran, *Winston Churchill*, p. 275.
25   See above, pp. 55–6.
26   Gar Alperowitz, *The Decision to Use the Atomic Bomb and the Architecture of an American Myth*, London, 1995, p. 260.
27   Bryant, *Triumph in the West*, pp. 373–4.
28   Woodward, *British Foreign Policy*, V, pp. 469–71.
29   Robert H. Ferrell (ed.), *Off the Record: The Private Papers of Harry S. Truman*, New York, 1980, pp. 79–80.
30   *The Times*, 6 March 1946.
31   David Carlton, ' The European Cold War and the Origins of the Problem of "Extended Deterrence"', in The Open University, *Nuclear Weapons: Inquiry, Analysis and Debate*, Milton Keynes, 1986, p. 17.
32   Eden to Cranborne, 15 March 1946, Avon Papers, in David Dutton, *Anthony Eden: A Life and a Reputation*, London, 1997, p. 233. For further details see also Carlton, *Anthony Eden*, ch. 8.

33 *Hansard*, 5 June 1946, vol. 423, cols. 2016–17.

34 Paul Preston, *Franco: A Biography*, London, 1993, p. 559n.

35 *Hansard*, 10 December 1948, vol. 459, col. 718.

36 *Ibid.*, 17 November 1949, vol. 469, col. 2225.

37 Gilbert, 'From Yalta to Bermuda and Beyond', in Muller (ed.), *Churchill as Peacemaker*, p. 332.

38 Henry Kissinger, *Diplomacy*, London, 1994, pp. 463–70.

39 J. W. Pickersgill and D. F. Forster (eds), *The Mackenzie King Record: Vol. III, 1945–1946*, Toronto, 1970, p. 236–7.

40 Moran, *Winston Churchill*, p. 315.

41 J. W. Pickersgill and D. F. Forster (eds), *The Mackenzie King Record: Vol. IV, 1947–1948*, Toronto, 1970, pp. 112–13, 116–17.

42 United States Department of State, *Papers Relating to the Foreign Relations of the United States, 1948: Vol. III: Western Europe*, Washington, DC, 1974, pp. 90–1.

43 Churchill to Eisenhower, 27 July 1948, Churchill Papers, in Gilbert, *'Never Despair'*, p. 422.

44 Lord Boothby, *My Yesterday, Your Tomorrow*, London, 1962, p. 212.

45 Churchill to Eden, 12 September 1948, Churchill Papers, in Gilbert, *'Never Despair'*, pp. 432–3.

46 *Ibid.*, p. 468.

47 *Hansard*, 23 January 1948, vol. 446, col. 561.

48 Robert Rhodes James (ed.), *Winston S. Churchill: His Complete Speeches, 1897–1963*, 8 vols, New York, 1974, vol. VII, pp. 7707–17. See also *The Times*, 11 October 1948; *New York Times*, 10 October 1948; and comments thereon in Marc Trachtenberg, *History and Strategy*, Princeton, New Jersey, 1991, p. 101.

49 *The Times*, 11 October 1948.

50 *Pravda*, quoted in V. G. Trukhanovsky, *Winston Churchill*, Moscow, 1978, p. 343.

51 Rhodes James (ed.), *Complete Speeches*, VII, p. 7800.

52 *Ibid.* Churchill spoke in similar terms at Massachusetts Institute of Technology on 31 March 1949. See *ibid.*, p. 7809. See also Churchill Papers, 5/24, Churchill College, Cambridge.

53 Gilbert, *'Never Despair'*, p. 464.

7

SUMMITRY AND THE PRIMACY
OF DOMESTIC POLITICS

1950–1955

As THE 1950s dawned Churchill's approach to the Soviet Union underwent a marked change. He no longer actively called, even in private, for a 'showdown' with Moscow. And he never again talked in public about Soviet Communism as he had done in New York City in March 1949. Why was this? A part of the explanation may be that he was influenced greatly by the news of a Soviet atomic bomb test carried out in August 1949 – at a much earlier date than had been expected in elite circles in the West. Churchill's increasing moderation could thus have been a logical consequence of the ending of the American nuclear monopoly, which had been the declared precondition underlying his earlier calls for a 'showdown'. True, the Soviet test did not at a stroke create conditions of effective nuclear parity or anything like it. Indeed, for several more years Washington would have a much larger stock of atomic and, later, hydrogen bombs than Moscow. And, more important, the Americans would be in a position, operating from bomber bases in Western Europe, to raze Soviet cities while their own cities would remain invulnerable because their potential adversaries as yet had no appropriate means of delivery. What had changed, however, was that Western European cities, including London, had become vulnerable to Soviet atomic strikes. In these circumstances, therefore, Churchill, as a British leader, could hardly be expected any longer to urge or even tacitly support any American desire to precipitate a 'showdown'. Or could he? Actually, to anticipate, it seems that in the ensuing years he was still occasionally tempted to think in ideological and internationalist terms rather than concern himself solely with the narrow national British interest. For example, on 4 May 1954 he said to Moran:

> The danger is that the Americans may become impatient. I know their people – they may get in a rage and say: ... Why should we not go it alone? Why wait until Russia overtakes us? They could go to the Kremlin and say: 'These are our demands. Our fellows have been alerted. You must agree or we shall attack you.' I think it would be all right. There is fear in the Kremlin. If I were an American I'd do this. Six years ago in my Llandudno speech I advocated a show-down. They had no bombs then.[1]

It should not of course be forgotten that Churchill frequently reflected that if his father and not his mother had been American he would probably have been an American and not a British politician. This may explain, for example, why he could so easily empathise with the Americans and why he was never tempted during the 1950s to adopt the 'Gaullist' outlook increasingly held by Eden. And certainly Churchill did not share unambiguously Eden's sense of urgency about the need to 'contain' the American threat to peace.[2] This was demonstrated when Eisenhower wrote to the Prime Minister on 9 February 1954 in these remarkable terms, which seem to show incidentally that he was no less a fanatical anti-Communist than Dulles (his Secretary of State):

> I am sure that when history looks back upon us of today it will not long remember any one of this era who was merely a distinguished war leader whether on the battlefield or in the council chamber. It will remember and salute those people who succeed, out of the greatness of their understanding and the skill of their leadership, in establishing ties among the independent nations of the world that will throw back the Russian threat and allow civilization, as we have known it, to continue its progress. Indeed, unless individuals and nations of our times are successful – soon – in this effort, there will be no history of any kind, as we know it. There will only be a concocted story made up by the Communist conquerors of the world.
>
> It is only when one allows his mind to contemplate momentarily such a disaster for the world and attempts to picture an atheistic materialism in complete domination of all human life, that he fully appreciates how necessary it is to seek renewed faith and strength from his God, and sharpen up his sword for the struggle that cannot possibly be escaped.
>
> Destiny has given priceless opportunity to some of this epoch. You are one of them. Perhaps I am also one of the company on whom this great responsibility has fallen.[3]

On seeing this message, Eden angrily demanded that Churchill challenge Eisenhower and ask him to acknowledge that he only had a spiritual and not a military 'struggle' in view. But Churchill eventually replied to Eisenhower only in this non-provocative fashion:

> I understand of course that in speaking of the faith that must inspire us in the struggle against atheistic materialism, you are referring to the spiritual struggle, and that like me, you still believe that War is not inevitable. I am glad to think that in your spirit, as in mine, resolve to find a way out of this agony of peril transcends all else.[4]

This low-key response on Churchill's part should of course be seen in the context of the fact that both men knew that the Prime Minister had been a fervent believer just half a decade earlier in both the inevitability and the desirability of a 'showdown' with Moscow.[5] Nor could Eisenhower have been unaware that Churchill was privately extremely critical of both himself and Truman for not doing more to confront the Soviets in the spring of 1945, when the future of Germany and much of Eastern Europe could have been seen as still in the balance. Indeed, it might even be that the President, in writing as he did in February 1954, had teasingly expressed himself in the kind of terms that could be seen as almost a caricature of Churchill's erstwhile line.

A second consideration that must surely have influenced Churchill's thinking as the 1950s dawned was that a general election was approaching. Labour's leaders, it is true, had been far from sympathetic to the Soviets during their term in office. But they had confronted them on specific issues – such as the future of of the Near East or Berlin – in much the same way as many nineteenth-century British Administrations had confronted Tsarist Russia. Indeed, in this respect they had antagonised Moscow more than Washington had done in the first months of peace. They had not, however, in increasing contrast to the Americans, seen fit at any stage to take a Manichean line based on ideological principles. For example, Bevin, who probably was only dimly aware of the ideological foundations of Soviet Communism, had seemingly supposed in 1945 that 'Left can speak to Left in comradeship and confidence'.[6] Nor had the Labour leaders sought to provoke a 'showdown'. In all this they had been supported by Eden and most other Conservative frontbenchers. But, as has been seen, Churchill's approach had been strikingly different. As the general election approached, however, he had no rational alternative, if he wished to continue to lead the Conservative Party, other than to move closer to Eden and to play down his sympathies with Cold War ideologues on the other side of the Atlantic.

An early sign that Churchill was moving in a new direction came with his decision not to oppose the Labour Cabinet's recognition of the new Communist Government of China – which was formally accorded on 6 January 1950. By contrast, the United States continued to recognise the former rulers who had had to retreat to Formosa (Taiwan). Churchill appeared to share Labour's view that recognition of a plain fact was simply sensible and did not signify approval – but this had assuredly not been his attitude towards the First Labour Government's recognition of the Soviet Union on similar grounds in 1924. Maybe for Churchill the Chinese case was different in that he may have hoped, like some in the Foreign Office, that a degree of appeasement of Peking would prevent Hong Kong from being overrun, and that it might be possible over time to influence the Chinese into refusing to behave as mere satellites of the Soviets. However that may be, the fact is that Churchill's line on Chinese recognition was unwelcome to most influential people in Washington.

Then, on 14 February 1950, during the general election campaign Churchill sprang another surprise: in a speech at Edinburgh he called for the West to 'parley' with Moscow. As he put it: 'The idea appeals to me of a supreme effort to bridge the gulf between the two worlds so that each can live their life, if not in friendship, at least without the hatreds and manoeuvres of the cold war ... It is not easy to see how things could be worsened by a parley at the summit if such a thing were possible.'[7] This was certainly a volte-face from the line he had hitherto taken as Leader of the Oppositon. For example, as early as 18 March 1946 he had told Halifax that meeting Stalin would be like 'going to see Hitler before the war'.[8] But perhaps his new line was dictated by a belief that he would soon be Prime Minister again and hence that that he, and not Attlee, would be participating in any possible summit. Moreover, he may have calculated that his own experience in attending various wartime conferences with Stalin would seem to the electorate to make him a better choice than Attlee for such a role and thereby garner some additional votes for the Conservative Party.

In the event, however, Labour narrowly won the general election of 1950 and as a result Churchill did not immediately get a chance to canvas his summit idea with Truman and Stalin. But it was widely thought that a further general election would soon have to be called. Churchill in these circumstances might have been expected at least to continue strongly to argue for a summit in the British domestic context. And he seemed to be heading in that direction on 28 March when he told the House of Commons: 'I cannot help coming back to this idea of another talk with Soviet Russia upon the highest level.' He added, no doubt hoping to conciliate sceptical Americans, that 'certainly we must seek to negotiate from strength and not from weakness'.[9] That he did not continue to press his case with any real vigour, however, is probably explained by the great worsening in the international climate that came on 25 June when Communist North Korea invaded West-leaning South Korea.

Throughout the West the general belief was that this was an act of aggression ordered and organised by the Soviets. This inevitably led to the Americans deciding to assist South Korea. They were, moreover, fortunate enough to be able to secure United Nations backing for their intervention – the Soviets being temporarily absent from the Security Council and hence unable to cast a veto. The upshot was that the Labour Government, despite being overstretched with other commitments throughout the world, stoutly backed the Americans with a sizeable contingent of troops; and then greatly increased general defence spending. In all this the Government naturally had the support of the Conservatives.

As the Korean War proceeded, however, tension developed between London and Washington. And this presented Churchill with some rather difficult choices. On 30 November 1950, for example, Truman reacted to Chinese intervention on the side of North Korea by making it clear in public that the use of atomic weapons in the Korean conflict had not been ruled out. Many Labour MPs expressed alarm on the same day in the House of Commons. And from the Conservative front bench Butler said: 'I want to express, at any rate on my own behalf, and I believe on behalf of a great many other hon. Members, my very great disquiet ... the horror that many of us would feel at the use of this weapon in circumstances which were not such that our own moral conscience was satisfied that there was no alternative.'[10] Earlier in the debate Churchill, for his part, had used words less critical of Truman but that were nevertheless ones that indicated that he was responding to the views of his colleagues:

> the United Nations should avoid by every means in their power becoming entangled inextricably in a war with China ... the sooner

the Far Eastern diversion – because, vast as it is, it is but a diversion – can be brought into something like a static condition and stabilised, the better it will be for all those hopes which the United Nations have in hand. For it is in Europe that the world cause will be decided ... it is there that the mortal danger lies.[11]

Attlee's response was to fly to Washington to urge restraint on Truman.

Churchill's reaction on the Prime Minister's return was to praise him, but at the same time he went out of his way to oppose any dogmatic renunciation by the United States of the right to make first use of nuclear weapons. As he told the House of Commons on 14 December:

> The argument is now put forward that we must never use the atomic bomb until, or unless, it has been used against us first ... That seems to me undoubtedly a silly thing to say and a still more imprudent position to adopt ... The Soviet power could not be confronted, or even placated, with any hope of success if we were in these years of tension through which we are passing to deprive ourselves of the atomic bomb, or to prevent its use by announcing gratuitously self-imposed restrictions.[12]

This indicated that that his desire to be seen as a 'dove' had its limits.

Again, Churchill found himself uneasy at the beginning of 1951 at the mounting criticism of the United States and of General Douglas MacArthur, the Commander-in-Chief of the United Nations Command, in particular. For example, he wrote privately to Eden on 8 January 'we should on no account approve any separation between our policy and that of the United States on the measures to be taken against China' even if this meant 'severing diplomatic relations and withdrawing recognition' from the Peking regime.[13] And he postponed a planned visit to the United States in order to avoid being drawn into the acute controversy that broke out there following the decision by Truman to dismiss MacArthur in April 1951.[14]

Nor was Korea the only issue that caused Churchill problems during 1951. Another was how far to identify himself with the argument that West German rearmament in some form was unavoidable. He had originally argued this case in March 1950 but it had not received a great deal of attention. But once this became the official line of the United States, after September 1950, Churchill's earlier approach became the subject of wide comment – especially when it emerged that there was likely to be much opposition in France and within the British Labour Party. He did not, however, attempt during

1951 to resile. And his strong condemnations of the Labour Government's 'policy of scuttle' in the wake of Iran's nationalisation of the Abadan oil refinery was also widely noted. The upshot was that by October 1951, when a further general election was held, Churchill was increasingly seen as a 'hawk' – despite his continuing notional support for the summit idea he had canvassed during the general election of 1950. Hence many individual Labour supporters and Labour newspapers insisted on describing him as a 'warmonger'. This culminated in the *Daily Mirror* asking on polling day: 'Whose Finger on the Trigger?'

In the event, the Conservatives managed to achieve an overall majority of 17 seats – just enough to give them a full term. But at the same time Churchill's authority was somewhat weakened by the fact that the Labour Party actually secured a larger share of the popular vote.

The point we need to consider here is whether Churchill returned to Number Ten with a coherent programme *vis-à-vis* the Soviet Union. In the view of one historian, John Young, his line in opposition had been reasonably consistent and defensible:

> There can be no doubt that the warmonger charge irked Churchill and made him more anxious to demonstrate his abilities as a peacemaker. Yet, such a desire was born long before the 1951 election. He may have been the original advocate of an Anglo-American alliance against the Soviets, yet he was no simple Cold Warrior bent on an anti-Communist crusade. As Opposition leader his speeches had shifted in emphasis, sometimes in favour of toughness towards Stalin, sometimes in favour of talks. However, the apparent shifts masked some remarkable consistencies especially the faith in an American alliance, the belief that military (including nuclear) power would pave the way for negotiation and the confidence that it was possible to deal with Stalin from strength. These beliefs were all deeply founded in Churchill's lifelong outlook on world affairs and the European tradition of *realpolitik*, where secret diplomacy, the balance of power and spheres of influence were acceptable tools of the international statesman. Indeed, he wished to replace the Cold War with a more traditional European balance of power relationship supplemented by Summit diplomacy. Such a desire was reinforced, especially after 1949, by his concern for Britain's vulnerability to Soviet atomic attack. Whatever was said during the 1951 election, Churchill was no warmonger.[15]

But this conclusion seems to underrate, above all, the extent of the extremism Churchill represented at least until 1949 in his calls for a 'showdown' with Moscow. Kissinger's verdict on this aspect is more persuasive than Young's: 'Had he not lost the 1945 election, he might well have given the emerging Cold War a different direction – provided that America and the other allies had been willing to risk the confrontation which seemed to underlie Churchill's preferred strategy.'[16] Moreover, Young's conclusion tends to ignore the ideological strand in Churchill's analysis of the character of the Soviet Union; and to downplay the possibility that his conduct during 1950 and 1951 was somewhat inconsistent and above all, motivated in aspects relating to the calls for a summit with Stalin by electioneering calculations.

We must now turn to Churchill's final period in office. He was exceptionally fortunate in that, when resuming the Premiership in October 1951, the international scene was much less disturbed than for many years past. The Korean War had not yet terminated. But its acute phase had ended in July 1951 when an apparent military deadlock had led to the opening of armistice talks which were destined to drag on until 1953. And in Europe the mere passage of time had made the two-bloc system, including even a divided Germany and a divided Berlin, begin to assume an appearance of stability and normality. True, Stalin still ruled in the Kremlin but few in the West expected him to launch any outright military attack on Western Europe now that the North Atlantic Treaty Organisation (NATO) had come into existence, with Eisenhower installed as the first Supreme Allied Commander. At all events, the Conservatives felt able over time to reduce the exceptionally high level of defence spending introduced in 1950 by their predecessors. And Churchill had no difficulty in publicly supporting these prospective defence cuts in terms that would have appealed to Neville Chamberlain: there could be no strength without firm economic foundations and the defence programme must be kept within the nation's strength.[17] He was also able in these relatively untroubled conditions to take his time before revealing the main drift of the international policies he intended to pursue.

In 1951 Churchill was unusual and perhaps unique among incoming Prime Ministers of the twentieth century in that he must have known with certainty that his colleagues would not countenance his leading them into another general election. His age (76), his deteriorating physical and mental condition, and the fact that Foreign Secretary Eden was impatiently waiting to succeed him, surely made that unthinkable even to Churchill. But what was less clear was whether Churchill would be allowed, if he so desired, to serve for the bulk of the Parliament. There was of course in those days no provision for the kind of vote among Conservative MPs that brought down Margaret Thatcher in 1990. All the same, as a practical matter, if enough Cabinet colleagues had been sufficiently determined, even Churchill could not have faced them down for long. Hence the suspicion has to be that his approach to every aspect of politics, and to relations with the Soviet Union in particular, soon came to be dominated by a desire to put off for as long as possible such a 'showdown' with his colleagues. From this point of view evidence of his growing frailty – deafness for example – was no doubt a problem from the outset. But only from the end of 1952 did the pressures on him markedly increase. For at that point he found himself reneging on the promise he had earlier given to Eden, according to the latter's authorised biographer, to hand over the premiership after a year.[18] Hence it is probably not chance that he thereafter increasingly relied on the prospect of a summit meeting along wartime lines as a means of putting off the naming of a retirement date. Operating in his favour was the fact that, in an age when intrusive televising of politicians was in its infancy, the general public was only dimly aware of his increasing senility. He accordingly seems to have had little difficulty in persuading most of his colleagues that if a summit were to be held he would be seen by the public as the obvious man to represent Great Britain – with corresponding benefits for the Conservative Party at home. In this writer's view, with the passage of time he consciously allowed this consideration to distort almost all his thinking about the Soviet Union and he unscrupulously attempted to manipulate other world leaders to serve his essentially selfish purposes.

Immediately after returning to Downing Street he could afford to be relatively relaxed. Hence, though he mentioned the desirability of a Big Three summit in vague terms in a House of Commons speech on 6 November 1951, he was not as yet minded to launch a crusade on the subject. And he seems to have gone to Washington in January 1952 for a series of meetings with Truman in this spirit also. For though he raised the possiblity of their seeking a summit with Stalin, the Prime Minister readily accepted Truman's opposition to the idea; and he did not even mention the option that he himself might go alone to meet Stalin. He appeared to agree that recent Soviet statements had been markedly unfriendly. And he seemingly recognised that in a Presidential Election year no US Administration could afford to give even the appearance of weakness – especially so with Senator Joseph McCarthy in the background. Hence Churchill told Truman that 'in this matter' he 'would not do anything ... to make things more difficult for the President'.[19] Moreover, on other issues than summitry the Prime Minister pleased his hosts by striking a much stronger anti-Communist note than did Eden. For example, Churchill went so far as to tell Truman that since Potsdam 'you more than any other man have saved Western civilisation'.[20] Again, Churchill made it evident that he did not share his Foreign Secretary's reluctance to support American moves in East Asia that might further antagonise Peking.[21] He wanted the British and the Americans to see each other as defenders of 'civilisation' against Communism. From this starting point he hoped that the Americans would back the British in the Middle East (where Iran and Egypt were being particularly troublesome) in return for British broad support for the Americans in East Asia. In short, he still appeared to see the world to a great extent through ideological spectacles. In practice, by 1952 the Americans were not interested in a partnership of this kind if it meant backing 'colonialism' in the Middle East. But they were even less attracted to Eden's view, which was that the supposed global ideological contest between the West and Communism was in no way central to the way in which the world actually worked. Hence of course he did not see Truman or any other American as a saviour of 'civilisation' on a global scale.

Throughout the rest of 1952 Churchill for his part continued to behave as if he saw world Communism as a threat to be unitedly resisted. For example, on 21 October he appeared to fall in with the American view of summitry. He told the House of Commons: 'I think the moment may well have been lost when such approaches [for a three-power summit] could have been made.'[22] And he at first backed the Americans against Eden when it came to handling the Korean armistice negotiations. The Chinese had indicated that a successful result was in sight, provided the West agreed to the forcible return of Communist prisoners-of-war held in South Korea. The Americans saw this as a price they were unwilling to pay, whereas the British Foreign Office, hesitantly supported by Eden, were inclined to give way or at least to seek a compromise. But Churchill, perhaps having a bad conscience about his wartime conduct *vis-à-vis* the Soviets on this kind of issue, supported the Americans. On 12 July 1952, for example, he privately minuted: 'In my view there can be no question of forcing any Chinese prisoners-of-war to go back to Communist China against their will. These are the ones above all others who carry with them the moral significance, as the ones who have opted for us would certainly be put to death or otherwise maltreated.'[23]

Meanwhile the Communist threat to French control over Indochina was causing mounting concern in Paris, London and Washington. At first the Truman Administration was hesitant about the extent of the support that it would be appropriate to give to an old-fashioned European colonialist regime. And this duly alarmed the British who feared that if Indochina fell to Communism, Malaya, with its vital resources of rubber and tin, might become increasingly vulnerable. But by early 1952 the Americans made it clear that they did see preventing the spread of Communism to Indochina as vital. They were understandably unenthusiatic, however, in the light of their exper-iences in Korea, about getting involved in another limited con-ventional war in East Asia. The American approach, therefore, increasingly became one of threatening to treat what was happening in Indochina as mainly a Chinese responsibility and accordingly being willing in the final analysis to bomb Chinese territory. This alarmed most of the British elite – led by Eden, by Foreign Office officials and by the Chiefs of Staff. For they feared that Hong Kong would become vulnerable in such circumstances. And, above all, they believed that the Soviet Union might be drawn in. As Air Chief Marshal William Elliot put it to the Prime Minister on 16 February 1952: 'We are opposed to general war against China or to action which we feel might (almost involuntarily) involve Soviet Russia and lead to global war.'[24] For his part, however, Churchill never fully accepted the premise that Moscow would allow the Chinese to act as catalysts to a general war. On 30 November 1951, for example, the minutes of a meeting of the Chiefs of Staff included the following

> THE PRIME MINISTER, however, considered that Russia would start World War III when she wanted to: she certainly would not do so merely to honour her pledge to China. He was, therefore, not unduly worried about bombing targets in Manchuria. As regards a war with China, he considered that China was not a country against which one declared war; rather a country against which war was waged.[25]

And Churchill was also somewhat predisposed on issues of substance like Asia's future, as distinct from his essentially cosmetic Soviet summit project, to hold that it was natural that the United States should take the leading role. This was a line that the Americans them-selves, reasonably enough, tried to sell to their allies – Dulles, for example, saying early in 1953 that the latter needed to display 'faith in the United States and show trust in the fundamental decency and moderation of American objectives'.[26] But Churchill was unable during his final term to win general support for these assessments among his colleagues. He became, therefore, increasingly reserved on Asian matters and especially so on Indochina. On 3 September 1952, however, he ventured to write to Eden urging 'don't let's fall out with US for the sake of Communist China'.[27]

If therefore Churchill had retired in October 1952, on the first anniversary of his return to Number Ten, there would have been little in his record to justify claims that he had become a crusader for *détente* or that his calls for a summit with the Soviets during 1950 and 1951 had been anything more than cynical electioneering. Indeed, the main discontinuity with the immediate post-war period would probably have been seen by historians as relating only to the desirability or not of having an immediate 'showdown' with Moscow – a discontinuity fully explained by British vulnerability to atomic attack following the Soviet test of 1949.

Churchill did not, however, keep the promise he had made to Eden to hand over the Premiership after a year in office. But this did not mean that the promise had been of no importance. For Eden (and others) soon began to press him on the matter. On 8 December 1952 Evelyn Shuckburgh, Eden's Principal Private Secretary, wrote in his diary:

> He [Eden] said to Winston that he must know something of his plans. PM made a solemn Winstonian speech to the effect that his intention was, when the time came, to hand over his powers and authority with the utmost smoothness and surety to Anthony. AE said, yes – but the point was when would that be? ... But the net result was no clear indication.[28]

Shuckburgh's diary contains many subsequent entries along these lines – stretching into early 1955.[29] And the papers and diaries of Eden himself and of many other contemporaries confirm that Churchill was under continuous pressure to name a date for retirement and they reveal also his endless evasiveness and duplicity in this connection.[30] Foremost among his excuses for delay was the prospect, which he was almost alone in perceiving, that he was about to win over the Americans and/or the Soviets to the holding of a summit at which he himself would play a key role in inaugurating a wholly new era of mutual 'easement'.

The watching world was thus soon led to believe that Churchill's Edinburgh speech of 1950 had not after all been a *volte face* performed only for electoral purposes but had marked a genuine conversion to a more sanguine view of what the Soviets represented. And many historians have also taken this line. Here, however, we shall trace Churchill's course on the assumption that he still believed what he had said in New York City in 1949, namely that the Soviets were 'quite as wicked but much more formidable than Hitler';[31] and that all the statements by him to the contrary between 1953 and 1955 were essentially insincere.

The news in November 1952 that Eisenhower had been elected as US President had mixed implications for Churchill as his reactions showed. On the one hand, he grasped that a Republican Administration was likely to be even more anti-Communist than Truman's had been, and thus on the face of it unlikely to create conditions in which his goal of posturing as a peacemaker could be easily achieved. On the other hand, Churchill had known Eisenhower well since the Second World War and evidently hoped to be able to manipulate him into approving the calling of a summit with the Soviets. Unsurprisingly therefore Churchill gave out confusing signals. For example, he spoke pessimistically to Colville: 'For your private ear, I am greatly disturbed. I think this makes war much more probable.'[32] Yet, according to one historian, Young:

> When Eisenhower's victory over Adlai Stevenson in the Presidential election was announced … Churchill could not hide his delight, sending a hearty message to his wartime colleague hoping for 'a renewal of our comradeship … for the same causes of peace and freedom as in the past'. Eden, fearful of offending the outgoing Truman administration, vainly tried to persuade the Prime Minister to change the message from 'sincere and heartfelt congratulations' to 'best wishes' but at this Churchill, as observed by Evelyn Shuckburgh, became extremely cross. For him the result not only broke the sense of deadlock in US foreign policy, inevitable in election year, but promised the opportunity of a close working relationship with the White House and the chance to pursue *détente* with American approval. Once again Eden and others had to face the possibility of a Roosevelt-style relationship between Prime Minister and President and the official biographer [Gilbert] notes that, from this moment on, Churchill gained 'a new sense of mission: to stay on … until he could bring about, by his own exertions, a reconciliation of the two Great Powers', America and the USSR.[33]

Churchill's expectations were to fluctuate greatly during his remaining years in office. But he never admitted that his quest was hopeless – hence enabling him to cling on longer than any of his entourage would have believed possible. The Prime Minister's first bout of optimism arose as a result of Eisenhower's decision to allow him to visit him in New York in January 1953, even before he had taken over from Truman. Their two meetings were extremely cordial. But on the issue of summitry Eisenhower gave Churchill both encouragement and discouragement as the former's report to London reveals:

> Eisenhower opened yesterday with much vigour about direct contacts with Stalin. I was quite welcome to go myself if I thought fit at any time. He thought of making it plain in his inauguration speech that he would go to, say, Stockholm to meet him, if Stalin were willing. Evidently he did not want Britain. ' That would involve asking France and Italy.'[34]

The good news for Churchill was that he could remind Eisenhower of this conversation in the event that, all else having failed, he wished to go alone to meet Stalin – provided of course that objections from his own Cabinet colleagues could be overridden. At least the Americans under the new Administration, in contrast to that of Truman, would not actually be able to oppose *à l'outrance* suggestions for such a visit. But the bad news for Churchill was that Eisenhower had signalled that a three-power heads of government summit on the model of Teheran, Yalta and Potsdam was unappealing to him. Great Britain thus faced unwelcome relegation: the Big Three, in other words, was to be replaced either by the Big Two – the superpowers as they later became known – or by the Big Four (or more). For Churchill, the idea of an Eisenhower-Stalin meeting in his absence would have been the worst outcome of all. He was wise enough, however, not to say so to the President – and in the event this option was not to be seriously mooted again during Churchill's Premiership.

If summitry dominated Churchill's thinking at this time, Eisenhower was more concerned at the inappropriateness of the Prime Minister's assumption that an exclusive 'special relationship' between the two of them could be created. As the President wrote in his diary on 6 January 1953:

> Winston is trying to relive the days of World War II.
> In those days he had the enjoyable feeling that he and our

President were sitting on some rather Olympian platform with respect to the rest of the world, and directing world affairs from that point of vantage ...

In the present international complexities, any hope of establishing such a relationship is completely fatuous.[35]

Fortunately for Churchill's peace of mind Eisenhower had been too polite to say this to his face.

While in New York Churchill also had a meeting with Dulles who had just been appointed to serve as Eisenhower's Secretary of State. In other circumstances the two men would presumably in the main have seen eye to eye. For both were fanatical but sophisticated anti-Communists. Indeed, it was for just such an ideological kindred spirit at the top of American politics that Churchill had looked in vain during the closing stages of the Second World War and during the early peacetime years – though Dulles was probably at that stage the less extreme of the two men. But during his final term as Prime Minister Churchill came to hate Dulles – believing, almost certainly mistakenly, that he was responsible for Eisenhower's unwillingness to treat Great Britain as an equal partner, and for his lack of enthusiasm for the kind of summitry with the Soviets that Churchill probably believed was necessary for his survival in Number Ten.

Returning to London at the end of January after a holiday in Jamaica, Churchill, now 78, spent the next weeks preparing for a 'showdown' with Eden over the date of his retirement. His hopes of survival were clearly receding – particularly as no early opportunity for calling a summit was in prospect. But then his luck changed: on 6 March Stalin's sudden death was announced. He was thus enabled to argue to his colleagues and to the Americans that a summit in one form or another should take place in order to discover whether there was to be a 'New Look' in Moscow. He had of course frequently argued in the past, as has been seen, that Stalin was more human and businesslike than those who stood behind him. But as such a view no longer suited his purpose he instantly argued that the new collective leadership, headed at first by Georgi Malenkov, represented a promising chance for 'easement'. Moran, for example, recorded on 7 March: 'The P.M. feels that Stalin's death may lead to a relaxation in tension. It is an opportunity that will not recur.'[36] Kissinger has also noted Churchill's lack of consistency:

Prior to Stalin's death, Churchill had urged negotiations because he had deemed Stalin to be the Soviet leader best able to guarantee the fulfillment of what he had promised. Now Churchill was urging a summit in order to preserve the hopeful prospects that had arisen after the dictator's death. In other words, negotiations were needed no matter what happened within the Soviet Union or who controlled the Soviet hierarchy.[37]

Hence as early as 11 March Churchill wrote to Eisenhower in these terms:

> I am sure that everyone will want to know whether you still contemplate a meeting with the Soviets. I remember our talk ... when you told me I was welcome to meet Stalin if I thought fit and that you intended to offer to do so. I understand this as meaning that you did not not want us to go together, but now there is no more Stalin I wonder whether this makes any difference to your view about separate approaches to the new regime or whether there is a possiblity of collective action.[38]

On neither side of the Atlantic did this line find favour with members of the policy-making elite. But Churchill calculated correctly that the general public, particularly in Great Britain and Western Europe, would think otherwise. Hence he was soon contemplating a proclamation to the House of Commons about his hopes for a relaxation of tension.

Churchill's renewed eagerness for summitry was made evident so soon after Stalin's death that it cannot possibly have been based on serious analysis of any emerging evidence about the intentions of the successors in Moscow. But Churchill predictably interpreted every subsequent news item relating to the Soviets in a way that favoured his thesis and bolstered his hopes. Malenkov had hitherto been primarily interested in Soviet domestic affairs and so this was seen as a sign that he would wish to lower the international temperature. But when Molotov, a Stalinist loyalist, was reinstated as Foreign Minister, that was considered to be irrelevant. When progress in the Korean armistice talks began to be made this was 'evidence' of a 'New Look' in Moscow; but when the Soviets crushed a rising in East Germany in June 1953 Churchill privately excused their conduct in these words: 'Is it suggested that the Soviets should have allowed the Eastern Zone to fall into anarchy and riot? I had the impression they acted with considerable restraint in the face of mounting disorder.'[39] And whenever Western leaders or officials took any actions that made summitry and a relaxation of tension more unlikely he was angered. He had no longer any patience with French hesitations about accepting

German rearmament under the auspices of the European Defence Community (EDC) scheme – lest any delay made American opposition to a summit with the Soviets more plausible. He disapproved of the Americans providing food parcels for East Germans in the aftermath of the rising there; and he objected to statements by British officials in Berlin that were critical of Soviet behaviour in East Germany (reminiscent of his objections to similar statements by British officials in Romania early in 1945). And he was uninfluenced by reports from the British Embassy in Moscow that discerned no serious changes in the Soviet outlook.

Another occasion when concern for the chances of what could be called his 'great matter' seems to have dominated Churchill's thinking came when Syngman Rhee, the right-wing authoritarian leader of South Korea, almost wrecked hopes for an armistice agreement by unilaterally releasing in late June 1953 large numbers of prisoners-of-war whose ultimate fate was under intense discussion with the Communists. Churchill wrote a minute to Lord Salisbury (formerly Cranborne), the Lord Privy Seal, on 2 July in astonishing terms:

> The first question is whether the United States can afford to leave Rhee to his fate and accept a Communist subjugation of Korea. It is purely a question of American sentimental pride ... Myself, I think the United States are so powerful that they can afford to be indifferent to a local Communist success. They could afford to let Rhee be squelched and Korea communised and spend the money saved on increasing their armaments ... If I were an American, as I might have been, I would vote for Rhee going to hell and taking Korea with him.[40]

This irresponsible outburst was presumably motivated in large part by a fear that if a Korean armistice was lost as a result of Rhee's action the chances of a summit would plummet simultaneously. By comparison, the sacrifices made by British forces during the Korean War seemingly meant little to him.

Churchill's growing obsession with summitry was welcome neither to his Cabinet colleagues nor to the Eisenhower Administration. But this was not surprising. For he offered no serious evidence that the Soviet ideology had changed or that any agreement on an issue of substance involving Moscow and the West was in prospect. Indeed, he had no specific agenda in view; what he apparently wanted was to take part in an unstructured but spectacular meeting of world leaders which would somehow produce a general 'easement'. This therefore

seemed to most of his elite contemporaries to be a call for summitry
for summitry's sake. Indeed, according to Kissinger, 'American leaders
unfairly ascribed Churchill's eagerness to negotiate to approaching
senility'.[41] And Eisenhower himself made his disapproval clear in a
message sent to Churchill on 11 March 1953. And that might have
been the effective end of the matter. For Churchill's colleagues, and
Eden in particular, certainly shared the President's scepticism about
the likely utility of any early summit.

Then Churchill had another stroke of good fortune: Eden became
seriously ill and was told on 4 April 1953 that he must undergo an
operation. Eventually this turned into no fewer than three separate
operations which kept the Foreign Secretary totally out of action until
October 1953. With alacrity Churchill made it known that he would
take charge of the Foreign Office in the interim – with Salisbury
assisting him. The upshot was that his crusade for a summit resumed
in earnest. From 5 April he began to bombard Eisenhower with a
series of messages on the subject. And when he met with no encouragement to expect any early American participation in a summit, the
Prime Minister boldly threatened a bilateral Anglo-Soviet version in
this message to the President despatched on 21 April: 'If nothing can
be arranged I shall have to consider seriously a personal contact. You
told me in New York you would have no objection to this.'[42]
Eisenhower replied on 25 April:

> The situation has changed considerably since we talked in New York
> and I believe that we should watch developments for a while longer
> before determining our further course. However, if you should find it
> necessary for some special local reason to seek a personal contact, we
> would hope for as much advance notice as you could possibly give
> us.[43]

The reference to 'some special local reason' suggests that Eisenhower
saw Churchill's conduct as being neither sincere nor the direct consequence of senility but as domestically-driven in essence. (That the
President was, incidentally, quite willing to risk giving offence in this
way is proved by the fact that when, on 6 May 1955, he was asked by
Prime Minister Eden to agree to hold a four-power summit with the
Soviets he replied: 'We appreciate the importance to you of this
project under existing circumstances and are naturally disposed to do
everything we can to further it. On the other hand, you will understand that we also have our local problems, including public opinion,
to consider.'[44] This was an obvious reference to the fact that Eden, who

was in the throes of a general election campaign, needed a speedy decision to boost his electoral prospects.)

Confronted by Eisenhower's opposition, Churchill did not now hesitate to seek public support for summitry. He gave the Commons a hint about his thinking on 20 April 1953.[45] But by early May he was determined to go much further. On the 3rd, for example, Dixon of the Foreign Office recorded:

> At luncheon yesterday the Prime Minister spoke to me about his ideas for establishing contact with the new Soviet regime. He thought that a meeting of the three Powers [the Soviet Union, the United States and Great Britain] would be best, but if President Eisenhower was not willing to take part, then Sir Winston Churchill's strong instinct was that he ought to offer himself. He would propose to offer to go to Moscow. He was thinking of making some references to this possibility in the foreign affairs debate next week.
>
> I said there were very serious objections to any Western initiatives for general talks with the Russians at the moment; and separate Anglo-Soviet talks would, in my view, be even more dangerous than tripartite talks. The Soviet Government would probably accept, but we could not rely in any way on their sincerity in doing so. Their object, I thought, would be to seize an opportunity of driving a wedge between us and the Americans. The whole world would, of course, be agape while the talks were going on, and everyone would mark time … My own feeling was that this was not the moment to make a direct high-level contact with the Soviet leaders. The present policy of collective defence in the West had had an effect on the Russians: we should surely do well to continue the same policy for some time yet until we were stronger.
>
> The Prime Minister said that he did not deny that risks were involved. We should not, however, underrate the good he might be able to do in an attempt to get back with the Soviet leaders on to the old wartime basis. He thought that they were largely actuated by fear and that he might be able to allay their suspicions.
>
> I asked what the Prime Minister's idea would be about the scope of the discussions. He said that in general he would try to get on terms with them, as indicated above. He would also show recognition of their desire for outlets to the sea. I said that I thought any encouragement of these desires would provoke a request for withdrawal of Norway and Denmark on the one hand, and Turkey, on the other from the North Atlantic alliance, since Russia had traditional ambitions in connexion with the Baltic and the Straits. We could be sure that one of the Russian objectives would be to dissolve the Atlantic alliance and the special relationship between Great Britain and the United States.[46]

William Strang, the Foreign Office's Permanent Under-Secretary, also attempted to influence the Prime Minister around this time. According to his own record:

> I said [to Churchill] that though there were strong arguments in favour of a visit there were also strong arguments against any talks with the Russians at the present stage, whether two or three or four Party. It would be better if the Bonn Treaties and a German defence contribution could be clinched before we opened such talks. For the Prime Minister to visit Moscow might be to open a series of individual visits, and the Russians would have an opportunity to deal with the Atlantic Powers one by one. The French in particular might be expected to follow suit, and a French visit to Moscow might be extremely dangerous, given the hankering at the back of the French mind for a Franco-Russian agreement against Germany.
>
> The Prime Minister said that he was aware of these risks, but he was confident that he could pay this visit without giving anything away. As for the French, they did not matter: if they would not ratify the E.D.C., Germany would have to enter N.A.T.O., and if the French raised objections to this we could withhold protection from them.[47]

Even Churchill's warmest admirers are unlikely to see much merit in the arguments adduced by him in these encounters with his Foreign Office advisers. In particular, how could it be possible to make Churchill's suggestion for appeasing the Soviets with respect to outlets to the sea compatible with his oft-repeated claims to favour peace through strength? At all events, Churchill himself seems never to have had the courage to mention this idea again – certainly not to the Americans who would surely have reacted with the utmost indignation. But perhaps he only mentioned it to Dixon in May 1953 because he felt the need to add something to his call for talks otherwise apparently designed merely to get his personal relations with the Soviets back 'on to the old wartime basis' – exemplified, above all, by the Moscow meeting of October 1944. As for this latter aim, it seems in retrospect to have verged on the absurd. In 1944–1945 the Americans had been proclaiming their intention to withdraw from Europe soon after Germany's surrender and that would have meant that at least for some considerable time Great Britain and the Soviet Union would have been the only great powers in the region. But by 1953 the geostrategic relationships had evolved in dramatically different fashion: NATO had emerged and the United States was now clearly the leading military power in the Western end of Europe – with Great Britain being no more than an auxiliary state. In these circumstances a visit by Churchill alone to Moscow would have stood no chance of restoring Anglo-Soviet relations to what they had been almost a decade earlier – not least because it was no longer open to the British to attempt to forge any bilateral deal along the lines of the 'percentages agreement'. And even the Prime Minister himself seems to have recognised these realities to some degree in the face of the arguments of his Foreign Office advisers. At all events, he decided at least for the present not to refer in public to the possibility of a bilateral British-Soviet summit. But he was not to be dissuaded from calling for a three-power version even though he knew that this would be unwelcome to the Americans. Accordingly on May 11, without having consulted the Cabinet, he created a public sensation by saying to the Commons:

> I must make it plain that, in spite of all uncertainties and confusion in which world affairs are plunged, I believe that a conference on the highest level should take place between the leading Powers without long delay. The conference should not be overhung by a ponderous agenda ... The conference should be confined to the smallest number of Powers and persons possible. It should meet with a measure of informality and a still greater measure of privacy and seclusion. It might well be that no hard-faced agreements would be reached, but there might be a general feeling among those gathered together that they might do something better than tear the human race, including themselves, to bits ...
> ... If there is not at the summit of the nations the will to win the greatest prize and the greatest honour ever offered to mankind, doom-laden responsibility will fall upon those who now possess the power to decide. At the worst the participants in the meeting would have established more intimate contact. At the best we might have a generation of peace.[48]

This speech was extremely popular, according to opinion polls, both at home and abroad. Hence, in the absence of Eden, no Cabinet Minister was to resign – though Salisbury almost did so. For their part, the dismayed American leadership was unsure how to proceed. For 78 per cent of the American public, according to a Gallup Poll, favoured a summit.[49] But opinion on Capitol Hill was broadly adverse to Churchill's initiative. Coral Bell has written:

> [Republican] Senator [Everett] Dirksen made threatening sounds on the subject of foreign aid, and the [Republican] Majority leader, Senator [William] Knowland, said that Britain was preparing a Far Eastern Munich which would make a third World War inevitable. A

Democrat, Senator Paul Douglas, accused Churchill of 'nudging the United States into a position where we will have to acquiesce in the main features of Communist proposals'. On the whole, both parties cast their comments in accents of dismay, anxiety and indignation.[50]

But by May 20 Eisenhower and Dulles had decided that the only way to contain Churchill, and to minimise his disruptive effects on the chances of France ratifying the EDC, was to propose the holding of a meeting of American, British and French Heads of Government in order to review the world scene in general and Soviet intentions in particular. Churchill cheerfully welcomed this proposal – hoping no doubt, as he hinted to the House of Commons, that a summit with the Soviets might then follow, notwithstanding initial American reservations.[51] With one and possibly two summits in prospect and Eden sick, he could thus now expect that his tenure of Number Ten would be indefinitely extended.

Churchill's plans appeared to receive a setback, however, just two weeks before the proposed Western Summit was due to open in Bermuda. For on 23 June he suffered a severe stroke and was obliged to ask for an indefinite postponement. The stroke cannot, it must be said, have come as a surprise to his immediate entourage. For he had been in visible decline for many months. Moreover, he frequently drank to excess. For example, on 3 May 1953 Dixon of the Foreign Office recorded in his diary: 'Lunched with W S C at No. 10 ... The lunch lasted for $3^{1}/_{4}$ hours. A varied and noble procession of wines with which I could not keep pace – champagne, port, brandy, cointreau: W. drank a great deal of all, and ended with two glasses of whisky and soda.'[52] Now, six weeks later, he had had a stroke which seemed certain to end his career. But Eden was at this time in Boston in order to undergo a third operation and hence could not immediately take over. It was therefore decided that Churchill, while not actually resigning, would take a complete rest and that the nature of his illness would be kept secret.

Astonishingly, by the time that Eden was fit to return to active politics in October 1953, Churchill had made a sufficient recovery to feel able to carry on a little longer. Naturally he was soon insisting that the projected Western summit in Bermuda be rescheduled; and Eisenhower felt unable to refuse. Accordingly the American, British and French leaders assembled there in early December. Meanwhile, on 9 November, Churchill stated at the Lord Mayor's Banquet in the Guild-hall that 'many people think that the best we can do is get used to the

Cold War like eels are said to get used to skinning'. But he intended to pursue 'peace through strength together – and mark this – with any contacts, formal or informal, which may be thought to be helpful'.[53]

Churchill may have believed that Bermuda was his last, best hope of manipulating the Americans into agreeing in principle to an eventual Heads of Government summit with the Soviets. But, if so, he reckoned without Eisenhower. Irritated by Churchill's unscrupulous use of public opinion, the President was now determined to resist the view that the Soviets might really have changed. To Churchill's arguments to this effect he replied with some brutality. According to Colville:

> Ike followed with a short, very violent statement, in the coarsest terms. He said that as regards the P.M.'s belief that there was a New Look in Soviet Policy, Russia was a woman of the streets and whether her dress was new, or just the old one patched, it was certainly the same whore underneath. America intended to drive her off her present 'beat' into the back streets.[54]

He added, according to the American record:

> He did not want to approach this problem on the basis that there had been any change in the Soviet policy of destroying the Capitalist free world by all means, by force, by deceit or by lies. This was their long-term purpose. From their writings it was clear there had been no change since Lenin.[55]

To Churchill this was most unwelcome – though he cannot have missed the irony that their roles had been reversed since 1945 when he had wished to race the Soviets for control of Eastern Europe and Eisenhower had favoured a more conciliatory approach. A consolation for the Prime Minister, however, was that the Bermuda meeting did confirm that the three Western Foreign Ministers should hold a meeting with Molotov early in 1954 to consider the German and Austrian questions. This meant that Eden was to be fully occupied and in the spotlight – thus making it less likely that he would press too strongly for the Prime Minister's immediate retirement.

Bermuda was also marked by Churchill's desire to bring intense pressure to bear on the French leaders, Joseph Laniel and Georges Bidault, to expedite ratification of the EDC scheme for West German rearmament.[56] In May 1953, his attitude, as has been seen, had been one of insouciane: the French did not matter because if they failed to ratify EDC West Germany would be brought into NATO whether they approved or not. He had also not even seemed worried about the possibility of German unification on the basis of neutralisation 'if the Germans wished, but only if they wished for this'.[57] But by the end of the year Churchill had concluded that if EDC finally failed, the Americans might well terminate their presence in the centre of Europe and hence the French in particular suddenly mattered greatly. As he put it privately to Eisenhower:

> Mr President, you are quite right. The French must be called to their duty. They must be spoken harshly to ... But not by me, Sir. By you. Not by me, because I hope to spend a portion of my declining years in the South of France.[58]

In the event, Churchill spoke out even more strongly than Eisenhower in the plenary session. And in doing so he revealed how afraid he still was concerning Soviet intentions in the contingency of an American withdrawal to the edges of the Eurasian landmass. His case for believing in a 'New Look' on the part of the Soviets and for holding a summit with them was, to say the least, hardly strengthened. But perhaps he was actually now so senile, following his major stroke, that he did not even realise how contradictory his line must have seemed. The historian is also fortunate in that Churchill dictated a minute to Eden on 6 December 1953 which unambiguously reveals that in some moods, he was still capable of expressing at least in private the visceral and apocalyptic anti-Sovietism which had been such a prominent feature of his outlook during the later 1940s:

> We are all agreed to press EDC through. President Eisenhower rejects the idea that if it continues to be indefinitely delayed an arrangement can be made to include a German army in NATO. It must be EDC or some solution of a 'peripheral' character. This would mean that the United States forces would withdraw from France and occupy the crescent of bases from Iceland, via East Anglia, Spain, North Africa, and Turkey, operating with atomic power therefrom in case of war. The consequence would be a Russian occupation of the whole of defenceless Germany and probably an arrangement between Communist-soaked France and Soviet Russia. Benelux and Scandinavia would go down the drain. The Americans would probably declare atomic war on the Soviets if they made a forcible military advance westward. It is it not foreseeable how they would deal with a gradual, though rapid and certain Sovietisation of Western Europe à la Czechoslovakia. It is probable that the process would be gradual so that Sovietisation would be substantially effective and then war came. Thus we should certainly have the worst

of both alternatives.

If the United States withdraws her troops from Europe, the British will certainly go at the same time. The approach of the Russian air bases and the facilities soon available to them west of the Rhine would expose us, apart from bombing, rockets, guided missiles etc., to very heavy paratroop descents. We must have all our available forces to garrison the Island and at least go down fighting.

The French should realise that failure to carry out EDC (unless they can persuade the United States to try the NATO alternative) would leave them without either any American or any British troops in Europe, and that a third World War would become inevitable. It would be conducted from American peripheral bases, and as the Russian armies would be in occupation of Western Europe all these unhappy countries would be liable to be American strategic bombing points. Whatever happens Great Britain will continue to resist until destroyed. In three or four months or even less after the beginning of atomic war the United States unless out matched in Air Power will be all-powerful and largely uninjured with the wreck of Europe and Asia on its hands.

No-one can guarantee that this unpleasant result may not occur even if we take the right course and follow the 'peace through strength' policy. We should however at least have a chance of escaping the doom which now impends upon mankind.[59]

In the light of this minute it is indeed difficult to take Churchill seriously as a pioneer of *détente* – at least as that term was later to be understood. Another incident at Bermuda also points to the Prime Minister being, at root, less than convinced about the merits of his 'New Look' thesis concerning the Soviets. For he reported to Moran that he and Eisenhower had had an extraordinary exchange on the subject of preventive war. Moran recorded in his diary on 5 December:

> Of course ... anyone could say the Russians are evil minded and mean to destroy the free countries. Well, if we really feel like that, perhaps we ought to take action before they get as many atomic bombs as America has. I [Churchill] made that point to Ike, who said, perhaps logically, that it ought to be considered.[60]

Kissinger has also found Churchill's espousal of *détente* somewhat puzzling – even though he does not question his sincerity. In particular, Kissinger, writing in 1994, could not easily understand the timing of Churchill's 'conversion', though he tried hard to do so. 'Churchill,' he wrote, 'had recognized that the difficulty with containment in its original version was that, however powerful its analysis, its practical implementation amounted to endurance for its own sake until that distant day when the Soviet system somehow transformed itself.' Yet Kissinger also saw that the basis for any meaningful settlement between East and West was far more difficult to conceive during the 1950s than had been the case immediately after the war:

> In 1945 Finnish-type regimes in Eastern Europe would have been a return to normalcy. In 1952, they could no longer have been established by negotiation: they could only have come about through a Soviet collapse or a major confrontation. That confrontation, moreover, would have had to be conducted over the issue of German unification – and no Western European country was prepared to run such a risk on behalf of a defeated enemy so soon after the war.[61]

And of course Kissinger would also have been aware that the West German Government of Konrad Adenauer, dominant in Bonn throughout the 1950s, would have been quite unwilling to have adopted the *détente* outlook that Willy Brandt's Germany voluntarily chose during the Presidency of Richard Nixon of the early 1970s, in which Kissinger played so prominent a part, first as National Security Adviser and then as Secretary of State. No wonder, then, that Kissinger in 1994 seemed unable to decide whether to applaud or dismiss Churchill's approach.

What is perhaps odd, however, is that so experienced an historian gave no consideration to the possibility that Churchill's may have been simply less than sincere. After all, it is not only Eisenhower and this writer who have questioned his motives. For example, the historian Peter Lowe has written: 'Part of the explanation for Churchill's zeal [for *détente* with the Soviet Union] probably lies in an elderly politician wishing to close his career on a note of triumph in addition to offering further justification for his continuance in office (as with [W. E.] Gladstone's emphasis on the importance of resolving Irish Home Rule from 1886).'[62] And even Shuckburgh, a contemporary official in heart of the Foreign Office, had been able to write in his diary on 24 July 1953:

> The more I think of it, the more I disapprove of W.S.C. fostering this sentimental illusion that peace can be obtained if only the 'top men' can get together. It seems an example of the hubris which afflicts old men who have power, as it did Chamberlain when he visited Hitler. Even if you do believe in the theory, surely you should keep this trump card in your hand for emergency and not play it out at a time when there is no burning need, no particularly dangerous tension (rather the reverse) and your opponents are plunged in internal

struggles and dissensions. It is hard to avoid the conclusion that W.S.C. is longing for a top-level meeting before he dies – not because it is wise or necessary but because it would complete the pattern of his ambition and make him the Father of Peace as well as of Victory. But it would do no such thing unless he were to make concessions to the Russians which there is no need to make, in return for a momentary and probably illusory 'reduction of tension'. After that splendid achievement he would die in triumph and we should all be left behind in a weaker position than before.[63]

By 17 March 1954 Shuckburgh was even more disillusioned about Churchill's likely motive for continuing to seek a summit with the Soviets: 'this mirage may give him an additional excuse for not resigning.'[64] And even John Young, whose major work on Churchill published in 1996 showed little sign of scepticism, flirted with similar views in the course of an article published eight years earlier:

The Prime Minister may not have sought detente purely in order to make a reputation as a great peace-maker, but there was a degree of vanity behind his interest in easing tensions with Russia and this blinded him to some of the problems with his policy – particularly the reaction his ideas would have on Adenauer's policy in Germany and on the French governments's efforts to secure EDC ... After mid-1953 he claimed that it was the hope of reaching a *modus vivendi* with Moscow that kept him in office, but it is difficult to know whether this was a reason or a rationalization for remaining as premier. In such an extraordinary character as Churchill the interplay of personal motives, political realism and visionary idealism was doubtless complex.[65]

That Kissinger abstained from similar speculation is, then, puzzling. But perhaps his own years in high office served to make him less cynical about fellow statesmen than would have been the case had he remained a mere academic historian.

Back in London, Churchill entered 1954 with shrinking hopes of putting off for much longer his overdue resignation. Yet he was to find one resourse after another that enabled him to survive through another entire year. The first respite came as a result of Eden being placated by representing Great Britain at the four-power meeting of foreign ministers held in Berlin during January and February to discuss the future of Germany and Austria. This meeting produced no noteworthy result. And for Churchill there was the further disappointment that none of the foreign ministers urged the merits of an early summit of heads of government. But a meaningful consolation for the Prime Minister was that Eden and Molotov agreed to try to arrange a second meeting of foreign ministers initially to address the problem of Korea. But this was soon transformed, against Dulles's better judgement, into a conference on Indochina – which was entering an acute phase. The difficulty was that to be meaningful, it would be necessary that Communist China's Foreign Minister should attend – something repugnant to the United States which continued to recognise the Nationalist regime in Taipei. In the event, however, the Americans relented once they had accepted that a collapse of French authority in Indochina was imminent. Hence between April and July, fortunately for Churchill, Eden was again fully occupied in stage-managing a protracted conference in Geneva.[66]

The conference resulted in July 1954 in a compromise which was largely seen as the outcome of the exercise of great diplomatic skills on the part of Eden. Indochina was effectively partitioned into four separate states: Communist North Vietnam; West-leaning South Vietnam; neutral Cambodia; and neutral Laos. The Americans were unhappy with this but had not felt able to intervene militarily without support from their major allies. That this support had not been forthcoming was due in large measure to a negative line adopted by the British Cabinet. And this in turn was mainly attributable to Eden's preference for a compromise arrangement. Churchill was at times somewhat inclined to urge understanding of the American view[67] – something that can only surprise those who see him as an apostle of *détente* rather than an unreconstructed anti-Communist. But his standing with his colleagues was no longer such that he could hope successfully to confront Eden on an issue of this importance – especially as the Chiefs of Staff and most of his Cabinet colleagues had consistently shown over a period of years their strong conviction that a general war with China could escalate to a global war involving the Soviet Union. Hence Churchill proved willing on 20 July 1954 to congratulate Eden on his role in achieving the Geneva compromise – stating that preventing a wider war had been the 'supreme objective'.[68] But maybe this was not particularly strongly felt on the Prime Minister's part. For he himself seemingly never really believed there was much risk of the problems of Indochina leading to such a 'wider war'.

More evidence that Eden had now achieved dominance over most matters concerning British foreign policy also emerged at the same period when the United States became actively involved in Guatemala to mastermind the overthrow of an allegedly Marxist regime. According to Colville, on June 28 he heard that the Prime Minister had been 'holding forth about the Guatemala revolution ... making the Foreign Secretary look rather small in argument (the F.S. being all for caution and the P.M. being all for supporting the U.S. in their encouragement of the rebels and their hostility to the Communist Guatemalan regime)'.[69] All the same it was Eden and not Churchill who had the last word. For Great Britain abstained on the issue when it came before the United Nations. (This was of course also an interesting episode because it reminds us of a similar disagreement between the two men over the much more important matter of the future of Spain in 1944 and it thus provides additional evidence that even in the closing stages of his career, Churchill still remained at root more of an anti-Communist than Eden.)

What Churchill was able to do in the summer of 1954 was to some extent to outmanoevre Eden on the matter of summitry. First, he succeeded in persuading Eisenhower that they should have a meeting in Washington. The Prime Minister proposed to 'survey the whole question of sharing information about the [h-] bomb' and to discuss the crisis in Indochina[70] – and given the sensitivity of both topics the French were not to be invited. No doubt Eisenhower and Dulles, in agreeing to this, hoped that Churchill would be more amenable than Eden on the Indochina issue. But as Eden insisted on accompanying his chief to the Washington conversations – which lasted from 25 to 29 June – the Americans were soon to discover that power with respect to this matter had effectively moved from Number Ten to the Foreign Office. Once in Washington, however, the duplicitous Churchill quickly revealed that his main interest lay of course in another direction: could he even at this late stage win over Eisenhower to his heads of government summit project? The answer turned out, after some wavering, to be a rather predictable negative so far as any American participation was concerned. But, as on previous occasions, the Americans politely tolerated Churchill's talk of possibly seeking a meeting à deux with Malenkov. On the way back to Great Britain on the Queen Elizabeth Churchill clearly realised that the time had thus now come to play his last ace. He accordingly decided to send a personal telegram directly to Moscow proposing an Anglo-Soviet summit. He thus by-passed the Cabinet – informing only Eden and Butler. Eden at first was strongly opposed – as might have been expected. But in the end he reluctantly acquiesced in Churchill's action. He later claimed, however, that he had made it clear to the Prime Minister that he expected the Cabinet to be consulted before any message was sent to Moscow – a condition which was not to be met. Shuckburgh recorded in his diary that everyone in the Foreign Office 'feels that A.E. [Eden] has made a disgraceful compact with the old man'.[71] And it does seem that Eden was indeed promised by Churchill that the handover of power would take place in September after the proposed meeting with Malenkov.[72]

Churchill's *fait accompli* caused deep anger in the Cabinet. Salisbury in particular held that the Prime Minister's action had been 'unconstitutional' – whatever that might have meant in a country which does not have a constitution. A series of fraught Cabinet meetings ensued. According to the diary of Harry Crookshank, the Lord Privy Seal, Churchill on 8 July was 'very shame faced' and 'he knew he had done wrong'. But by the 23rd, according to the same source, the Prime Minister was in a more combative mood on the issue: 'terrible Cabinet … Bobbety [Salisbury] threatened to resign – also Winston.'[73] Churchill in fact urged on this occasion that he be allowed to offer Molotov possible dates and places for a meeting with the Soviet leaders. But this led to renewed dispute about the way in which the Prime Minister had already effectively pre-empted the decision by his earlier behaviour. He then offered what seems to have been a prepared statement to his colleagues that could have formed the basis of a public appeal to the nation in the event that he did not get his way and had to resign. According to the Cabinet minutes

> The Prime Minister said that when, in the course of the return journey from his visit to Washington, he had reached the conclusion that the time was ripe for suggesting such a meeting, he had thought it better that he should himself take the responsibility for making the first informal approach to the Soviet Government. He had thought it would be preferable that the Cabinet should not be in any way committed at that stage, and that he should first explore the possibility on a purely personal basis. He had thought, and still thought, that it was perfectly proper for him to do this without prior consultation with the Cabinet. For the idea of such a meeting was not novel. It had been mentioned in his speech to the House of Commons on 11th May, 1953. More recently in the debate in the House of Commons on 8th April, 1954, the Government had accepted an Opposition motion welcoming 'an immediate initiative' by the Government to bring about a meeting between the Prime Minister

and the Head of Administrations of the United States and the Soviet Union. The Prime Minister circulated a paper containing some extracts from speeches made in the debate, and drew particular attention to the Foreign Secretary's statement, in winding up, that when the Government thought there was the least chance of such a meeting being fruitful they would not hesitate to go for it. In the light of this it had seemed natural that he should explore the possibility of proceeding with a project which, as his colleagues well knew, has been in his mind for some time past; and he was not prepared to admit that there was anything unconstitutional in the course which he had taken in making his preliminary approach to M. Molotov on a purely personal basis. Before sending his message he had discussed the matter with the Foreign Secretary and had gained the impression that, while he would not have initiated this project, he did not disapprove it. If he had disapproved, he could have insisted that the matter should be referred to the Cabinet.[74]

Even the most fervent admirers of Churchill must surely find it difficult to defend the line taken here. First, in claiming that there was no novelty involved he deliberately conflated two things: the possibility of a summit at which the United States would be a willing participant and a bilateral Soviet–British summit from which the Americans would exclude themselves. As everyone in the Cabinet Room knew, the facts were that the latter was what he was now promoting and this had never been approved by the Cabinet and had never been canvassed by any Government spokesman in Parliament. But, above all, Churchill ruthlessly misrepresented Eden's position. For, as the Foreign Secretary himself had to tell the Cabinet, that while willing to aquiesce in the face of the Prime Minister's insistence, he had had no belief that a bilateral summit would prove fruitful and, moreover, 'it had been his view that the Cabinet should be consulted before the message [to Moscow] was sent, and he had made this clear to the Prime Minister'. This led on, not for the first time, to acrimony concerning whether Butler should or should not have called a Cabinet to discuss the matter while Churchill and Eden had still been at sea.[75] With the Cabinet of 23 July thus brought to disarray, resignations might easily have occurred. Indeed, Churchill himself may actually have been trying to manipulate the situation so that he could quit in such a way as to leave his colleagues, including Eden, greatly discredited. For it seems that he fantasised around this time about the possibility of forming a 'national' coalition government with Labour support – something Labour's Shadow Cabinet and National Executive

Committee, with their bitter memories of 1931, would surely not have taken seriously on an issue as insubstantial as a possible visit by Churchill to Moscow to discuss nothing in particular. But if Churchill was seeking a 'showdown' with his colleagues on 23 July he was frustrated by Eden, who rather unconvincingly argued that no decision should be reached until it was seen to what extent the Soviets responded to the outcome of the Geneva Conference with hostile propaganda against the West in general, and against the Americans in particular, in the light of the latter's evident discomfiture at the compromises that had been involved. The Cabinet hastily backed Eden – leaving Churchill further time for reflection. In the event, Malenkov duly obliged Eden by calling for a conference involving all European powers, the United States and a Chinese observer – a transparent and clumsy attempt to isolate the Americans and to delay West German rearmament. The entire Cabinet, with Churchill's acquiescence, was thus able to save face by claiming that in the new situation any bilateral summit would be inappropriate.[76]

Now Churchill's career was effectively over. But even so he found another pretext for delay: he would stay to receive public tributes on the occasion of his 80th birthday on 30 November. His colleagues could scarcely refuse. The formalities involved were agreeable enough. But Churchill managed, perhaps inadvertently, to provoke renewed controversy concerning his attitue towards the Soviet Union just a week before his birthday. For on 23 November, in a speech in his Woodford constituency, he decided to reminisce about his views in the spring of 1945. He stated that he had sent a telegram to Bernard Montgomery, then British Commander, to order him 'to be careful in collecting the German arms, to stack them so that they could be easily issued again to the German soldiers whom we should have to work with if the Soviet advance continued'.[77] It soon emerged that no record of this telegram could be found. Churchill was then forced to concede in the House of Commons that his memory could have been at fault. But he maintained that the telegram, even if it had never existed, was not 'contrary to my thoughts'.[78] This was of course credible enough. But what Churchill did not satisfactorily explain was why he had deliberately reminisced along these lines in November 1954. It certainly cannot have strengthened the hands of Soviet 'doves', if any existed, anxious to respond positively to Churchill's apparent desire for 'easement'. For it followed just a few months after the publication of the diatribe against the Soviet Union that had been such a notable feature of the last volume of his memoirs of the Second World War – provocatively entitled *Triumph and Tragedy*. All in all, it was as if in his increasing senility he had momentarily forgotten that he was now supposed to be an advocate of a relaxation of tension. But of course, if his main motive for adopting this posture had been to prolong his time in Number Ten, there was no longer much point in continuing the charade now that his early eviction from office had become a certainty. By 7 December, however, he was confusingly back to his summitry obsession – telegraphing plaintively to Eisenhower:

> I still hope we may reach a top level meeting with the new regime in Russia and that you and I may both be present ... It is in the hope of helping forward such a meeting that I am remaining in harness longer than I wished or planned. I hope you will continue to look to it as a goal in seeking which we could not lose anything and might gain an easier and safer co-existence – which is a lot. When I had my last audience with The Queen she spoke of the pleasure with which she would welcome a State visit by you to London. This might be combined in any way convenient with a top level meeting.[79]

Eisenhower's reply was predictably discouraging:

> I have always felt, as you know, that it would be a mistake for you and me to participate in a meeting which was either essentially social or exploratory. A social meeting would merely give a false impression of accord which, in our free countries, would probably make it more difficult to get parliamentary support for needed defense appropriations. Within the captive world it would give the impression that we condone the present state of affairs. And if there are to be exploratory talks, should they not be carried out by our Foreign Ministers, so that Heads of Government would come in only if some really worthwhile agreement is in likely prospect?
>
> The latter, I fear, is not an early possibility ... So, I am bound to say that, while I would like to be more optimistic, I cannot see that a top-level meeting is anything which I can inscribe on my schedule for any predictable date.[80]

Thus Churchill entered 1955, the terrible year in which he would have to retire. Soon he was virtually forced by Macmillan and others privately to name a date. This was fixed for 6 April – though at first none could be certain that he would stick to it. His last serious possibility of postponement was blocked, however, at the end of February when a farewell dinner to be attended by the Queen was privately arranged for 4 April. But to the end he continued to thrash around in the desperate hope that a miracle would occur.[81] Would the Cabinet, for example, not want him to stay on until May when Eisenhower was considering a possible visit to Europe to Commemorate V-E Day with maybe some chance of a meeting with a Soviet leader? Naturally his colleagues were not interested. And so on 6 April 1955 Churchill finally quit.

One of Eden's first moves after taking over was not without irony. For, having usually resisted Churchill's summitry designs, he now decided, after calling an early general election, to seek an increase in the Conservative vote by, if possible, arranging the announcement of a four-power summit at which he would represent Great Britain if he survived as Prime Minister. Eager to see the Conservatives re-elected, Eisenhower fell in with Eden's wishes. Nikita Khrushchev and Nikolai Bulganin, who had replaced Malenkov earlier in 1955, proved willing to attend on behalf of the Soviet Union. And naturally the French were eager to be represented. With the British Conservatives re-elected with an increased majority on 26 May the way was thus open for Eden to attend the Geneva summit of July 1955. How did Churchill react? He said pointedly to Moran on 11 May: 'Anthony has changed his tune about top-level talks; he is pressing for them now, though it was he and Bobbity [Salisbury] who were so much against them when I wanted them. I am quite cool about it all.'[82] To Macmillan he had spoken in an even more sour vein on 5 May: 'How much more attractive a top-level meeting seems when one has reached the top.'[83] And when the summit actually took place Churchill seems to have taken little serious interest in the proceedings. But his feelings can easily be imagined when he received this transparently insincere message from Eisenhower on 15 July 1955 on the summit's eve:

> As you know I feel sure that the Western nations could not, with self-respect, have earlier consented to a Four Power Summit Meeting. Yet I cannot escape a feeling of sadness that its delay brought about by the persistent hostile Soviet attitude towards NATO has operated to prevent your personal attendance at the meeting.[84]

It needs only to be added that the Geneva summit achieved nothing of a concrete nature and that Churchill made no notable public proclamations on the subject before or during it; nor did he subsequently call for further summits. It is tempting of course to argue from this that here is decisive proof that Churchill had no enduring interest in summitry and its supposed merits once it was of no further domestic political utility to him. But that may be unfair.

For by now he was over 80 and in rapid mental decline. If he did not continue to crusade for summits nor did he continue to crusade against Communism. In short, though he did not die until January 1965, his political life was effectively over. And he wrote no further memoirs after finally leaving office. Historians can therefore only base their judgments on his record in the Cold War on his periods as Leader of the Opposition and as Prime Minister. They appear unlikely to arrive at a consensus on the subject.

NOTES

1   Moran, *Winston Churchill*, p. 545. See also Gilbert, *'Never Despair'*, pp. 635–6, for similar thoughts expressed in Paris on 10 September 1951.
2   The insight that Eden actually saw himself during the Eisenhower Presidency as primarily engaged in 'containing' the United States is to be found in Kevin Ruane, '"Containing America": Aspects of British Foreign Policy and the Cold War in South-East Asia, 1951–54', *Diplomacy and Statecraft*, VII, 1996.
3   Eisenhower to Churchill, 9 February 1954, in Peter G. Boyle (ed.), *The Churchill–Eisenhower Correspondence, 1953–1955*, Chapel Hill, North Carolina, 1990, p. 121.
4   Eden minute, 2 March 1954, in Ruane, '"Containing America"', p. 161; and Churchill to Eisenhower, 9 March 1954, in Boyle (ed.), *The Churchill–Eisenhower Correspondence*, p. 124.
5   See above, p. 156.
6   Conservative and Unionist Central Office, *General Election, 1950: Campaign Guide*, London, 1950, p. 16.
7   *The Times*, 15 February 1950.
8   Halifax Diary, 18 March 1946, in Ponting, *Churchill*, p. 777.
9   *Hansard*, 28 March 1950, vol. 473, col. 199.
10 *Ibid.*, 30 November 1950, vol. 481, col. 1435.
11 *Ibid.*, col. 1344.
12 *Ibid.*, 14 December 1950, vol. 482, col. 1376.
13 Churchill to Eden, 8 January 1951, Eden Papers, in John Charmley, *Churchill's Grand Alliance: The Anglo-American Special Relationship, 1940–57*, London, 1995, p. 239.
14 Gilbert, *'Never Despair'*, p. 605 n.
15 Young, *Winston Churchill's Last Campaign*, p. 40.
16 Kissinger, *Diplomacy*, p. 507.
17 Coral Bell, *Negotiation from Strength: A Study in the Politics of Power*, London, 1962, p. 59. See also *Hansard*, 30 July 1952, vol. 504, cols 1272–1403, 1491–1612.
18 Robert Rhodes James, *Anthony Eden*, London, 1986, pp. 343, 358.
19 United States Department of State, *Papers relating to the Foreign Relations of the United States, 1952–1954: Vol. VI: Western Europe and Canada*, Washington, DC, 1986, p. 849.
20 David McCullough, *Truman*, New York, 1992, p. 875.
21 See Young, *Winston Churchill's Last Campaign*, pp. 75–6; and Carlton,

Anthony Eden, pp. 302–4.

22 *Hansard*, 21 October 1952, vol. 505, col. 863.
23 Minute by Churchill, 12 July 1952, FO 371/99581/409, PRO, in Peter Lowe, *Containing the Cold War in East Asia: British Policies towards Japan, China and Korea, 1948–53*, Manchester, 1997, p. 253.
24 PREM 11/369, PRO, in Ruane, '"Containing America"', p. 147.
25 PREM 11/112, PRO, in Lowe, *Containing the Cold War in East Asia*, p. 246.
26 FO 371/105180, PRO, in Ruane, '"Containing America"', p. 156.
27 Minute by Churchill, 3 September 1952, PREM 11/301, PRO, in *ibid.*, p. 254.
28 Evelyn Shuckburgh, *Descent to Suez: Diaries, 1951–56*, London, 1986, p. 66.
29 See *ibid.*, *passim*.
30 See Dutton, *Anthony Eden*, ch 8.
31 See above, p. 159.
32 Colville, *The Fringes of Power*, p. 654.
33 Young, *Winston Churchill's Last Campaign*, p. 110.
34 Churchill to London, 8 January 1953, PREM 11/422, PRO, in Gilbert, '*Never Despair*', p. 790.
35 Eisenhower Diary, 6 January 1953, in Carlton, *Anthony Eden*, p. 333.
36 Moran, *Winston Churchill*, p. 403.
37 Kissinger, *Diplomacy*, p. 511.
38 Churchill to Eisenhower, 11 March 1953, PREM 11/422, PRO, in Gilbert, '*Never Despair*', p. 806.
39 Churchill to William Strang, 19 June 1953, FO 371/1083842/124, PRO, quoted in M. Steven Fish, 'After Stalin's Death: The Anglo-American Debate Over a New Cold War', *Diplomatic History*, X, 1986, p. 341.
40 Churchill to Salisbury, 2 July 1953, FO 371/105508/626, PRO, in Lowe, *Containing the Cold War in East Asia*, p. 259.
41 Kissinger, *Diplomacy*, p. 507.
42 Churchill to Eisenhower, 21 April 1953, in Boyle (ed.), *The Churchill–Eisenhower Correspondence*, p. 46.
43 Eisenhower to Churchill, 25 April 1953, in *ibid.*, p. 47.
44 Eisenhower to Eden, 6 May 1955, PREM 11/893, PRO.
45 *Hansard*, 20 April 1953, vol. 514, col. 650.
46 Dixon Minute, 3 May 1953, Avon Papers, FO 800/821, PRO.
47 Strang Minute, 4 May 1953, *ibid*. It should be noted that during Churchill's final term he appears to have wished to do little to keep the traditions of the Franco-British entente in good repair and most French leaders were similarly unenthusiastic. See Maurice Vaisse, 'Churchill and France', 1951–55, in Parker (ed.), *Winston Churchill*.
48 *Hansard*, 11 May 1953, vol. 515, cols 897–8.
49 Bell, *Negotiation From Strength*, p. 102.
50 *Ibid.* The author (in n.2) lists five further Senators who spoke critically in the Senate on 14 May 1953 against Churchill's initiative.
51 *Hansard*, 21 May 1953, vol. 515, cols 2262–3.
52 Dixon Diary, 3 May 1953, in Carlton, *Anthony Eden*, p. 328.
53 *The Times*, 10 November 1953.
54 Colville, *The Fringes of Power*, p. 683.
55 Gilbert, '*Never Despair*', p. 923.
56 For the EDC aspect of the Bermuda Conference see Young, *Winston Churchill's Last Campaign*, pp. 227–8. See also John W. Young, 'Churchill, the

Russians and the Western Alliance: The Three-Power Conference at Bermuda, December 1953', *The English Historical Review*, CI, 1986.

57   Minute by William Strang, 19 May 1953, FO 371/103660, PRO, in Hans-Peter Schwarz, 'Churchill and Adenauer', in Parker (ed.), *Winston Churchill*, p. 181. For further evidence that in May 1953 Churchill might have been willing at least in principle to countenance German unification, even on the basis of neutralisation, see Saki Dockrill, *Britain's Policy for West German Rearmament, 1950–1955*, Cambridge, 1991, pp. 124–6.

58   Livingston Merchant Recollections, Columbia University Oral Project, New York City, in Carlton, *Anthony Eden*, p. 336.

59   Churchill to Eden, 6 December 1953, PREM 11/618, PRO. This important minute does not appear in Gilbert, *'Never Despair'*.

60   Moran, *Winston Churchill*, p. 505.

61   Kissinger, *Diplomacy*, p. 508.

62   Lowe, *Containing the Cold War in East Asia*, p. 257.

63   Shuckburgh, *Descent to Suez*, pp. 91–2.

64   *Ibid.*, p. 149.

65   John W. Young, 'Cold War and Detente with Moscow', in John W. Young (ed.), *The Foreign Policy of Churchill's Peacetime Administration, 1951–1955*, Leicester, 1988, p. 75. The same author fails to develop this line of analysis in his *Winston Churchill's Last Campaign*.

66   For details on the origins of the Geneva Conference see Kevin Ruane, 'Anthony Eden, British Diplomacy and the Origins of the Geneva Conference of 1954', *The Historical Journal*, XXXVII, 1994, pp. 153–72.

67   For details on Churchill's hesitant search for 'a meeting of minds with the Americans' over Indochina and Eden's resistance to this see Geoffrey Warner, 'The Settlement of the Indochina War', in Young (ed.), *The Foreign Policy of Churchill's Peacetime Administration*, p. 252.

68   Churchill to Eisenhower, 13 May 1954, in Boyle (ed.), *The Churchill–Eisenhower Correspondence*, p. 141.

69   Colville, *The Fringes of Power*, p. 694. For Eden's perspective on the Guatemalan issue see Anthony Eden, *The Eden Memoirs: Full Circle*, London, 1960, pp. 133–8.

70   PREM 11/650, PRO, in Ruane, '"Containing America"', p. 168.

71   Evelyn Shuckburgh Diary, 6 July 1954, in Carlton, *Anthony Eden*, p. 353. This sentence does not appear in Shuckburgh, *Descent to Suez*.

72   Rhodes James, *Anthony Eden*, p. 381.

73   Crookshank Diary, 8 and 23 July 1954, Bodleian Library, Oxford, in Henry Pelling, *Churchill's Peacetime Ministry, 1951–55*, London, 1997, pp. 127, 133. See also Young, *Winston Churchill's Last Campaign*, pp. 273–5.

74   Cabinet Minutes, 23 July 1954, CAB 128/27, PRO.

75   *Ibid.*

76   *Ibid.*, 23 and 26 July 1954; and Young, *Winston Churchill's Last Campaign*, pp. 283–6.

77   *The Times*, 24 November 1954.

78   *Hansard*, 1 December 1954, vol. 535, col. 174. For more details see Arthur L. Smith, *Churchill's German Army: Wartime Strategy and Cold War Politics, 1943–1947*, Beverly Hills, California, 1977, *passim*; Gilbert, *'Never Despair'*, pp. 1078–81; and Young, *Winston Churchill's Last Campaign*, pp. 294–5.

79   Churchill to Eisenhower, 7 December 1954, in Boyle (ed.), *The Churchill–*

Eisenhower Correspondence, p. 180.

80 Eisenhower to Churchill, 14 December 1954, in *ibid.*, pp. 181–2.

81 For further details see, for example, Gilbert, 'From Yalta to Bermuda and Beyond'.

82 Moran, *Winston Churchill*, p. 655.

83 Harold Macmillan, *Tides of Fortune, 1945–1955*, London, 1969, p. 587.

84 Eisenhower to Churchill, 15 July 1955, in Boyle (ed.), *The Churchill–Eisenhower Correspondence*, p. 213.

Conclusion

'It is a riddle wrapped in a mystery inside an enigma.' The writer began this volume began by quoting Churchill's famous verdict on the Soviet Union and by speculating that the Soviets must have felt at times much the same way about him. In these pages an attempt has been made to provide a 'solution' to the 'enigma' concerning Churchill. But it is not one that will appeal to everyone. For those who wish to do so will certainly find ammunition here to make the case that Churchill's approach to the Soviet Union and Communism was throughout essentially self-serving and hence frequently opportunist and insincere. Others will substitute 'serving the interest of his country' for 'self-serving', while not denying his opportunism and insincerity. In other words, they may in effect echo what Churchill himself added to his 'enigma' description of the Soviet Union: 'but perhaps there is a key. That key is Russian national interest.'[1] Yet other readers may see Churchill as simply bewilderingly and inexplicably inconsistent while being, at least most of the time, fundamentally sincere in the line he took about the Soviet Union: in other words for them the 'enigma' will remain 'unsolved'. But those who find themselves in general sympathy with the present work will reject all these broad approaches. For the conclusion has been reached that ideologically-based anti-Sovietism and anti-Communism were Churchill's most abiding obsession for some forty years and that apparent somersaults were mere digressions and often only tactical in character. In short, the extremism of his anti-Soviet utterances and behaviour at various points, separated by great distances of time, seem to be incompatible with any other explanation – even after making every allowance for the fact that his was a mind of great sophistication that readily recognised the complex nature of the global developments with which he was concerned. During 1919 and 1920, for example, he became almost demented on the subject of Bolshevism and thereby placed his political career in obvious jeopardy – with his patron Lloyd George showing great forebearance in the face of much provocation. Interestingly, Churchill's call for resistance to Germany in the late 1930s was in comparison measured and statesmanlike in tone; and his use of imagery concerning the Nazis was relatively restrained – with no references, for example, to baboons or vampires. And he expressly stated in 1937 that he would 'not pretend that, if I had to choose between Communism and Naziism, I would choose Communism'. Again, during 1948 he imprudently demanded in effect the initiation of a preventive war against the Soviet Union at a time when even most American 'hawks' could see that the necessary democratic support for such a contrived 'showdown' would have been absent in every Western country. And in 1949 he told a New York City audience, still no doubt reeling from the recent Holocaust revelations, that Soviet Communism was 'quite as wicked but much more formidable than Hitler'.[2] Whatever else it may have been, this kind of reckless conduct was surely not that of a mere self-serving opportunist.

Why, then, did Churchill hate Communism in this visceral fashion? Probably the most convincing short explanation he ever gave was one he presented to the House of Commons on 8 July 1920:

> I yield to no one in my detestation of Bolshevism and of the revolu-tionary violence which precedes it ... my hatred of Bolshevism and Bolsheviks is not founded on their silly system of economics, or their absurd doctrine of an impossible equality. It arises from the bloody and devastating terrorism which they practice in every land into which they have broken, and by which alone their criminal regime can be sustained.[3]

He further believed that the Bolsheviks were irreconcilable enemies of civilisation itself. As he wrote on 22 June 1919: 'Theirs is a war against civilised society which can never end ... between them and such order of civilisation as we have been able to build up since the dawn of history there can, as Lenin rightly proclaims, be neither truce nor pact.'[4] Again, on 20 January 1920 he prepared a draft memorandum for Lloyd George which was not actually sent but which included this passage: 'I regard the Bolshevik danger as the most formidable that has ever threatened civilisation. It is a movement which will deluge in blood every country to which it spreads, and if it triumphed it would extinguish, perhaps for long centuries, the whole prosperity and genius of mankind.'[5] In June 1940 he also claimed to see a Nazi German victory over Great Britain as threatening the world with a return to 'a new dark age'.[6] But somehow the language he employed, even at a time when hyperbole was surely to be expected, seems more restrained than that which he frequently used about Communism throughout four decades. Just five months earlier, for example, he had said that if the Soviets quenched the 'light of freedom' in Finland, 'it might well herald a return to the Dark Ages, when every vestige of human progress during two thousand years would be engulfed'.[7] This was of course at a point when Great Britain was at war with Nazi Germany and when the Soviet Union was neutral between them. And we have noted the apparent evidence of his somewhat unheroic pliablity during War Cabinet discussions about a possible compromise peace with Germany in May 1940 during the Dunkirk crisis. Finally, he seemingly confirmed in 1949 that he saw Nazism as having been less threatening to civilisation *per se* when he stated: 'Hitler had only the Herrenvolk stuff and anti-Semitism. Well, somebody said about that – a good starter, but a bad stayer.'[8]

How was it, then, that Churchill seemed to stray so strikingly from the anti-Communist fold between 1938 and 1945 and again between 1953 and 1955? The latter is in some respects easier to explain than the former. For it was an apparent aberration which took place at a time of relative international tranquillity, at least in comparison with the earlier period, and one which was seen at the time as likely to have no seminal consequences. It appears to have been largely motivated by a desire to postpone a retirement that was being regularly pressed upon him by Conservative Cabinet colleagues, eager to see Eden established in Number Ten before a general election was judged to be imminent. In any case, Churchill's project was essentially lacking in substance. He held, as he put it at a news conference in Washington in June 1954, that 'jaw-jaw is better than war-war'.[9] But this had not been a line he had taken *vis-à-vis* Nazi Germany during the late 1930s. And in October 1948 he had told the Conservative Party Conference:

> I will not encourge you with false hopes of a speedy, friendly settlement with Russia. It may be that some formula will be found, or some artificial compromise effected, which will be hailed as a solution or a deliverance. But the fundamental danger and antagonisms will remain. The 14 men in the Kremlin, who rule 300 million human beings with an arbitrary authority never possessed by any Tsar since Ivan the Terrible, and who are now holding down nearly half Europe by Communist methods, these men dread the friendship of the free, civilized world almost as much as they would its hostility … we should not delude ourselves with the vain expectation of a change of heart in the ruling forces of Communist Russia.[10]

Now in the early 1950s he appeared to have been converted to a contrary evaluation. At the same time, however, he did not expect or even advocate that the West should make any concessions to the Soviets and their allies on any of the great issues of the day such as German rearmament, nuclear and conventional arms control, Indochina and Formosa. Nor were any important surrenders from the Soviet side considered by him to be in prospect. It was as if Neville Chamberlain had called for a series of meetings with Hitler in 1938 without either party having anything to offer the other. No wonder, then, that the Americans found Churchill's approach during the early 1950s unattractive: summitry for summitry's sake would do no good and might actually do harm in that it might lead the French to delay further their acceptance of German rearmament (which Churchill of course fervently claimed to favour at the West's Bermuda Conference of 1953). But Eisenhower seems to have concluded that this was a case of the primacy of *Innenpolitik* (domestic politics). Indeed, as has been seen, he rather scornfully indicated to Churchill that he had guessed that the Prime Minister needed to seek 'a personal contact' with the Soviets 'for some special local reason'.[11] Some later analysts, for example Henry Kissinger, Sir Michael Howard and John Young, have been rather less clear-sighted. For they have solemnly depicted Churchill as to some degree a thoughtful precursor of the kind of *détente* with the Soviets that came about in the early 1970s. Kissinger saw Churchill as sharing 'the reasoning behind the later detente policy of Nixon'; Howard prepared a lecture on the subject which he later turned into an article entitled 'Churchill: Prophet of Detente'; and Young wrote an entire book, entitled *Winston Churchill's Last Campaign*, in which he consistently assumed that his subject was indeed engaged in a genuine struggle to create world 'easement'.[12] In reality, however, some meaningful relaxation of tension in the Cold War only proved feasible in the era of Nixon, Brezhnev, Brandt and Kissinger himself precisely because 'jaw-jaw' was accompanied by some concrete agreements of the kind that Churchill evidently did *not* have in view. These included the First Strategic Arms Limitation Talks Treaty (SALT I) between the two superpowers; and various European agreements arranged by Brandt that brought mutual recognition of the two German states, the opening of West German diplomatic and trading relations with various states in Eastern Europe and increasing contact between West and East Berlin. (It should be noted, however, that those aspects of so-called global *détente* between the superpowers during the 1970s which were *not* based on precise agreements soon broke down amid mutual recriminations over Angola and later over Afghanistan.) And similarly the enormous improvement in East–West relations that materialised in the late 1980s was based not on any personal chemistry between Gorbachev and Presidents Ronald Reagan and George Bush but on a series of Soviet surrenders on matters of central significance symbolised, above all, by Moscow's acquiescence in the pulling down of the Berlin Wall and in the disbanding of the Warsaw Treaty Organisation. The fact is that Churchill at no time had expectations that developments of this radical kind would occur in his era. This point was indeed grasped by Kissinger when he wrote: 'In the 1950s Churchill never spelled out the details of the global settlement he was urging.' But Kissinger thought he understood what motivated Churchill in that period: 'True to British tradition, Churchill sought a more tolerable coexistence with the Soviet Union by way of near-permanent negotiations.'[13] In reality, however, Churchill was not much of an optimist about the likely benefits of negotiating with, or even attempting 'co-existence' with Moscow. Indeed, he remained privately convinced that the Soviet Union still aimed at spreading Communism throughout continental Europe – hence his remarkable memorandum of 6 December 1953 expressing acute fear of the consequences he expected to follow if the Americans opted for a 'peripheral defence' strategy. And, most strikingly, as has been seen, the half-American Churchill indicated to Moran on 4 May 1954 that 'if he were an American' he would sympathise with those in Washington who wanted to present their 'demands' to the Kremlin[14] – evidence that throws into question his supposedly genuine belief in the possible benefits of 'easement' for the West as a whole. In short, Churchill's straying from the anti-Communist fold during the 1950s was more apparent than real and based almost entirely on domestic pressures concerning Great Britain's particular vulnerability to nuclear attack and on his own career interests. His senility may also have played a part – but mainly in providing the reason why, in the absence of the prospect of summitry, Churchill expected his colleagues to insist on his immediate retirement.

Much more seminal and seemingly also more sincere was Churchill's apparent apostasy between 1938 and 1945. Certainly he was well aware that his co-operation with the Soviets during much of this period had indeed the appearance, in Colville's words, of bowing down in the House of Rimmon.[15] Yet he claimed that his new obsession was simply to see the destruction of Nazi Germany. But, if so, was it the Nazi or the German component that dominated his thinking?

On one view it was ideological hostility to the Nazis that caused Churchill to swing away from anti-Sovietism during the 1930s. The difficulty with this explanation is that he was in no sense a consistent enemy of other forms of right-wing authoritarianism. Indeed, as has been seen, he himself may even have come close to getting involved in something of the sort for Great Britain in 1920 when, Henry Wilson, Trenchard and others were in despair at Lloyd George's alleged appeasement of the extreme Left, both at home and abroad. But apart from that affair, he had made no secret of his admiration for Italian Fascism: in 1927 he had praised it for having 'rendered a service to the whole world ' and for 'providing the necessary antidote to the Russian poison'.[16] Likewise, during the Spanish Civil War his sympathies lay with the rebels who were being supported by Fascist Italy and Nazi Germany; and in 1944 and then again at the Potsdam Conference he strove successfully to prevent both his own compatriots and his allies taking steps to destabilise Franco's regime which had shrewdly stayed neutral during the Second World War. None of this is to suggest that Churchill was any kind of convinced Fascist. On the contrary, he wholeheartedly favoured British-style Parliamentary Democracy wherever it could be found and sustained. But whereas Neville Chamberlain, at least prior to September 1939, appears to have considered all variants of Fascism as lesser evils than Soviet Communism, Churchill is usually assumed to have seen the Nazis from the outset as in a category quite distinct from other types of Fascists, as being as bad or worse than the Soviet Communists and hence deserving of his unequivocal hostility. But doubts about this deserve to be considered. True, in June 1934 he wrote of Nazi Germany that 'we are confronted with the monstrosity of the totalitarian state'. But he qualified this by adding: 'A despotism has been erected *only less frightful* than the Russian nightmare. Its aims are different, its forms are opposite, but its methods are the same.'[17] [Italics added.] Then, in 1935, he wrote a brief essay on Hitler, republished two years later in a volume entitled *Great Contemporaries*. It was certainly critical in tone. But Churchill strikingly failed to denounce Hitler in the unequivocal language he had used about Lenin and the other early Bolsheviks. On the contrary, he wrote of those who had met Hitler 'finding a highly competent, cool, well-informed functionary with an agreeable manner, a disarming smile, and few have been unaffected by a subtle personal magnetism'. Churchill also acknowledged that 'he [Hitler], and the ever-increasing legions who worked with him, certainly showed' during the Nazis' rise to power 'in their patriotic ardour and love of country, that there was nothing that they would not do or dare, no sacrifice of limb or liberty that they would not make themselves or inflict on their opponents'. But this was as far as Churchill was prepared to go. Above all, he was silent about the Nazis' role as a provider 'of the necessary antidote to the Russian poison', which had been his enthusiatic verdict on Italian Fascism. He was silent, too, about the ideological content of Nazism. What Churchill did again emphasise, however, was an essentially non-ideological objection to Hitler and the Nazis, namely that they were guilty of 'frightful' conduct. Hitler's rise to power had, he stated, been marked by 'frightful methods'. And Hitler in power had 'loosed these frightful evils' associated with 'the Totalitarian State' including the persecution of the Jews of Germany and the cowing of opponents in concentration camps.[18] 'Frightfulness' was actually something Churchill had memorably condemned on a previous occasion: he had told the House of Commons on 8 July 1920 that it was what in essence had been wrong about General Reginald Dyer's conduct during the notorious Amritsar Massacre.[19] The question at issue, then, is whether Churchill thought that the Nazis' 'frightfulness', like that of Great Britain in India in 1920, was something that might presently be repudiated or regretted by the Nazis themselves; or whether he considered Nazi Germany to be simply the incarnation of evil. The evidence suggests that in 1935 at least he was still undecided on this point. 'We cannot tell,' he wrote, 'whether Hitler will be the man who will once again let loose upon the world another war in which civilization will irretrievably succumb, or whether he will go down to history as the man who restored honour and peace of mind to the great Germanic nation and brought it back serene, helpful and strong, to the forefront of the European family circle.'[20] This uncharacteristic tentativeness on Churchill's part thus surely makes it impossible to say that he had at this stage definitely formed a conviction, at least on ideological grounds, that he must be prepared in principle to desert the anti-Communist camp for that of the anti-Nazis. And, as has been seen, the outbreak of the Spanish Civil War in 1936 seemed for a time at least to drive him back towards the thinking of long-standing anti-Communist allies like Tudor. He was clear, above all, that forging Popular Fronts with Communists was likely to be a fatal step for democrats in any kind of domestic politics. As he wrote for the *Evening Standard* of 4 September 1936:

> When we survey all these hideous evils which have come upon the world directly and indirectly through Communism, it is surely necessary to point out how Communism wins its victories. The preliminary to Communist victory is the establishment of what is called the Popular Front. First instal weak, well-meaning Radical or Socialist Governments in office; then spread about the doctrine that all liberal-minded men and all progressives mean the same thing. Thus destroy the resisting powers of patriotism, Conservatism and Liberalism, and finally seize violently the power from enfeebled or puppet hands. Here is the path by which Kerensky led Russia to her doom. Here is the path by which [President Manuel] Azana has brought Spain to her awful plight. Here is the path upon which the feet of reluctant, and now thoroughly alarmed France, have already been set. Here is the path which British high-browed intellectuals or calculating politicians indicate to our own people. The monstrous dogma 'No enemies to the Left' has been the undoing of many famous states. The masses of good-hearted citizens of all classes are assured that all can be happily adjusted in a friendly way and by constitutional means. A facade of respectability covers the advance of terror, and at the appointed hour the Communist, armed with the automatic, appears as the master of the event.
>
> Britain must arm herself against dangers from abroad. She must also discern and unmask the many false pretences under which Communism advances among her continental friends, and even tries to rear its head at home.[21]

There is certainly not much evidence here to suggest that from an ideological standpoint Churchill had softened his hostility to Communism in the wake of the rise of Nazism.

So did hostility to Germany *per se* dwarf ideological concerns in Churchill's thinking in the late 1930s? Certainly many recalled at this time that as a Liberal Cabinet Minister he had been an enthusiatic supporter of resisting what he saw as Germany's bid for European mastery when many of his colleagues were hesitating between war and peace in August 1914. Nor had he ever been tempted by proposals for a compromise peace that emerged in 1917 as the slaughter on the Western Front intensified. And he had first modified his opposition to diplomatic dealings with the Soviet Union as early as 1934 – when renewed signs of the potential aggressiveness of Germany had begun to manifest themselves with respect to Austria. Yet Churchill was by no means a consistent Germanophobe in outlook and was never apparently persuaded that Great Britain and Germany were destined to have a relationship of permanent enmity. As has been seen, on the eve of the Armistice of 1918 he urged in the War Cabinet that 'we might have to build up the German Army, as it was important to get Germany on its legs again for fear of the spread of Bolshevism'.[22] Nor did he favour French efforts during the Paris Peace Conference to impose a Carthaginian Peace on Germany. Then, on 24 March 1920, he urged Lloyd George to work for 'early revision of the Peace Treaty by a Conference to which New Germany shall be invited as an equal partner in the rebuilding of Europe'.[23] By 28 July of the same year he was expressing the hope in the *Evening News* that Germany would 'build a dyke of peaceful, lawful, patient strength and virtue against the flood of red barbarianism flowing from the East'.[24] Nor was Churchill eager to ally solely with France during the 1920s. On the contrary, in 1925, as Chancellor of the Exchequer, he strongly opposed Foreign Office plans for such an arrangement. His actual preference apparently was for Great Britain to remain aloof from European commitments.[25] But he finally acquiesced in the Locarno Treaties which involved Great Britain, France and Germany in a system of mutual security guarantees – something most welcome to the Germany of Gustav Stresemann. Churchill again showed magnanimity towards Germany after the collapse of the Nazi regime. Indeed, in a remarkable echo of the line he had taken in 1918, he sensationally recalled in 1954 that he had actually ordered Montgomery in 1945 'to be careful in collecting the German arms, to stack them so that they could be easily issued again to the German soldiers whom we should have to work with if the Soviet advance continued'.[26] Admitting later that his precise recollection was probably false, Churchill stated, however, that this had not been contrary to his thoughts at the time. And by March 1950 he had become one of the first West European leading figues to call for West German rearmament. It is thus difficult to see how Churchill can be accused of having visceral anti-German feelings. In this he was thus less of a 'Blimp' than most of his fellow Conservatives. Yet many of the latter were much slower than he was in the Nazi era to see the merits of seeking British alignment with the Soviet Union; and indeed some of them in their hearts were never really to agree with him about this.

What Churchill undoubtedly did believe about Germany in the

mid-1930s, however, was that it could soon achieve such military strength as to be capable of making a renewed bid for the mastery of all Europe. He accordingly, as is well-known, became an early advocate of rapid British rearmament. But that was also to be the line of Neville Chamberlain who strove hard both as Chancellor of the Exchequer and as Prime Minister to achieve rearmament at as fast a rate as domestic political realities permitted. Indeed, Churchill and Chamberlain were in broad agreement on much else in the mid-1930s: they were both in normal circumstances neo-isolationists *vis-à-vis* continental Europe but they intended if necessary to resist any bid by either Moscow or Berlin for total mastery; neither at this stage was particularly committed to preserving the territorial *status quo* in Eastern Europe; they favoured friendship with Fascist Italy; they were suspicious of Hitler but also seemingly hopeful that he might mend his ways; they were ideologically more anti-Communist than anti-Fascist and hence desired to see a victory for Franco in the Spanish Civil War; and neither of course had ever up to that stage even contemplated a formal British alliance with the Soviet Union. Is it, then, too far-fetched to speculate that had Chamberlain, on becoming Prime Minister in May 1937, made Churchill his Foreign Secretary the two men might easily have worked in as close a partnership during the late 1930s as they were actually to do in the summer of 1940? Some will ask if Chamberlain could not work with the Foreign Secretary he actually appointed in 1937, namely Eden, how could he possibly have worked with Churchill? But Eden, inherited form Baldwin, was much more of a Tory 'wet' than Churchill; he was opposed to co-operating with Fascist Italy (the issue on which he resigned in February 1938); and he was, above all, not a fanatical enemy of Communism or the Soviet Union.

Why, then, did not Chamberlain in 1937 consider offering Churchill the Foreign Office or indeed any Cabinet post? The likelihood is that the principal doubt was about Churchill's predictability and personal loyalty rather than about his views – though India had been a major issue on which he had differed from all his senior colleagues during the early 1930s. And in any case, we know that Chamberlain feared that Churchill would be uncollegial. The Prime Minister, for example, once told Leslie Hore-Belisha: 'If I take him into the Cabinet he will dominate it. He won't give others the chance of even talking.'[27] But in or out of office Churchill might have been expected to welcome Chamberlain as an improvement on the lethargic

Baldwin in matters relating to foreign policy and defence. And probably at first he did so. Yet the two men diverged fundamentally during 1938 and 1939 on the related issues as to whether or not to go to war in an attempt to maintain the territorial *status quo* in Eastern Europe and whether or not to seek an alliance with the Soviet Union. It is difficult to believe that these particular differences could have been at all widely foreseen by contemporaries in, say, 1937. And maybe Churchill's radical new course was adopted only after much private hesitation. Here, for example, it has been argued that the evolution of the Spanish Civil War may have made a substantial difference to his thinking. For had pro-Soviet forces emerged as the likely winners by 1938 Churchill would presumably have had to give his long-held ideological anti-Communist concerns greater weight during the Sudeten Crisis. In any case, even had there been no Spanish complication, there would still be some mystery about why Churchill had in effect by 1938 rejected Baldwin's argument, made in 1936, that 'if there is any fighting in Europe to be done, I should like to see the Bolshies and the Nazis doing it'.[28] Did he, in short, really suppose that Great Britain and France by allying with Czechoslovakia, or later with Poland, could restore the military balance in *Mitteleuropa* and thereby deter or check a possible German bid for European mastery – even in the absence of any assurance concerning Soviet intentions? After all, he himself had stated in public in July 1936 that 'the progress of German fortifications in the Rhineland cuts off the small states of eastern and central Europe from the possibility of effective French assistance'.[29] Would it not, then, thereafter have made more military sense for the Western Powers, by that juncture benefiting from a rearmament drive, to have in effect allowed Germany a free hand in that region while retaining the option of intervening in any subsequent Soviet–German war in order to try to prevent a European hegemon arising? True, the policy Churchill actually urged was belatedly and reluctantly adopted by Chamberlain in March 1939. But it only had the consequence that Great Britain and France found themselves involved in a hopeless endeavour to save Poland in circumstances that allowed the Soviet Union to remain neutral. Of course Churchill claimed to want to see the Soviet Union, in a Grand Alliance with the Western Powers, coming to the assistance of its neighbours in the event of a German attack on them – though he did not make a Soviet undertaking to join such a Grand Alliance a precondition for Anglo-French willingness to go to war for Czechoslovakia or Poland.

But can he really have believed that such an arrangement would have appealed to Moscow – given, as has been seen,[30] that as recently as 30 October 1936 he had written in the *Evening Standard* that 'Soviet Russia has taken not a few steps likely to render difficult, if not impossible, her association with the western democracies, and with the League of Nations'? It was surely much more likely that, as actually happened, Stalin would apply the logic of Baldwin to the situation and in effect say: 'If there is any fighting in Europe to be done, I should like to see the Western bourgeois democracies and the Nazis doing it.' In short, can Churchill ever have been genuinely convinced of the likelihood of the Soviets going to war for the sake of capitalist Czechoslovakia or for neo-Fascist Poland? Or was he just an old man in a hurry?

This leads us back to another dimension previously considered here. It is Churchill's sense of frustration at being denied office of any kind by Chamberlain. He was already 63 at the beginning of 1938 and would have been a wholly unusual politician if he had not asked himself how, if at all, he could hope to return to a position of power. Loyalty to Chamberlain cannot have looked likely to pay off. So why not risk all by playing the anti-German card *à l'outrance*? True, this would involve abandoning neo-isolationism and even accepting in principle collaboration with the Soviet Union in the unlikely event that this would turn out to be on offer. But he had perhaps been preparing the ground for such a metamorphosis for some time – by, for example, associating himself cautiously with the Arms and the Covenant campaigners and by holding occasional meetings with the Soviet Ambassador in London. And maybe such opportunism or 'boxing the compass', if true, need not unduly surprise us. Churchill was, after all, a professional politician. On this occasion, moreover, no floor-crossing was to be involved!

The ironic outcome, if the foregoing broad interpretation has merit, is that the leader who eventually gained a unique reputation as the one above all others who came to symbolise successful resistance to Hitler and Nazism would probably have found it at least as congenial – and probably more so – to have been remembered instead for having led a successful crusade on behalf of world civilisation to eliminate Soviet Communism. But Churchill was initially frustrated in this regard in 1919 and 1920; and he was subsequently deflected in a totally different direction by the vicissitudes of international and particularly British politics. In short, having rather fortuitously had the chance to give the lion's roar and having spoken of his country's finest hour in 1940, Churchill may soon have found himself yearning to see an end to what may have been for him but a second-order crusade so that he could return to his true path of destiny, as he saw it, namely that of taking on the ultimate barbarians in the Soviet Union. At first of course it looked as if it would fall to Nazi Germany see off the Soviet Union – hence perhaps Churchill's rather frivolous and contradictory remarks in private at the time of the initial German attack.[31] But by 1943 it had become obvious that the Soviets would be victorious on the Eastern Front and might indeed be able eventually to dominate all Europe. Hence Churchill was soon seen by many of his intimates to be devoting at least as much of his attention to frustrating Soviet designs, real or imaginery, as to defeating Germany. Of course he rejoiced unreservedly at the destruction of Hitler and the Nazi regime – and there are surely today few indeed who regret that this was one of the outcomes of the Second World War. But for Churchill himself it was seemingly by no means enough.

On this interpretation, the final decade or so of Churchill's political life was to be marked by much frustration. First, it had become obvious to him by 1943 at the latest that the Soviet Union would emerge from the Second World War as not only a victorious power but as one with armies on a scale that Great Britain would be unable to match in the post-war world. This in turn forced Churchill to recognise that any anti-Soviet crusading on his part would henceforth have to be in a joint partnership with the President of the United States. But during the closing stages of the European War he was further compelled to realise that neither Roosevelt nor Truman was minded to confront the Soviets at his behest. Roosevelt made this tolerably clear at the Teheran Conference – driving Churchill himself into the cynical bilateral bargaining with Stalin that culminated in October 1944 in the 'percentages agreement'. And Roosevelt went even further at Yalta by openly stating he expected that American troops would be withdrawn from Europe within two years of the surrender of Nazi Germany. Then, Truman, after some initial hesitation, also definitely showed himself by May 1945 to be willing to appease Stalin rather than risk a confrontation over Poland in particular. The detailed British contingency planning for an early Anglo-American war against the Soviet Union, drawn up at the Prime Ministers's behest, thus could never even be shown to the American Joint Chiefs of Staff let alone put into operation. Churchill's frustration was further compounded in July

1945 when he had to hand over the Premiership to Attlee following Labour's landslide general election victory.

Churchill did not, however, even now abandon his grand design. For he seems to have expected that as an *éminence gris* he would gradually be able to steer both Truman and Attlee in the desired direction. Immensely encouraged by the emerging East–West tension and by signs of increasing American robustness, he accordingly risked his reputation with the dramatic warning about Communism that he issued to the world at Fulton in March 1946. But, as has been seen, his apparent call for containment there was misleading. For he actually was developing a hidden agenda, namely for the West to move rapidly from containment to contrived confrontation. In this he was, perhaps unconsciously, following the much-condemned precedent set, according to many historians, by Germany in 1870 and 1914. Hence by 1948 he was privately urging on the Americans a course that was likely to culminate in a preventive atomic war being waged against the Soviet Union. But Truman was unimpressed – as he was to be by similar arguments advanced by Bertrand Russell between October 1946 and November 1948.[32] And so the optimum moment for Churchill's most favoured crusade was missed. For by the time Churchill himself returned to power in 1951 the Soviets had successfully tested an atomic bomb of their own and this inevitably meant that even he, as the leader of a country now vulnerable to nuclear bombardment, could no longer plausibly call for a decisive 'showdown' with the ultimate enemies of civilisation in Moscow. The rest of his time in politics was thus, on this reading, to be merely a sad anticlimax.

Some authorities will no doubt hold that this kind of analysis of Churchill is greatly oversimplified – particularly with respect to the war years. They will presumably argue that he was by no means consistently set on an ultimate crusade against the Soviet Union. For did he not frequently make public statements and gestures during the years of the Grand Alliance that pointed in a contrary direction? And did he not during the same period even speak privately to intimates such as Moran and Eden in admiring fashion about Stalin? For some analysts this will surely suggest that Churchill had come at least for a time sincerely to believe in his new role as a friend of the Soviets. Howard, for example, has taken this view of Churchill's approach as late as the occasion of the Fulton speech:

Churchill was no cold warrior. Wary as he had been of Soviet ambitions and objectives, he had gone to extreme lengths – in the eyes of some, too extreme – to conciliate his wartime ally. He had established – so he believed – a warm relationship with Marshal Stalin. He was sensitive to the security needs of the Soviet state. Most of all, he had a deep respect and affection for the Russian people and a grateful recognition for all they had suffered in the common cause.[33]

And Eden reflected in retirement:

It has to be remembered that his [Churchill's] record [*The Second World War*] was written, tho' not his minutes, after Soviet policy had revealed itself in all its stark brutality. W's attitude to Stalin in conference and conversation was not so consistently stern or firm. He fell at intervals under S's spell.[34]

Then there is the historian Roy Douglas, who has written of Churchill's 'one-war-at-a-time mentality'. He added:

Right at the root of Churchill's character was a deep psychological need to be at the very thick of some conflict or other; to devote every ounce of energy to that conflict, and to ignore all other considerations, however vital for the future. It was agony to him that he could do little to assist the great and decisive battles which were being played out on the Soviet plains in 1942 and 1943; that a Second Front at that time would have been an act of futile suicide; that he must even suspend the Arctic convoys. By a strange and archaic logic, which he may not have understood fully himself, Churchill sought to discharge the moral debt which he felt to the Soviet people in the only way which came to his mind: by backing the political aspirations of their Government, at the expense of so many other peoples. This fits in well with the corporate ethic which was deeply ingrained in men of the Prime Minister's class and generation.[35]

There may be some truth in all this – but probably not much. For Churchill's private remarks to his intimates during the war period were frequently bitterly anti-Soviet and probably represented his deepest convictions better than when he addressed them in a contrary vein. On 8 May 1944, for example, he minuted to Eden: 'I fear that very great evil may come upon the world … The Russians are drunk with victory and there is no length they may not go.'[36] And to Moran he said at Potsdam, according to the latter's diary of 22 July 1945:

The Russians have stripped their zone [of Germany] and want a rake-off from the British and American sectors [*sic*] as well. They will grind their zone, there will be unimaginable cruelties. It is indefensible except on one ground: that there is no alternative.[37]

As for his wartime 'concessions' to the Soviet Union, the fact is that few could in any case actually have been avoided and were doubtless usually seen by him as 'terrible and even humbling submissions' that had to be made to the general aim.[38] And we have noted the relish with which he undertook his anti-Communist intervention in Greece in 1944 and the enduring joy this achievement brought him. Important also is the way in which in the same year, in the context of disagreement with Eden about the future of Franco's Spain, he went so far as to accuse the Foreign Office of seeking to promote Communism.[39]

Churchill, then, could come in due time to be widely recognised as someone who wished, above all, to be remembered primarily as an anti-Communist crusader. If so, what may we expect future historians to say about this? First, his reputation will to some extent rest, along with those of other notable anti-Communists of the twentieth century, on whether Communism comes to be seen to have had many redeeming features and to have been at least a lesser evil than Fascism (and Nazism in particular). It seems to this writer unlikely that this view will prevail and hence that Churchill will to some extent benefit from this. In short, his judgment of 1949 that the Soviets 'were quite as wicked but much more formidable than Hitler' may tend to be upheld.[40] For the death toll arising from the courses pursued by Lenin, Stalin, Mao, Pol Pot *et al.* was simply massively greater even than that arising from Nazism/Fascism and this fact alone is likely to impress uninvolved posterity. At the same time, it may well come to be widely believed that Communism was so frightening a phenomenon to middle-class people everywhere that it served as the decisive factor enabling the Extreme Right to come to power in many countries. This may, for example, have been true of Italy in the 1920s, of Germany and Spain in the 1930s, of Greece in the 1960s and of Chile in the 1970s. As Churchill's friend Tudor wrote to him on 14 November 1936 in the context of the Spanish Civil War: 'I hope in any case that *we* shall not fight for communism against fascism. Fascism was forced on the nations by Russia with her communistic intrigues. If one must have despotism, I certainly would prefer to be governed by the educated and upper classes, than by the dregs of the population.'[41] And then there is the argument, strongly canvassed by the historian Richard Pipes, that 'examination of the origins of right-radical movements in interwar Europe quickly reveals that they would have been inconceivable without the precedent set by Lenin and Stalin':

Influences are treacherous terrain for the historian because of the risk of falling into the *post hoc ergo propter hoc* fallacy: 'after it, therefore because of it.' Communism cannot be said to have 'caused' Fascism and National Socialism, since their sources were indigenous. What can be said is that once antidemocratic forces in postwar Italy and Germany gathered sufficient strength, their leaders had a ready model at hand to follow. All the attributes of totalitarianism had antecedents in Lenin's Russia: an official, all-embracing ideology; a single party of the elect headed by a 'leader' and dominating the state; police terror; the ruling party's control of the means of communication and the armed forces; central command of the economy. Since these institutions and procedures were in place in the Soviet Union in the early 1920s when Mussolini founded his regime and Hitler his party, and were to be found nowhere else, the burden of proving there was no connection between 'Fascism' and Communism rests on those who hold this opinion.[42]

Thus the Bolsheviks may come, fairly or not, to be held directly responsible for the Gulags and indirectly responsible for the Holocaust! But the credibility of this argument may be much affected by the extent to which liberal democracy flourishes and the authoritarian and racist Right languishes in the Marxist–Leninist-free decades that now seem likely to be ahead of us. Again, much may turn on whether the 'globalisation' process now evolving brings mass impoverishment to the peoples of the developed world. If it does, then Soviet-style Communism will presumably not be judged, at least by many of the victims of such impoverishment, to be so economically indefensible as is now the fashion. But if, on the other hand, the majority of European countries that experienced Communism continue for decades to have economies that languish behind such European counterparts as experienced only Fascism, then Communism may gradually come to be seen as having left much the more deplorable economic legacy for posterity. This would naturally tend to bolster the reputations of leading anti-Communists of the twentieth century.

Meanwhile we should perhaps only judge Churchill according to whether or not he served with distinction the anti-Communist cause whatever we may think of that cause's relative merits or demerits in comparison with anti-Fascism. By this standard, it is not obvious, analysing with the advantage of hindsight, that he did particularly well. Let us consider first Churchill's role in seeking to promote large-scale intervention against the early Bolsheviks in Russia in 1919 and 1920. Many anti-Communists will of course say that his heart was decidedly in the right place. But the fact is that he soon achieved a public reputation as a wild fanatic on the subject. And there was probably some merit in Lloyd George's contention that if his counsel had been heeded by the British Cabinet it would have been 'the road to bankruptcy and Bolshevism in these islands': it would do 'more to incense organised labour than anything I can think of; and what is still worse, it would throw into the ranks of the extremists a very large number of thinking people who now abhor their methods.'[43] Of course there were those like Henry Wilson who suspected that Lloyd George was a traitor and who accordingly contemplated a military coup to overthrow him. And with these extremists Churchill seemingly came near in 1920 to associating himself. But there were many other anti-Communists in Lloyd George's Cabinet, such as Balfour and Austen Chamberlain, who took a more measured view of what the British people could be expected to undertake by way of involvement in a Russian Civil War in the immediate aftermath of the 'war to end wars'. And it is difficult, with hindsight, to deny that they seem to have had the better of their exchanges with Churchill on these matters.

As for Churchill's role in the approach to and the course of the Second World War, it is only by rather tortuous arguments that one can make a case for his having actually been a more effective anti-Communist than the more straightforward Neville Chamberlain. But those wishing to argue along these lines could stress that Churchill's course at least ensured that an anti-Communist of a sort took over the Premiership on Chamberlain's 'inevitable' fall in May 1940. Let us suppose, arguing counterfactually, that Churchill had died in 1937 but that history had otherwise unfolded in much the same way as it actually did. Then who would have become Prime Minister after the Norwegian catastrophe? Possibly Halifax or even Eden would have emerged. But would either subsequently have been as alert as Churchill about the rising menace of the Soviet Union as the war proceeded? Probably not. And that could have meant that, for example, neither Greece nor Spain would have been saved from Communism. Though this argument clearly has much to commend it, it depends ultimately on the acceptance of the dubious argument that Chamberlain's fate was foreordained. What, for example, would have happened if, to offer just one other counterfactual ingredient, Chamberlain had called a general election immediately after his triumph at Munich and thereby decisively weakened the challenge of the Conservative 'wets'? Would the fateful 'guarantee' to Poland ever have been given and, if not, might not the European War of the period then have been between Germany and the Soviet Union with the Western Powers neutral and rearming? Again, in the same counterfactual spirit, some may wish to argue that Halifax or Eden, in contrast to Churchill, might have failed to court Roosevelt with sufficient ardour during 1940 and 1941 and hence that the United States might have have stayed out of the war altogether – with possibly catastrophic implications for containing the spread of Soviet influence in post-war Europe. But there is a major problem with this particular counterfactual argument. It is that it was not Churchill but another rather unpredicatable anti-Communist who actually rendered the signal service to the anti-Communist cause of bringing the Americans, as matters turned out, decisively and permanently into European affairs. This was of course Hitler, whose declaration of war on Washington in the aftermath of Pearl Harbor was one of the most seminal deeds of the twentieth century.

We know of course that Churchill himself speculated a good deal along counterfactual lines and he was far from consistently confident about how future historians would judge him in the light of the Soviet domination of East-Central Europe that his crusade against Nazi Germany had seemingly helped to bring about. We have already noted Macmillan's recollection that, as early as 1943, Churchill was comparing himself to Cromwell, who, obsessed by fear of the power of Spain, failed to observe the rise of France. But Boothby too later recorded something of a similar character:

> He [Churchill] once talked to me, when the war was over and he was out of power, about the position he would ultimately occupy in history; and I said that nothing could take away from him the fact that he had saved Britain in 1940. He then said, rather sadly: 'Historians are apt to judge war ministers less by the victories achieved under their direction than by the political results which flowed from them. Judged by that standard, I am not sure that I shall be held to have done very well.'[44]

This brings us finally to the immediate post-Nazi era. And here again Churchill's record as an anti-Communist looks far from impressive. For he reverted for a time, certainly in private and to an extent in public, to the impractical extremism that had marked his 1919-1920 phase. To borrow from Lloyd George, we might even say that his 'obsession' concerning the Soviet Union was again 'upsetting his balance'.[45] Churchill first vainly and persistently urged both Roosevelt and Truman in the spring of 1945 to 'race' the Soviets for possession of Prague and even Berlin; and to refuse to respect agreed zonal demarcation lines in Germany unless and until the Soviets gave ground over disputed issues in the Eastern European region which they had already occupied and which they saw as the inalienable fruit of their hard-won victory over Nazism. Above all, by 1948–49, now perhaps a very old man in a hurry, Churchill was bluntly to demand a Western 'showdown' with the Soviet Union while the Americans still had a nuclear monopoly. In short, he was convinced, as he told the US Ambassador in London, that 'when the Soviet develop the atom bomb, war will become a certainty'.[46] This was an extraordinarily dogmatic prediction for an experienced world statesman to make. Fortunately it was falsified by events – like many similar forecasts made by his Marxist–Leninist adversaries. But the policy prescription that Churchill saw as flowing from it, in effect a willingness to wage preventive nuclear war, will presumably be condemned by a majority in future generations – however critical of Communism they may be. And this condemnation will presumably be greatly accentuated if any future national leaders, sincerely impressed by Churchill's beguiling logic, should contrive to initiate preventive wars involving the 'first use' of weapons of mass destruction.

Each year since 1979 at Fulton, Missouri, a lecture is delivered to commemorate the occasion in March 1946 when Truman took the chair while Churchill denounced Soviet-style Communism. The chosen lecturers, usually Britishers possessing peerages or knighthoods, invariably heap compliments on Churchill but few say much about Truman. Sir Michael Howard, for example, when his turn came, only mentioned Truman to point out that the President 'had to deny that his presence on the platform [at Fulton] in any way indicated official endorsement of Churchill's remarks'. Howard then saw fit to end his offering with these ringing words:

> Never despair of victory. Never despair of peace. That is the Churchill we celebrate here today. May God rest that great and noble soul.[47]

But the present author, in the doubtless unlikely event of being asked to deliver one of these Fulton lectures, would, by contrast, concentrate praise not on the distinguished principal speaker in 1946 but on his self-effacing chairman. For two years later Truman, in rejecting Churchill's advice to seek a contrived atomic 'showdown' with Moscow, showed decisively which of these two commited anti-Communists had the greater maturity, steadiness and sense of proportion.

NOTES

1   *The Times*, 2 October 1939.
2   See above, p. 57 and pp. 156–9.
3   *Hansard*, 8 July 1920, vol. 131, col. 1729.
4   *Weekly Dispatch*, 22 June 1919, in Gilbert, *World in Torment*, p. 903.
5   Gilbert, *Churchill: IV, Companion*, p. 1024.
6   *Hansard*, 18 June 1940, vol. 362, col. 60.
7   See above, p. 72.
8   See above, pp. 77–81; and p. 159.
9   *New York Times*, 28 June 1954, in Bell, *Negotiation from Strength*, p. 111.
10 Rhodes James (ed.), *Collected Speeches*, VII, p. 7707.
11 See above, p. 179.
12 Kissinger, *Diplomacy*; Michael Howard, 'Churchill: Prophet of Detente' in R. Crosby Kemper III (ed.), *Winston Churchill: Resolution, Defiance, Magnanimity, Good Will*, Columbia, Missouri, 1996, pp. 177–88; and Young, *Winston Churchill's Last Campaign*.
13 Kissinger, *Diplomacy*, pp. 507, 508.
14 See above, pp. 185–6 and 163.
15 See above, p. 84.
16 See above, pp. 37–8.
17 *Pearson's Magazine*, June 1934, in Gilbert, *Churchill's Political Philosophy*, p. 93.
18 Winston S. Churchill, *Great Contemporaries*, London, 1937, pp. 203–10.
19 *Hansard*, 8 July 1920, vol. 131, col. 1728.
20 Churchill, *Great Contemporaries*, p. 203.
21 Winston Churchill, 'Enemies to the Left', article for *Evening Standard*, 4 September 1936, as preserved in Churchill (Chartwell) Papers, 8/543, Churchill College, Cambridge.
22 See above, p. 5.
23 Churchill to Lloyd George, 24 March 1920, Churchill Papers, in Gilbert, *Churchill: IV, Companion*, p. 1054.
24 *Evening News*, 28 July 1920, in Gilbert, *World in Torment*, p. 418.
25 Carlton, *Anthony Eden*, p. 19.
26 See above, p. 193.
27 R. J. Minney, *The Private Papers of Hore-Belisha*, London, 1960, p. 130.
28 See above, p. 49.
29 Gilbert, *Prophet of Truth*, p. 763.
30 See above, p. 56.
31 See above, pp. 84–5.
32 For Russell see Trachtenberg, *History and Strategy*, p. 103. See also John Lewis Gaddis, *We Now Know: Rethinking the Cold War*, Oxford, 1997, p. 91.
33 Howard, 'Churchill: Prophet of Detente', p. 179.
34 Avon Diary, 1 January 1968, in Dutton, *Anthony Eden*, pp. 214–15.
35 Douglas, *War to Cold War*, p. 187.
36 Churchill to Eden, 8 May 1944, Avon Papers, FO 954/20, PRO. Churchill had used identical words with respect to the early Russian Bolsheviks, namely that very great evils would come upon the world, in a letter to Henry Wilson dated 31 December 1919. See Gilbert, *World in Torment*, p. 362.
37 Moran, *Winston Churchill*, p. 278.

38 See above, p. 118.
39 See above, pp. 120 and 125.
40 See above, p. 159.
41 Tudor to Churchill, 14 November 1936, Churchill (Chartwell) Papers, 2/260, Churchill College, Cambridge. Churchill does not appear to have replied. It is right to add that many historians do not accept that 'Fascism was forced on nations by Russia'. Sir Michael Howard, for example, considers that during the interwar years 'fear of Bolshevism everywhere provided *an excuse* for reactionary authoritarianism'. [Italics added.] See his book review in *International Affairs*, LXXV, 1999, p. 161.
42 Richard Pipes, *Russia under the Bolshevik Regime, 1919–1924*, London, 1994, pp. 241, 245.
43 See above, p. 12.
44 See above, pp. 103–4; and Lord Boothby, *Recollections of a Rebel*, London, 1978, pp. 183–4.
45 See above, p. 18.
46 See above, p. 156.
47 Howard, 'Churchill: Prophet of Detente', pp. 178, 188.

Bibliography

Alperowitz, Gar, *The Decision to Use the Atomic Bomb and the Architecture of an American Myth*, London, 1995

Andrew, Christopher, 'British Intelligence and the Break with Russia in 1927', *The Historical Journal*, XXV, 1982

Aster, Sidney, *1939: The Making of the Second World War*, London, 1973

Avon, The Earl of, *The Eden Memoirs: Facing the Dictators*, London, 1962

—, *The Eden Memoirs: The Reckoning*, London, 1965

Barker, Elisabeth, *Churchill and Eden at War*, London, 1978

Barnes, John and David Nicholson (eds), *The Empire at Bay: The Leo Amery Diaries, 1929–1945*, London, 1988

Beaverbrook, Lord, *The Decline and Fall of Lloyd George*, London, 1963

Bell, Coral, *Negotiation from Strength: A Study in the Politics of Power*, London, 1962

Bell, P. M. H., *John Bull and the Bear: British Public Opinion, Foreign Policy and the Soviet Union*, London, 1990

Bethell, Nicholas, *The Last Secret: Forcible Repatriation to Russia, 1944–7*, London, 1974

Boadle, D. G., *Winston Churchill and the German Question in British Foreign Policy, 1918–1922*, The Hague, 1973

Boothby, Lord, *My Yesterday, Your Tomorrow*, London, 1962

—, *Recollections of a Rebel*, London, 1978

Boyle, Peter G. (ed.), *The Churchill–Eisenhower Correspondence, 1953–1955*, Chapel Hill, North Carolina, 1990

Bryant, Arthur, *The Turn of the Tide: A Study Based on the Diaries and Autobiographical Notes of Field-Marshal The Viscount Alanbrooke*, London, 1957

Carlton, David, *Anthony Eden: A Biography*, London, 1981

—, 'Churchill and Eden: An Uneasy Partnership', *The Listener*, 6 August 1981

—, 'The European Cold War and the Origins of the Problem of "Extended Deterrence"', in The Open University, *Nuclear Weapons: Inquiry, Analysis and Debate*, Milton Keynes, 1986

—, 'Churchill in 1940: Myth and Reality', *World Affairs*, CLVI, 1993–94

Charmley, John, *Churchill: The End of Glory: A Political Biography*, London, 1993

—, *Churchill's Grand Alliance: The Anglo-American Special Relationship, 1940–57*, London, 1995

Churchill, Randolph S., *Winston S. Churchill: Vol. I: Youth, 1874–1900*, London, 1966

—, *Winston S. Churchill: Vol. II: Young Statesman, 1901–1914*, London, 1967

Churchill, Winston S., *The Aftermath*, London, 1929

—, *Great Contemporaries*, London, 1937

—, *Step by Step, 1936–1939*, London, 1939

—, *The Second World War*, 6 vols, London, 1948–54

Colville, John, *The Fringes of Power: Downing Street Diaries, 1939–1955*, London, 1985
Conservative and Unionist Central Office, *General Election, 1950: Campaign Guide*, London, 1950
Cosgrave, Patrick, *Churchill at War: Vol. I: Alone, 1939–40*, London, 1974
Costello, John, *Ten Days That Saved the West*, London, 1991
Cowling, Maurice, *The Impact of Hitler: British Politics and Policies, 1933–1940*, Cambridge, 1975
Crozier, Andrew J., *The Causes of the Second World War*, Oxford, 1997
Crozier, Brian, *Franco: A Biographical History*, London, 1967
Dilks, David (ed.), *The Diaries of Sir Alexander Cadogan, 1938–1945*, London, 1971
—, *Neville Chamberlain: Vol. I, Pioneering and Reform, 1869–1929*, Cambridge, 1984
Djilas, Milovan, *Conversations with Stalin*, New York, 1962
Dockrill, Saki, *Britain's Policy for West German Rearmament, 1950–1955*, Cambridge, 1991
Douglas, Roy, *From War to Cold War, 1942–48*, London, 1981
Dutton, David, *Austen Chamberlain: Gentleman in Politics*, Bolton, 1985
—, *Anthony Eden: A Life and Reputation*, London, 1997
Eden, Anthony, *The Eden Memoirs: Full Circle*, London, 1960
Edmonds, Robin, *The Big Three: Churchill, Roosevelt and Stalin in Peace and War*, New York, 1991
Fish, M. Steven, 'After Stalin's Death: The Anglo-American Debate Over a New Cold War', *Diplomatic History*, X, 1986
Ferrell, Robert H. (ed.), *Off the Record: The Private Papers of Harry S. Truman*. New York, 1980
Gaddis, John Lewis, *We Now Know: Rethinking Cold War History*, Oxford, 1997
Gilbert, Martin, *World in Torment: Winston S. Churchill, 1917–1922*, London, 1975
—, *Prophet of Truth: Winston S. Churchill, 1922–1939*, London, 1976
—, *Finest Hour: Winston S. Churchill, 1939–1941*, London, 1983
—, *Road to Victory: Winston S. Churchill, 1941–1945*, London, 1986
—, *'Never Despair': Winston S. Churchill, 1945–1965*, London, 1988
—, *Winston S. Churchill: Companion Volumes* to the above, London, dated between 1972 and 1982
—, *Winston Churchill: The Wilderness Years*, London, 1981
—, *Churchill's Political Philosophy*, Oxford, 1981
—, 'Churchill and the European Idea', in R. A. C. Parker (ed.), *Winston Churchill: Studies in Statesmanship*, London, 1995
—, 'From Yalta to Bermuda and Beyond: In Search of Peace with the Soviet Union', in James W. Muller, *Churchill as Peacemaker*, Cambridge, 1997
Glenny, M. V., 'The Anglo-Soviet Trade Agreement, March 1921', *Journal of Contemporary History*, V, 1970
Gorodetsky, Gabriel, *The Perilous Truce: Anglo-Soviet Relations, 1924–27*, Cambridge, 1977
Griffiths, Richard, *Fellow Travellers of the Right: British Enthusiasts for Nazi Germany, 1933–9*, London, 1980
Grigg, John, 'Churchill and Lloyd George', in Robert Blake and Wm. Roger Louis (eds), *Churchill*, Oxford, 1993
Harbutt, Fraser, J., *The Iron Curtain: Churchill, America and the Origins of the Cold War*, Oxford, 1986

Harriman, W. Averill and Elie Abel, *Special Envoy to Churchill and Stalin, 1941–1946*, New York, 1975

Harvey, John (ed.), *The War Diaries of Oliver Harvey, 1941–1945*, London, 1978

Haslam, Jonathan, *The Soviet Union and the Struggle for Collective Security in Europe, 1933–39*, London, 1984

Hochman, Jiri, *The Soviet Union and the Failure of Collective Security, 1934–1938*, Ithaca, New York, 1984

Howard, Michael, 'Churchill: Prophet of Detente', in R. Crosby Kemper III (ed.), *Winston Churchill: Resolution, Defiance, Magnanimity, Good Will*, Columbia, Missouri, 1996

—, book review of Mark Mazower's *The Dark Continent: Europe's Twentieth Century*, in *International Affairs*, LXXV, 1999.

Irving, David, *Churchill's War: Vol. I: the Struggle for Power*, Western Australia, 1987

Kettle, Michael, *Churchill and the Archangel Fiasco, November 1918–July 1919*, London, 1992

Kimball, Warren F. (ed.), 'Naked Reverse Right: Roosevelt, Churchill, and Eastern Europe from TOLSTOY to Yalta – and a Little Beyond' *Diplomatic History*, IX, 1985

—, 'Churchill, Roosevelt and Post-war Europe', in R. A. C. Parker (ed.), *Winston Churchill: Studies in Statesmanship*, London, 1995

—, *Churchill and Roosevelt: The Complete Correspondence*, 3 vols, Princeton, New Jersey, 1984

—, *Forged in War: Churchill, Roosevelt and the Second World War*, London, 1997

Kissinger, Henry, *Diplomacy*, London, 1994

Kitchen, Martin, *British Policy towards the Soviet Union during the Second World War*, New York, 1986

Lamb, Richard, *Churchill as War Leader: Right or Wrong?*, London, 1991

Leahy, William, *I Was There*, London, 1950

Lees, Michael, *The Rape of Serbia: the British Role in Tito's Grab for Power 1943–1944*, San Diego, 1990

Lloyd George, David, *The Truth about the Peace Treaties*, London, 1938

Lowe, Peter, *Containing the Cold War in East Asia: British Policies towards Japan, China and Korea, 1948–53*, Manchester, 1997

McCullough, David, *Truman*, New York, 1992

Macfarlane, L. J., 'Hands Off Russia: The British Labour Movement and the Russo-Polish War, 1920', *Past and Present*, no. 38, December 1967

Macmillan, Harold, *Tides of Fortune, 1945–1955*, London, 1969

Maisky, Ivan, *Spanish Notebooks*, London, 1966

Manchester, William, *The Caged Lion: Winston Spencer Churchill, 1932–1940*, London, 1988

Martin, David, *The Web of Disinformation: Churchill's Yugoslav Blunder*, New York, 1988

Miliband, Ralph, *Parliamentary Socialism: A Study in the Politics of Labour*, London, 1961

Minney, R. J., *The Private Papers of Hore-Belisha*, London 1960

Moran, Lord, *Winston Churchill: The Struggle for Survival*, London, 1966

Morrison, Lord, *An Autobiography*, London, 1960

Mowat, Charles Loch, *Britain Between the Wars, 1918–1940*, London, 1955

Nicolson, Nigel (ed.), *Harold Nicolson: Diaries and Letters, 1930–1939*, London, 1966

—, *Harold Nicolson: Diaries and Letters, 1939–1945*, London, 1967

Parker, R. A. C. (ed.), *Winston Churchill: Studies in Statesmanship*, London, 1995

Pelling, Henry, *Churchill's Peacetime Ministry, 1951–55*, London, 1997

Pickersgill, J. W. and D. F. Forster (eds), *The Mackenzie King Record: Vol. III, 1945–1946*, Toronto, 1970

—, *The Mackenzie King Record: Vol. IV, 1947–1948*, Toronto, 1970

Pipes, Richard, *Russia under the Bolshevik Regime, 1919–1924*, London, 1994

Pombeni, Paolo, 'Churchill and Italy, 1922–40', in R. A. C. Parker (ed.), *Winston Churchill: Studies in Statesmanship*, London, 1995

Ponting, Clive, *1940: Myth and Reality*, London, 1990

—, *Churchill*, London, 1994

Pratt, Lawrence R., *East of Malta, West of Suez: Britain's Mediterranean Crisis. 1936–1939*, Cambridge, 1975

Preston, Paul, *Franco: A Biography*, London, 1993

Reynolds, David, 'Churchill and the British "Decision" to Fight On in 1940', in Richard Langhorne (ed.), *Diplomacy and Intelligence during the Second World War*, Cambridge, 1985

Riddell, Lord, *Lord Riddell's Intimate Diary of the Peace Conference and After*, New York, 1934

Rhodes, James, Robert (ed.), *Memoirs of a Conservative: J. C. C. Davidson's Memoirs and Papers, 1910–37*, London, 1969

—, *Churchill: A Study in Failure, 1900–1939*, London, 1970

—, *Anthony Eden*, London, 1986

—, *Chips: The Diaries of Sir Henry Channon*, London, 1967

— (ed.), *Winston S. Churchill: His Complete Speeches, 1897–1963*, 8 vols, New York, 1974

Roberts, Andrew, *'The Holy Fox': A Biography of Lord Halifax*, London, 1991

—, *Eminent Churchillians*, London, 1994

Roberts, Geoffrey, *The Soviet Union and the Origins of the Second World War: Russo-German Relations and the Road to War, 1933–1941*, Basingstoke, 1995

Rose, Norman (ed.), *Baffy: The Diaries of Blanche Dugdale, 1936–1947*, London, 1973

—,'Churchill and Zionism', in Robert Blake and Wm. Roger Louis (eds), *Churchill*, Oxford, 1993

—, *Churchill: An Unruly Life*, London, 1994

Roskill, Stephen, *Hankey: Man of Secrets: Vol. II, 1919–1931*, London, 1972

Ruane, Kevin, 'Anthony Eden, the Foreign Office and War in Indo-China, 1951–54', unpublished Ph.D. thesis, University of Kent, 1991

—, 'Anthony Eden, British Diplomacy and the Origins of the Geneva Conference of 1954', *The Historical Journal*, XXXVII, 1994

—, '"Containing America": Aspects of British Foreign Policy and the Cold War in South East Asia, 1951–54', *Diplomacy and Statecraft*, VII, 1996

Sainsbury, Keith, *The Turning Point: Roosevelt, Stalin, Churchill, and Chiang-Kai-Shek, 1943: The Moscow, Cairo, and Teheran Conferences*, Oxford, 1985

Schwarz, Hans-Peter, 'Churchill and Adenauer', in R. A. C. Parker (ed.), *Winston, Churchill: Studies in Statesmanship*, London, 1995

Shuckburgh, Evelyn, *Descent to Suez: Diaries, 1951–56*, London, 1986

Smith, Arthur L., *Churchill's German Army: Wartime Strategy and Cold War Politics, 1943–1947*, Beverly Hills, California, 1977

Soames, Mary (ed.), *Speaking for Themselves: The Personal Letters of Winston and Clementine Churchill*, London, 1998

Stafford, David, *Churchill and the Secret Service*, London, 1997

Stewart, Graham Somerville, 'Winston Churchill and the Conservative Party, 1929–1937', unpublished Ph.D. thesis, University of Cambridge, 1995

Sulzberger, C. L., *The Last of the Giants*, New York, 1970

Taylor, A. J. P., *The Origins of the Second World War*, London, 2nd edn., 1963

—, *English History, 1914–1945*, Oxford, 1965

— et al., *Churchill: Four Faces and the Man*, London, 1969

— (ed.), *Lloyd George: A Diary by Frances Stevenson*, London, 1971

Tedder, Lord, *With Prejudice*, London, 1966

Thomas, Hugh, *Armed Truce: the Beginnings of the Cold War, 1945–46*, London, 1986

Thompson, John M., *Russia, Bolshevism and the Versailles Peace*, Princeton, New Jersey, 1966

Thompson, Neville, *The Anti-Appeasers: Conservative Opposition to Appeasement in the 1930s*, Oxford, 1971

Tillman, Seth P., *Anglo-American Relations at the Paris Peace Conference of 1919*, Princeton, New Jersey, 1961

Tolstoy, Nikolai, *Victims of Yalta*, London, 1977

Trachtenberg, Marc, *History and Strategy*, Princeton, New Jersey, 1991

Trukhanovsky, V. G., *British Foreign Policy during the Second World War*, Moscow, 1970

—, *Winston Churchill*, Moscow, 1978

Vaisse, Maurice, 'Churchill and France, 1951–55', in R. A. C. Parker (ed.), *Winston Churchill: Studies in Statesmanship*, London, 1995

Warner, Geoffrey, 'The Settlement of the Indochina War', in John W. Young (ed.), *The Foreign Policy of Churchill's Peacetime Administration, 1951–1955*, Leicester, 1988

White, Stephen, *Britain and the Bolshevik Revolution: A Study in the Politics of Diplomacy, 1920–1924*, London, 1979

—, *The Origins of Detente: The Genoa Conference and Soviet–Western Relations, 1921–1922*, Cambridge, 1985

Winant, John G., *A Letter from Grosvenor Square*, London, 1947

Woodward, Llewellyn, *British Foreign Policy in the Second World War*, 5 vols, London, 1970–76

Yergin, Daniel, *Shattered Peace: The Origins of the Cold War*, London, 1978

Young, John W., 'Churchill, the Russians and the Western Alliance: The Three-Power Conference at Bermuda, December 1953', *The English Historical Review*, CI, 1986

—, 'Cold War and Detente with Moscow', in John W. Young (ed.), *The Foreign Policy of Churchill's Peacetime Administration, 1951–1955*, Leicester, 1988

—, *Winston Churchill's Last Campaign: Britain and the Cold War, 1951–55*, Oxford, 1996

Young, Kenneth, *Churchill and Beaverbrook: A Study in Politics and Friendship*, London, 1966

— (ed.), *The Diaries of Sir Robert Bruce Lockhart, 1939–1965*, London, 1980

PRINCIPAL PRIMARY SOURCES

British Government archives housed at the Public Record Office, Kew

Chartwell and Churchill Papers housed at Churchill College, Cambridge; and material from this archive reproduced in Martin Gilbert's authorised multi-volume biography of Churchill and in the numerous Companion Volumes of documentation

Hansard

The Times

United States Department of State, *Papers Relating to the Foreign Relations of the United States*, Washington, DC

Index

Note: No entries for Winston Churchill, Great Britain or the Soviet Union appear in this index because they would relate to virtually every page; n. after a page reference indicates the number of a note on that page.